I0165505

MARKED BY TIME

Marked by Time

How Social Change
Has Transformed Crime
and the Life Trajectories
of Young Americans

ROBERT J. SAMPSON

THE BELKNAP PRESS
OF HARVARD UNIVERSITY PRESS

Cambridge, Massachusetts
London, England

2026

Copyright © 2026 by the President and Fellows of Harvard College
All rights reserved
Printed in the United States of America

First printing

EU GPSR Authorised Representative
LOGOS EUROPE, 9 rue Nicolas Poussin, 17000, LA ROCHELLE, France
E-mail: Contact@logoseurope.eu

Cataloging-in-Publication data available from the Library of Congress

ISBNs: 978-0-674-98754-8 (alk. paper);
978-0-674-30380-5 (ePub); 978-0-674-30381-2 (pdf)

No man ever steps in the same river twice, for it's not the same river and he's not the same man.

—ATTRIBUTED TO THE PHILOSOPHER HERACLITUS (CIRCA 500 BC)
(PLATO, CRATYLUS, 402A)

The members of any cohort are entitled to participate in only one slice of life—their unique location in the stream of history. Because it embodies a temporally specific version of the heritage, each cohort is differentiated from all others.

—DEMOGRAPHER NORMAN RYDER (1965)

Born under a bad sign
I been down since I began to crawl
If it wasn't for bad luck,
You know, I wouldn't have no luck at all.

—BLUESMAN ALBERT KING (RECORDED IN 1967 BY STAX RECORDS)

Contents

MARKED BY TIME

Born under a Good Sign?

By conventional measures, Darnell Jackson's future looked bleak. Born in 1995 to a single mother on welfare in an impoverished and racially segregated neighborhood on Chicago's South Side, he entered a world marked by near-record murder rates and surging incarceration.

Yet Darnell was lucky in ways that no one at the time predicted. The year of his birth marked a turning point: Violence had begun a dramatic decline that would continue throughout his childhood, not just in his neighborhood but across Chicago. Lead contamination—known to impair child development—had dropped even more sharply. Crime-related arrests had started falling around 1995, and by the time Darnell reached his mid-twenties—the typical age for first imprisonment—incarceration rates had sharply decreased. While Darnell was born into harsh circumstances, time's arrow bent unexpectedly in his favor at crucial developmental stages.

Andre Lewis was likewise raised by a single mother living in poverty in the same impoverished and racially segregated neighborhood on the South Side, but in 1995 he was already fifteen years old and less graced by history. Andre's early childhood unfolded during the chaos of the late 1980s crack epidemic and rising gang violence among the young, and his local neighborhood was a hot spot of lead contamination. While adolescence is a turbulent time for any boy, Andre's early teenage years aligned with Chicago's peak murder rates, when violence and fear defined daily life. As he recalled in an interview: "I had two friends who they say killed themselves. I think they were murdered by a friend." Aggressive drug policing dominated his young adulthood, and incarceration rates peaked just as Andre reached his mid-twenties.[1]

Like Darnell and Andre, we do not choose our times or how they will change. And yet changes in society, like shifting police enforcement or underlying rates of violence, powerfully influence how likely we are to face some of life's harshest consequences, like being arrested or shot. The unrelenting and often unpredictable torrent of large-scale social change will be in the foreground of my investigations in this book, even though these and other changes remain background settings for many leading narratives about the courses of individual lives.

Those who study crime, punishment, and more broadly the development of individual character often focus on personal traits (like self-control), demographic characteristics, and family resources that shape our life paths. These factors matter, of course, but this view misses something crucial: the impact of social change. This blind spot stems from how we commonly study trajectories of human development. Typically, a long-term research project, especially in the study of criminality, follows just one age cohort—a sample of children growing up simultaneously. This approach has a fundamental limitation: It fails to consider how similar children born in different years might mature under drastically different conditions.

On the flip side, the studies that do examine society-wide shifts in crime and its control—"period effects," as researchers call them—typically set aside how such changes differently affect people at various life stages. While macro-level analyses offer valuable insights, they miss crucial dynamics; the individuals themselves are changing as society changes around them. Moreover, the complex patterns of crime, punishment, and inequality over recent decades defy simple explanations of the rise of mass incarceration or America's great crime decline.

The core puzzle I address is the link between individual development and social change. The two are intertwined, and the question has challenged thinkers for millennia. Around 500 BCE, the philosopher Heraclitus captured this truth in his aphorism that no man ever steps in the same river twice, for it's not the same river and he's not the same man.[2] To focus exclusively on the individual or societal level is to miss the fact that as we age, time marches on. While this interplay seems obvious in hindsight, scholars of crime, character, and human development have struggled to study systematically how one's specific moment in history's flow shapes one's life path.

This book combines original, long-term data on multiple birth cohorts to tackle the long-standing challenge of disentangling individual from large-scale social change. It does so by tracing the lives of over a thousand children from Chicago who, by the lottery of when they were born, grew up at different times during the remarkable transformation of crime, punishment, and social inequality that started in the latter third of the twentieth century and that continues today. By following children like Andre and Darnell over twenty-five years—examining both their origins and life trajectories into early and mid-adulthood—I show how individual lives and historical change intersect. In the strongest form, I argue that *when* we are makes us *who* we are.

We will see, for example, that the chance of being arrested in life among people born in the mid-1980s is more than double that of those born just a decade later, in the mid-1990s. This large arrest inequality does not arise from early-life individual, family, or local neighborhood characteristics. It arises from the larger and highly divergent socio-historical contexts in which the children grew through adolescence into adulthood. Andre and Darnell were similar in all the usual respects, but only Andre became entangled with the criminal justice system. Individual qualities like resilience did not distinguish these two boys; social change did.

Personal character, family, and neighborhood still shape our lives—but their influences aren't fixed. Neither is the influence of an individual's race or class. By comparing people born at different times, we see how these familiar factors gain or lose power as society changes around them. Looking at the life course from birth through adulthood, my research shows, for example, that those who grew up poor in older cohorts were more likely to accumulate a criminal record than those who grew up equally poor in more recent cohorts. The arrest rate of poor African Americans declined rapidly over time as well. Perhaps most surprising, social change was so substantial between older and younger cohorts that it rendered the high self-control children of the older cohort just as likely to be arrested as the low self-control children of the cohort born just one decade later. That is, the most impulsive children of one cohort were arrested just as often as the best-behaved children of another cohort. The shifting import of classic factors like low self-control and poverty betrays the limits of individual and family qualities in predicting criminal futures.

Contrary to leading macrostructural accounts of social change, moreover, crime and its punishment, and many other features of inequality in American life, have unfolded over time in countervailing and unexpected ways that defy the dueling historical narratives of linear decline versus linear progress. Social change continues to catch us unaware and defy not only our expectations, but also our theories and policy assumptions about how lives progress.

TIME'S CHARACTER TRAP

The powerful forces of social change challenge the long-standing emphasis in American culture on individual character and family upbringing as foundations of success or failure in life. Ralph Waldo Emerson, the popular nineteenth-century essayist and philosopher, captured the national ethos when he declared that character is nature in its highest form, and that "no change of circumstances can repair a defect of character."[3] This ethos runs through familiar stories of rags to riches, or any success against the odds, from the athletic or musical to the political, that highlight features of inner character such as self-control, fortitude, and moral rectitude. Today's psychologists and economists talk more about "grit" and "soft skills" than character per se, but these more empirically grounded concepts still encircle the idea of character with reference to traits like self-control.[4] The veneration of character as the ultimate source of achievement and upward mobility builds on a grand tradition going back at least to Aristotle's emphasis on moral virtue.[5]

Everyday definitions of character and everyday decisions of legal authorities continue to focus on the mental and moral qualities of individuals. But defining character in this way can lead to what I call the *character trap*. By attributing life failures to an individual's low self-control or weak moral character, we typically assume character is fixed and internal. When someone is labeled as having a bad character, society often responds with contempt and harsh punishment, believing rehabilitation is futile since character is supposedly unchangeable. This creates a destructive cycle: Punishment often involves denying resources, dignity, and respect—actions that can reinforce the negative behaviors they're meant to eliminate, which can then lead to more negative behavior, confirming the original judgment and triggering yet harsher punishment. This spiral can make future misconduct more likely while seemingly validating the assumption of inherently flawed character. The trap is particularly powerful because character is such a capacious concept—institutions readily interpret various words and actions as evidence of character flaws, further strengthening this self-fulfilling cycle.

Criminal is a master institutional label in American society that is used to express an individual's moral character. In the most influential work of philosophy in the liberal tradition in the past half-century, John Rawls put it this way: The propensity to break the law, at least in a society perceived to be just, is a "mark of bad character."[6] This widely held view underscores the morally charged nature of crime and its attribution.

To be labeled by institutions of criminal authority also produces a public credential—a record that further traps and shapes an individual's life course. Here, criminality is externally and officially imposed, with a permanence that evokes the ancient Greek origins of the term *mark*—an instrument of engraving and a stamp used for indelibly marking coins. A criminal record is difficult to expunge, and considerable research shows that having one undermines future opportunities.[7] Common examples are the uses of criminal arrest histories to predict employment potential and the probability of recidivism. Assumptions about stable, intrinsic character and the persistency of the criminal label thus work hand in hand to build the confines of the character trap. But who exactly is caught in this trap depends in part on who is predicted to continue offending, and thus for whom additional punishment is justified—beginning (or continuing) the cycle of punishment and repeated criminality. In the criminal justice context, the prediction of future offending is essentially a judgment of bad character.

The idea that those individuals who will wreak disproportionate havoc on society can be predicted and potentially neutralized has long roots. An influential study published in 1972 put hard numbers on it, arguing that just 6 percent of children born in Philadelphia in 1945 accounted for more than half of the criminal offenses recorded for this cohort through age eighteen.[8] Evoking the idea of moral character, just three years later, the political scientist James Q. Wilson famously concluded: "Wicked people exist. Nothing avails except to set them apart from innocent people."[9] This separation was soon attempted on a large scale, including multiple efforts to selectively identify and incarcerate "chronic offenders" and, in the late twentieth century, alleged "super-predators" and what one study eventually called "ravenous wolves."[10] Yet not only chronic offenders or the allegedly incorrigible few were swept up. The chronic few became the many as the net of criminal punishment widened, leading to what we now call mass incarceration.

Important studies have found that various problem behaviors beyond outright criminality are also concentrated among a relatively small number of individuals who exert outsized influence on the future. In long-term research based on a birth cohort from New Zealand, 20 percent of the sample accounted for over half of the adult behaviors that inflict economic and social costs on society, including welfare dependency, fatherless child-rearing, and criminal convictions (at 97 percent of all convictions). Individual differences in low self-control measured at age three predicted which children joined this high-burden group.[11] But as noted earlier, if social change causes high self-control in one cohort to be just as valuable as low self-control in another, it is time to challenge the value of single-cohort studies that suggest easy connections between self-control and a stable, intrinsic character.

The most individualist of approaches to identifying future criminal character reach deep into the body. Students of crime have long read with fascination about the attempts of the Italian physician Cesare Lombroso in the 1800s to identify depraved criminals by examining the skulls of dead prisoners.[12] That approach sounds a bit silly today, but modern science forges ahead with new methods along similar lines. The neuro-criminologist Adrian Raine claims that we can predict violence using improved techniques of early brain imaging.[13] Similarly, psychologists have pointed to advances in neuroimaging indicating that self-control is detectable by immature brain structures in adolescents, with neuroscience promising a "biologically informed jurisprudence."[14] The authors of the New Zealand study report that brain health differences among three-year-olds predicted which cohort members became the adult members of the high-cost group in their society.[15] Other accounts reach even earlier in life, claiming that low self-control and related dispositions to destructive behavior can be predicted, and individualized treatments can be delivered, based on advances in polygenic scoring—the DNA of our character, as it were.[16]

Both historically and today, then, the tantalizing ideas that individuals with defects of character and a propensity to criminality produce the bulk of society's problems, and that we can accurately identify them before they emerge (that is, *ex ante*), have exerted a powerful hold on academics and the public. This predictive ideal is widespread and not limited to any one theoretical, ideological, or policy framework. Concepts of antisocial propensity and low self-control, and predictions thereof, are put forth in multiple theories of social mobility, human capital development, and crime over the life course. In the control of crime, both defense and prosecution rely on measures of criminal propensity to argue for innocence or guilt in trials and in the determination of criminal sentences among those judged guilty. Even at pretrial points, such as police encounters with citizens or bail decisions, evaluations of criminal propensity loom large. Meanwhile, analysts of "big data" advocate predictive algorithms based on criminal histories and other administrative records to inform official decision-making, purportedly satisfying the demands of both crime control and social justice.[17]

The lure of prediction has led many proponents of ending mass incarceration, conservative and liberal alike, to assume that we can divide the criminal population into two camps: those deserving of forgiveness (let's call them the redeemables) and the perceived smaller group of career criminals and violent offenders (the apparent irredeemables). It is the latter who are seen as deserving of prison time; meanwhile, their counterparts, the minor or nonviolent offenders, can be pegged for rehabilitation in a free society. A criminal justice reformer in Texas offered this succinct summary: "The intent is to be tough on career criminals, and try to reform the others."[18] Accelerating this process, the bipartisan criminal justice reform bill of 2018 called for the development of new risk assessment and prediction tools.[19] While the emphasis on prediction and the use of official records to ascertain criminal propensity has long been part of the criminal justice practice, mission creep has led to the widespread adoption of individual criminality as a predictive marker of character in the late twentieth and early twenty-first centuries.

This book challenges the turn to prediction and asks a different set of questions than traditional theories of crime, justice, and character: What if similar individuals born into the same economic or family conditions nonetheless face significantly different trajectories of crime or later-life outcomes because they were born in different years? If so, precisely what social changes could explain this shift, and what do they mean for our conception of character as stable and intrinsic? I show that the changing social environment looms large, in the form of historical turning points that reconfigure the very meaning of classic concepts such as self-control, criminal propensity, and social disadvantage over the life course. Indeed, my evidence shows that the traditional set of indicators used to gauge criminal character has been a function of social change as much as of individual propensities and personal and family traits. I also show how social change fundamentally undermines traditional tools of prediction.

Focusing on *when* we are rather than *who* we are, however, requires a systematic theoretical shift in intellectual perspective and a departure from business-as-usual research approaches. This book makes that shift by conceptualizing, identifying, measuring, and quantifying the power and mechanisms of social change in shaping crime and punishment in the lives of children of different birth cohorts. I seek to reveal, with long-term empirical data, how the birth lottery of history shapes the life course of children.

CONTOURS OF CHANGE

The world changed over the last half-century in ways that were as dramatic and unexpected as they were complex. We often think of criminalization and crime over the life course as shaped by penal policy, surrounding levels of violence, and inequalities in developmental risks faced by young people. All three sets of changes are implicated in America's social transformation.

Chapter 1 traces how violence in the United States began an unpredicted, decades-long ascent starting in the 1960s, rising over 400 percent before reaching historic proportions by the 1990s. It is no exaggeration to say that violence was epidemic in American society, affecting the minds and bodies of children at unprecedented levels. Neighborhoods in many cities resembled war zones and were written off as beyond salvation.

Incarceration began its ascent later but was no less powerful in its velocity and broad reach, also marking a generation of children's lives. The chronic offenders and the allegedly incorrigible few were not the only ones affected. Entire groups in society were caught in nets of violence and criminal punishment, fueled by the character trap and multiplying its severity, with the greatest impact on the poor and racial minorities. Homicide was and still is the leading cause of death among young Black males, for example, and nearly 60 percent of Black males who were born in the late 1960s and dropped out of high school were estimated to have served time in prison by the end of the 1990s, compared to only 17 percent of Black high-school dropouts who were born between 1945 and 1949.[20]

But there is another side to the story that is underappreciated. The unexpected and profound drop in violence since the 1990s meant that, by the luck of when they were born, some cohorts of children—regardless of their individual dispositions and even among the poorest of the poor—entered a different, more peaceful world. African Americans benefited the most from the declines in violence, as the sociologist Patrick Sharkey has shown, reaping major gains in life expectancy.[21] More broadly, and conflicting with frequent warnings that things are getting worse, many trends in the lives of American adolescents have run in positive directions in recent decades, including less substance use, less unprotected sex, and fewer automobile accidents.[22] Child poverty also declined dramatically from the mid-1990s to 2020.[23] Even juvenile detention and adult incarceration dropped and rather fast—reaching a twenty-five-year low by 2020.[24] Based on these measures, life has never been better for children and adolescents—of all races.

Yet the times changed again, and this time more abruptly. In 2020, protests erupted around the country over police brutality. Aggressive policing tactics against African Americans and officer-involved shootings have long been a scourge, but the video of George Floyd's death under a police officer's knee triggered explosive reactions among diverse racial groups, catalyzing protests that engulfed cities in ways the country had not seen since the 1960s. While disagreement remains regarding the ultimate effects of these protests, whether on reforming police behavior or inciting political backlash, the social changes in attitudes they reflected were large and sudden.

Around the same time, the decades-long trend of decreasing violence suddenly reversed in important ways. Murders, for example, especially by firearms, saw a substantial rise from 2019 to 2021, in some cities surpassing the heights of the 1980s and early 1990s.[25] Mass shootings in America climbed as well, as did car accidents and road rage shootings.[26] As of 2025, murders have declined substantially from the heights reached in 2019 to 2021—even in much-maligned Chicago—but no one knows if this will continue.[27] The only sure thing to expect is continual change.

Crime and its control are not the only aspects of society that have changed. Inequality in America increased sharply in the last fifty years.[28] Prospects for upward mobility, a tenet of the American Dream, fell despite improvements in other conditions of life. According to a well-publicized study, 90 percent of Americans born in the 1940s went on to earn more than their parents had, but among those born in the 1980s, only 50 percent were likely to do so.[29] The odds of mobility are also shaped by where a child grows up—another kind of birth lottery having nothing to do with a child's choosing or psychological makeup.[30] Social change is unevenly experienced, in other words, overlaid on neighborhood inequality and racial segregation. Theories of individual character are mostly silent in the face of such forces.

There are still other influences of the environment that are less visible and that are rarely studied in a multi-cohort perspective. Consider the many children exposed during the critical years of their development to forms of environmental degradation, such as extreme levels of lead poisoning and exposure to industrially polluted neighborhoods. These interrelated conditions give rise—in the same way that exposure to violence does—to poisoned development, as toxic environments shape children's cognition, self-control, expectations for longevity, and long-term patterns of behavior that fall under the societal definitions of character. But, like exposure to violence and incarceration, exposure to environmental toxins varies dramatically by time and place, and hidden toxins remain highly disparate by neighborhood. While lead exposure has fallen steeply in the last twenty-five years, its danger lingers. Meanwhile, climate change and exposure to air pollution pose new risks to child development.[31]

Inequality was further laid bare by the sudden arrival of COVID-19 in early 2020. The highly contagious virus upended nearly every aspect of everyday life, including the nature of work, childcare, social interactions, the economy, and crime. There is evidence that the experience of the pandemic years even altered the personalities of young people.[32]

MY AIMS AND APPROACH

The vast social changes in crime, punishment, and inequality of the last few decades, for good and for ill, demand a fresh account of growing up in the late twentieth and early twenty-first centuries—and of the meaning

of individual character, especially as it is defined by criminality and per-
petuated through the use of predictive tools. This book takes aim at this
goal both theoretically and empirically, guided by a unique, long-term
study of the life experiences—from birth to early adulthood—of over a
thousand children born in Chicago who grew up during different stages
of the contemporary transformations of crime, punishment, and inequality
in America. The oldest of these children, like Andre, were born around
1980, and the youngest, like Darnell, in 1995, coinciding with the study's
launch. The children were then followed over the same period, from 1995
to 2024, with data being collected about many aspects of their lives, families, neighborhoods, criminal justice contacts, and other social contexts.
Leveraging this unique dataset, I am now able to take the life trajectory as
my unit of analysis. Rather than society writ large, that is, the primary en-
tity being studied is the course of individual lives, and how that course
varies across youth from different birth cohorts who came of age in different social worlds.

My approach in no way denies that the indicators commonly used to
assess character capture real variability among individuals. Nor do I deny
the importance of morality, individual capacity, self-control, family dynamics, or the structural limits imposed by race and class inequality. On
the contrary, I take these distinctions to be an essential part of the story—
just not in the ways typically asserted. I measure individual and family differences directly, from self-control to temperament, and from family stability to family troubles with mental health and substance abuse. Rather
than duck individualist or family-background theories of criminality, in
other words, I put them to a strict empirical test to discover the extent to
which certain individual and family characteristics can explain differences
in crime and criminalization between cohorts.

The results provide fresh insight into how social change exerts power
over what we typically consider to be quite personal and interior characteristics. This temporal influence simultaneously shapes the salient features
of racial and class inequality in society. Furthermore, studying multiple
birth cohorts growing up in different times enables us to identify which
individual or family factors remain immune to the vagaries of social change.

As I engage with such questions, I take antisocial behavior seriously.
Moral evaluations of the actors aside, violent and destructive behaviors certainly inflict real damage. Some accounts of punishment seem to minimize

the harms of criminal behavior by viewing official criminality solely from the perspective of discrimination by the criminal justice system. The damage inflicted by violent, predatory, and destructive behavior is real, however, and is itself a form of inequality and an important part of the story of how individuals become trapped by the criminal justice system. Troubled families exist, as well, and often extend across multiple generations—as revealed by this study's recording of criminal behaviors and conflicts with the law among the subjects' parents, grandparents, aunts and uncles, cousins, siblings, and other relatives. It is essential that we acknowledge these realities as part of the larger picture of crime and criminality.

*　*　*

Using original data to examine how the birth lottery of history and the mark of time shape life chances, this book recasts the concepts of character and criminal propensity in a way that transcends the liberal-versus-conservative binary currently dominating discussions. One may wonder about the goal of studying historical change given a temporal window of just over a quarter-century. Looked at differently, however, the fact that large differences have occurred in such a small window of change, in some cases a few years, is important in its own right. Scholars and the public alike typically think in terms of the *longue durée* of history, typically spanning centuries, but short-term social change turns out to be an equally powerful force in shaping our lives.

As we try to form judgments about other people's character and who they really are, we routinely ask questions like How are you? and Where are you from? But by the end of this book, I hope to show that finding out when someone came of age—what moment in history left its mark on them—is just as telling as whatever those questions might elicit. I want to show, in short, how focusing on *when* rather than *who* transforms our understanding of human development, crime, and justice.

PART I

WHEN WE ARE

CHAPTER 1

Changing Lives, Changing Times

Each of us belongs to a birth cohort—the set of people born around the same time who share our historical context. Our lives unfold within specific, ever-changing historical moments. While timing's influence might be hard to prove in any single life, following multiple birth cohorts reveals something crucial: how historical changes and social structures shape group destinies.

In a static world, successive birth cohorts would meet the same fate. But our world is dynamic. On the cusp of the Great Depression, sociologist Karl Mannheim highlighted how changing sociohistorical environments gave young people distinctive shared experiences that influenced both older and future cohorts.[1] In the mid-1960s, as landmark Civil Rights legislation began transforming American society, demographer Norman Ryder declared the birth cohort to be a central concept for studying social change. He articulated the principle of cohort differences in aging: As we age, our individual experiences intertwine with social change, and when that change is substantial, it distinguishes different birth cohorts' life experiences.[2]

This way of thinking, called by C. Wright Mills the "sociological imagination," compels us to grasp both history and biography, and their interrelations within society.[3] Glen Elder Jr.'s *Children of the Great Depression* exemplifies this approach, showing how family economic hardships affected children differently depending on their age during that tumultuous time. Young children proved more sensitive to economic disruption than older ones.[4] Birth cohorts illuminate social change's impact even within single generations. As Elder later argued, individual and cohort life courses are embedded in and shaped by the times and places they experience.[5] Birth cohorts distinctly position people in time, allowing us to track the interplay of history and society across their lives.

This temporal positioning becomes crucial because both people and their available roles change as society changes, making each birth cohort different from its predecessors—sometimes subtly, sometimes profoundly. Economist Richard Easterlin showed that even birth cohort size can have enduring consequences for a generation's shared economic well-being.[6] Less appreciated is the two-way causation: Even as individuals are shaped by their world, they also shape it. As gerontologist Matilda White Riley explained, successive cohorts age in new ways, generating future changes in social structure.[7] Social change thus distinguishes what it means to grow up for different birth cohorts, the members of which then go on to transform the very structures in which they age.

Surprisingly, leading accounts of life-course change in crime and character have not widely applied this cohort-analytic approach. This oversight is significant. Even Ryder noted, with evident mockery, that traditional developmental accounts emphasizing early personality crystallization in childhood become "embarrassing" in the face of social change.[8] If personality is stable, how do we explain profound societal changes reshaping lives and personalities within single generations? Understanding the life course requires more than biological or psychological development theories, or even empirical studies of individuals over time or between generations. I take up Mills's challenge to link social change and social structure to changing lives—to biography—and ultimately to the very personal qualities of character.

AS THE WORLD TURNED

No one predicted it at the time, but American children born near the end of the twentieth century were destined to come of age during a paradoxical and profound societal transformation. Their lives would be shaped by an

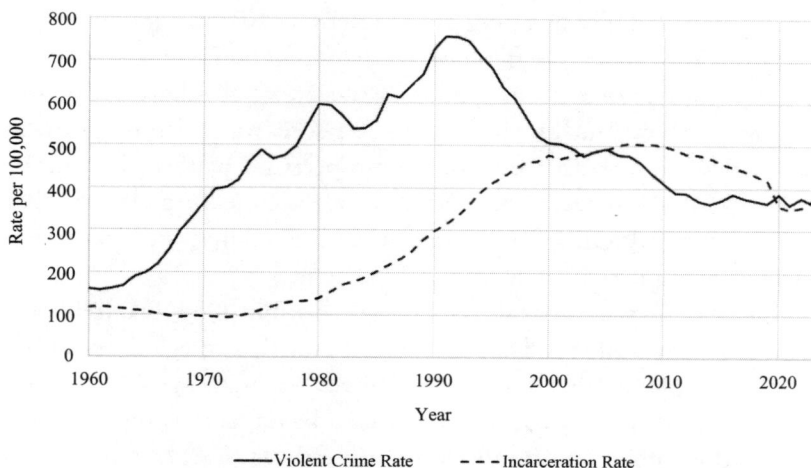

Figure 1.1. Transformation of American Violence and Incarceration, 1960–2023. Violent crime is here defined as murder / nonnegligent manslaughter, rape, robbery, and aggravated assault per 100,000 residents. Incarceration rate is defined as the number of sentenced prisoners under state or federal correctional jurisdiction per 100,000 residents. *Data sources:* Bureau of Justice Statistics; Uniform Crime Reporting System (2019, 2024).

era of crime, punishment, and inequality fundamentally different from that of birth cohorts just a decade earlier. Figure 1.1 illustrates two trends that reveal the drastic nature of this historical transition. Starting in the mid-1960s, the country experienced almost continuously rising violence for nearly three decades. Rioting, population flight from urban neighborhoods, deindustrialization, fiscal collapse, environmental degradation, and growing perceptions of social disorder combined with exploding crime rates to reinforce the idea that America's cities were dying—especially older eastern and midwestern Rust Belt cities.[9]

The increase in violence in the 1960s and early 1970s preceded the rise of what we now know as mass incarceration, which, as Figure 1.1 shows, didn't begin its climb until 1975. Later, it rose most sharply in concert with the eruption of urban violence in the late 1980s and early 1990s.[10] The violence epidemic was a turning point in American history. The nation's largest city, New York, topped 2,200 murders in 1990. It is no accident that the "broken windows" theory of urban decay and aggressive policing, which emphasizes the targeting of minor crimes (such as graffiti and loitering) in order to increase the appearance of neighborhood order and lawfulness, appealed to and was applied by the city's politicians and police.[11] The violence, combined with the city's response, was a defining time for young New Yorkers. In Chicago, the prospects for children born in the 1980s and 1990s appeared even grimmer at the time. Incarceration there had also climbed quickly, and more than fifty children aged fourteen or under were murdered in Chicago in 1992 alone.

One death in particular shook Chicago. Born in 1985, Dantrell Davis spent his early childhood in a poor and racially segregated neighborhood—the infamous Cabrini-Green Homes—on Chicago's Near North Side. Although conditions were known to be dangerous on the streets around this public housing project, the city was shocked when seven-year-old Dantrell, holding hands with his mother as he walked to school on a sunny October morning, was gunned down by a gang member aiming to take out a rival nearby. Dantrell's death made national news and became a tragic symbol of public housing in Chicago. "Killing Our Children," a Pulitzer Prize–winning series by the *Chicago Tribune,* captured the mood. As one observer of Chicago puts it: "Dantrell Davis changed Chicago forever."[12] The urban crisis, especially among those dubbed by William Julius Wilson the "truly disadvantaged," did not just take place in Chicago or New York.[13] Nearly every city in America witnessed many of the same trends, especially rising violence, increasing concentrated poverty, and rising incarceration.

The case of Freddie Gray, born in 1989 in the Sandtown-Winchester neighborhood of Baltimore, is another story of growing up in this turbulent era—but with additional turns. In 2015, his name became a byword not for gang violence but for aggressive policing tactics in America's poor Black communities. Less well known is that, before his death in the back of a Baltimore police van, Gray had suffered a lifetime of setbacks. Among early adversities, he grew up in a severely impoverished neighborhood and was diagnosed in infancy with dangerous levels of lead exposure; in a test before he turned two, his blood was found to contain a remarkably high 37 micrograms of lead per deciliter.[14] (Current standards from the US Centers for Disease Control and Prevention call for the monitoring of children with just 3.5 micrograms per deciliter.) A lawsuit brought on behalf of the boy and his sisters in 2008 sought (and won) damages from their landlord for lead poisoning after Freddie's impulsivity, aggression, and suspensions from school led to a diagnosis of Attention Deficit Hyperactivity Disorder (ADHD). According to the suit, his two sisters also had damaging lead levels in their blood, which caused multiple educational, behavioral, and medical problems. Freddie dropped out of high school after numerous suspensions and was arrested over a dozen times before his death.

Life-altering challenges like these defined the experience of growing up and coming of age for children born in the 1980s and early 1990s, especially for disadvantaged and minority children. Whether marked by arrest, imprisonment, exposure to violence, school suspensions, or toxic lead exposure, children growing up in US inner cities, like Dantrell Davis and Freddie Gray, faced dim prospects from the very start of their lives. In the case of Dantrell, the violence was so pervasive it swept up even the most innocent. For Freddie, it was the violence of the police, piled on top of a literally poisoned childhood. Dantrell's plight was an especially pernicious aspect of the broader urban crisis that at the time seemed intractable and terrifying. I remember this personally because, as a resident of the Chicago area in the mid-1990s, I and most people I knew had little hope that things would turn around anytime soon.

I was wrong, as we all were. Instead of the widespread predictions of urban collapse, the opposite happened. Violence plummeted and cities that had been hemorrhaging residents began to grow. The dramatic drop in violence portrayed in Figure 1.1 reflects what the criminologist Franklin Zimring called "the great American crime decline."[15] The well-being of children also improved, and mortality rates declined. Incarceration rates started to decrease around 2010 and have been declining ever since, and lead exposure rates fell. In New York City, rates of violence dropped to levels not seen since the late 1950s, puzzling even the experts. Chicago boomed, too, at least in its central core, and Baltimore's Inner Harbor filled with activity. These cities are not unique: In the 2000s, a new vibrancy emerged in scores of cities and, at least in some neighborhoods and even during the COVID-19 crisis, renewal took hold beyond the downtown glimmer, often in the heart of areas long considered doomed.

In Chicago, this renewal led to the demolishing of the projects in Dantrell's Cabrini-Green neighborhood—as directed by the Plan for Transformation launched in 2000 by the Chicago Housing Authority.[16] New housing, most of it private, rose in their place. Today, one of the last

Figure 1.2. Dantrell Davis Way, Chicago, March 2025. A recent photograph shows the transformation of the former Cabrini-Green Homes and the block on which Dantrell Davis was murdered. © Robert J. Sampson.

vacant lots, on the block where Dantrell was murdered and presumably a site for future redevelopment, faces a street renamed Dantrell Davis Way. This grassy expanse, pictured in Figure 1.2, sits at a halfway point on the path from the deep poverty and tragic violence of Dantrell's youth and a hopefully revitalized community in the future. Sandtown-Winchester, Freddie Gray's childhood neighborhood in Baltimore, was also targeted for revitalization.[17] An era of urban peace arrived, at least relative to the urban crisis of the 1980s and 1990s.[18] Were Dantrell Davis born on his home street today, his life prospects would be radically different.

Or maybe not. One of the sobering facts that we will come to see in the data is that while violence can abate, it can also return. For example, although Chicago's overall rate of murder is lower than it was in the early

1990s, 2020 witnessed a decisive surge in killings, up 50 percent from the prior year, and in the spring of 2021, the shootings of young children like Dantrell again made the national news. On a Sunday afternoon in April, Jaslyn Adams, age seven, was shot to death in her father's car while waiting in a McDonald's drive-thru in Chicago's North Lawndale neighborhood. A few weeks earlier and less than a mile-and-a-half south, in the city's Little Village neighborhood, thirteen-year-old Adam Toledo was killed by gunfire in an alley by a police officer called to investigate possible shootings. Perhaps most shocking, one-year-old Sincere Gaston was shot to death riding in his mother's car in the city's Englewood neighborhood on a particularly violent Saturday in June, the same day that a ten-year-old girl was killed when a stray bullet ripped through a window at her home. Arbitrary lethal gun violence is especially tragic, and gun homicides reached historic highs in Chicago and other cities in the early 2020s, surpassing accidents as the leading cause of death among children.[19] Despite falling homicide rates since that time, guns remain a singular danger to child well-being in the United States.

But social change goes beyond gun violence. Income inequality grew sharply and unexpectedly in the twenty-first century, and criminal justice crises erupted anew with high-profile aggressive patrol tactics and killings by the police, followed by widespread protests in African American communities—notably including both Chicago and Baltimore. The large-scale unrest prompted by the Chicago police killing of Laquan McDonald and its cover-up by city leaders, for example, preceded the George Floyd protests by three years. The suburbanization of poverty and its correlated adversities increased as well, and an opioid epidemic emerged, although this one, unlike the crack cocaine ravages of the late 1980s, also hit predominantly white communities. The net result is that American cities today are simultaneously better and worse off than just twenty-five years ago.

Dantrell Davis never lived to experience these sweeping and contradictory changes, so we will never know how an altered environment might have changed his life course. Freddie Gray made it into his twenties, but his life was marred by misfortune at each step along the way. Virtually all the adversities that marked Freddie's development—concentrated poverty, bodily poisoning from lead, exposure to violence in his early life, and various struggles in adulthood—were exacerbated by harms inflicted by criminal justice interventions, despite the great decline in violence. Dantrell

and Freddie's birth cohorts, children of the late 1980s and early 1990s, encountered historical circumstances radically different than those faced by
children growing up just a decade later. Both cohorts and their resulting
circumstances were shaped by changing structures of policing, violent
crime, environmental toxicity, behavioral norms, and other salient features
of growing up, which in turn were influenced by the life courses of earlier
cohorts. In this interplay of influences, we see the often defining impact
of when you are born on what sort of life you live.

Andre Lewis, to recall a name from the Introduction, was a contemporary of Freddie Gray and a bit older than Dantrell Davis; he was an
African American male born and raised as one of the truly disadvantaged
in the 1980s and early 1990s. Yet Andre was at least fortunate enough to
live to see adulthood. When my research team first interviewed him in
1995, he was fifteen years old. He was raised in the racially segregated West
Englewood neighborhood on the South Side, which at the time had a
poverty rate over 30 percent. The rate of single-parent families was even
higher, at 50 percent. Andre was raised in a single-parent family of nine
with an annual income of less than $5,000—near the very bottom of the
socioeconomic distribution. These childhood conditions are a virtual
stereotype of predicted failure later in life, and indeed Andre was arrested
at age nineteen, like many of his birth-cohort peers.

Darnell Jackson, also featured in the Introduction, shared with Andre
the same neighborhood and risk factors in childhood. Growing up a decade
later, though, Darnell was lucky to be born under a better sign, so to
speak—one that helped spare him a criminal record. This contrast highlights a crucial point: Birth year itself shapes outcomes, even when other
background factors remain similar. This is not to say that birth year is de-
terministic. Many factors shape our lives, and when we identify children
from similarly troubled (or privileged) backgrounds and follow them forward in time, we find considerable heterogeneity in their outcomes. This
variation exists for children in all walks of life, challenging our ability to
predict individual behavior, especially amid ongoing social change. This
book examines the powerful societal transformations that influenced the
lives of children like Dantrell, Freddie, Andre, and Darnell.

Very often the search for why children turn out differently is cast in
terms of race or class, which for these boys was the same. Or it is cast in
individual terms of personal character, such as whether one has sufficient

"grit." But does showing grit—the dogged work ethic and self-control often believed to presage success—bring similar rewards in different times, as social change rewrites the standards for success? A narrow focus on the American narrative of individual mobility is another form of the character trap, not only because meaningful upward mobility from severe disadvantage—especially through the fabled triumphs of "beating the odds" and "escaping from poverty"—is not the norm, but also because a focus on individual striving deflects our attention from the broad and powerful impacts of social change at the population level. Blaming downward mobility on individual character flaws—a common attribution—similarly obscures underlying structural constraints such as changing economic conditions.

We can avoid the character trap by focusing our attention on birth cohorts and the evolution of their life courses within varying historical periods and social structures. We can learn a lot, in other words, by foregrounding the temporal counterfactual perspective, considering people born in Andre's shoes but at a different time—people like Darnell.

A MULTI-COHORT STRATEGY

Selecting individuals who beat the odds, or fall from grace, and then looking backward to discern the exceptional individual properties or personal narratives that led to their fates is a popular but misguided strategy. We can discover more about the larger forces shaping all lives within and across cohorts by focusing on the broad spectrum of lived experience in a population-based sample of multiple birth cohorts—prospectively and through changing times.

This book presents the results of such a study, based on a unique longitudinal endeavor that began back in the mid-1990s—the Project on Human Development in Chicago Neighborhoods (PHDCN). This long-term study records the lives of children like Dantrell, Freddie, Darnell, Andre, and many others of their diverse birth cohorts—the well-off, middle-class, and poor, the Black, white, and brown, the male and female, the immigrant and native-born, the ostensibly smart and not so smart—who grew up at different moments during the social transformation of crime, punishment, and inequality in America in the late twentieth and early twenty-first centuries. These structural changes, especially in community violence, policing, and environmental inequality, provide a theoretical umbrella to study cohort variation. Reaching beyond the narratives of a few unique individuals, I examine a representative sample of children who were born between 1980 and 1995 and who came of age at different times from 1995 to the early 2020s, a period when all three sets of changes were in play.

To achieve the aims of the book, I push beyond the two major lines of inquiry in my scholarly research over the last three decades: the course of crime in individual lives, and the course of neighborhood inequality and change. Although I did not realize it at the time, my research with John Laub on the crime and punishment of Boston adolescent males transitioning to adulthood in the mid-twentieth century was critiquing, in a different language, the idea of character early on. Drawing on ideas and findings about these young men from two previous books coauthored with Laub, *Crime in the Making: Pathways and Turning Points through Life,* and *Shared Beginnings, Divergent Lives: Delinquent Boys to Age 70,* I bring the "criminology of character," as it were, to the forefront of growing up today. I might disagree with the interpretation that the great philosopher John Rawls gave it, but criminal behavior—and more so, being officially labeled criminal—is central to how our society defines character. But so, too, are family and neighborhood processes central to understanding character— another theme of my research in criminology and later on urban and community sociology in *Great American City: Chicago and the Enduring Neighborhood Effect* and associated articles.

Character has been missing as a critical component of my earlier research because it is only now, with decades of rich, historical, multi-cohort data, that I can show how children have differentially experienced societal transformations of criminality and environmental challenges in the course of growing up during the past quarter-century. Also central to understanding character are family and neighborhoods, which can carry marks of criminality and violence—and in the case of the latter, toxic contamination. A narrow and individualistic understanding of character causes us to miss essential facts. Tying together individual development, family life, the environment, and societal change is the unfinished business of my research—and, I would argue, much social inquiry. Looking across cohorts over time provides a wider analytical window which, generatively, leads back to many of society's core assumptions about what we often conceive of as the narrowest and most individual of attributes, character.

I take this approach by leveraging original data from five waves of interviews and records—a coordinated set of follow-ups with multiple birth cohorts sampled by the PHDCN. Thus, to refer to this full, three-decade effort, I use the acronym PHDCN+. These contemporary data, described more fully in Chapter 3, contrast sharply with the white and working-class males of *Crime in the Making* who grew up in Boston during an earlier era of social transformation, a time without mass incarceration and present-day inequalities, and with a sample very unlike the racially diverse cohorts, equally male and female, in Chicago.

For one cohort, the original study started literally at birth, as pregnant mothers and infants were enrolled soon after delivery, which alone is rare in the social sciences, particularly when it comes to the study of crime and punishment. I track this representative infant cohort, not one selected from administrative records or on a specific trait, from 1995 through the course of childhood and late adolescence, over twenty-five years in all. But equally relevant, I pair this infant cohort with the study of three adolescent cohorts—centered on children aged nine, twelve, and fifteen at the beginning of the study and again representative of their respective ages—studied at the same time, with data collected on these cohorts into their mid- to late thirties and early forties. Figure 1.3 sketches in visual form the design of this longitudinal and multi-cohort research spanning five waves of data collection. A vast amount of information was collected, allowing for

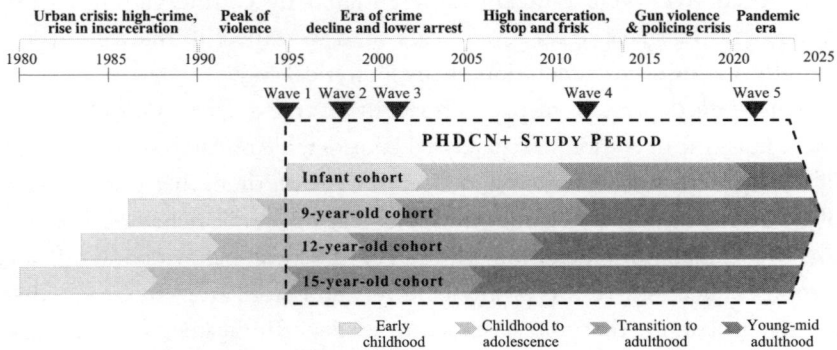

Figure 1.3. Multiple Birth-Cohort Design of the PHDCN+. The Project on Human Development in Chicago Neighborhoods and Its Extensions (PHDCN+) was designed to track the life course of study cohorts in a changing crime, punishment, and inequality landscape.

measurement of respondents' individual qualities and at the same time permitting careful examination of family, social, and especially historical context.

Integrating these data, I can view the children's experiences longitudinally, or over time, with each cohort aging through a distinct moment of history. Brief descriptors of key temporal patterns in the extended PHDCN+ are included at the top of Figure 1.3, reflecting the varied forms of toxic and harsh environments in which cohorts grew up, and which infiltrated their minds and bodies. The longitudinal and multi-cohort aspect of this research design thus allows me to examine how life events such as official criminality and violence simultaneously vary by individual age and historical location, independent of traditional risk factors. Going back centuries, for example, an oft-noted pattern is that criminality increases from adolescence to the late teens or early adulthood, after which it declines in what criminologists call "desistance" from crime. This pattern often evokes a developmental or even biological account, but aging and history are fundamentally intertwined and march together. By studying multiple cohorts who live through the same slice of history but at different ages, I shed new light on the life-course processes by which criminal character is differentially imposed by society.

Notably, mine is not a generational account. All the children in my study are members of the so-called Millennial generation. But they are not united or of a piece, and they do not share a common identity. As will become clear, their lives were radically differentiated by countervailing social changes in the space of far fewer years than we expect to matter so profoundly. Cohort, not generation, is my analytical tool.

This work departs from prior efforts in several other ways. While the era of mass incarceration has generated considerable research on the effects of having a criminal conviction and serving prison time, that research has often been disconnected from criminological studies of behavior. Precursors to incarceration, including criminal or antisocial behavior and official responses such as arrest, typically emerge well before an individual's first imprisonment. Furthermore, compelling evidence indicates that behaviors leading to punishment are concentrated among a relatively small number of individuals and families, both concurrently and across generations. These patterns complicate any simple portrayal of the contemporary criminal justice system as merely discriminatory. Though the system certainly can be

and often is discriminatory in many ways, incarceration as a societal phenomenon is too large and complex to be reduced to the actions—whether
malicious or inadvertent—of individuals within the justice system. Broader
social forces are at work.

A nuanced examination of criminalization requires both widening our
focus beyond incarceration and studying criminal justice involvement
across individual life courses and historical periods. Criminal justice operates as a sequential system of actions, with incarceration serving as a key
endpoint, but the process begins—officially, at least—with arrest. This
entry point matters profoundly across justice systems worldwide. In his
searing account of Soviet imprisonment, Aleksandr Solzhenitsyn opens *The
Gulag Archipelago* with a chapter simply titled "Arrest." In it, he writes: "Arrest! Need it be said that it is a breaking point in your life?"[20] While incarceration is severe, as it certainly was for Solzhenitsyn, the process leading
up to it is itself a form of punishment, reflected in the stigmatizing effects
of arrest on later outcomes. Having a criminal record not only precedes
incarceration but strongly influences it, as prosecutors routinely cite prior
arrests to justify harsher sentencing. Understanding the changing conditions of how people first enter the legal system must therefore be a primary
consideration.

Figure 1.4 gives an early glimpse of my approach that traces the official
criminal records of individuals in the study through 2020, allowing a composite picture of criminalization and its changes over the life course.[21] We
can first see the similar rise and fall of arrests by age for two of the birth
cohorts, born in 1980 and 1995 (other cohorts will be introduced in later
chapters). Yet simultaneously, we can see the distinctive experiences of each
cohort, with sharply different magnitudes of arrest (in the varying heights
of the curves) and ages at which arrest continues to occur (in the varying
widths of the curves). The probability of arrest rises sharply for both cohorts in adolescence, for example, but around age eighteen, those born in
1995 experienced a decline. By contrast, the probability of arrest continues
to rise for a few more years into early adulthood for those born in 1980. At
the peak of official criminality, twenty-year-olds in 2000 were arrested at
more than double the rate of twenty-year-olds in 2015. Short-run history
apparently makes a very large difference.

After their respective peaks, this cohort divergence continues. The chances
of arrest for the mid-1990s cohort declines to a low at age twenty-five that

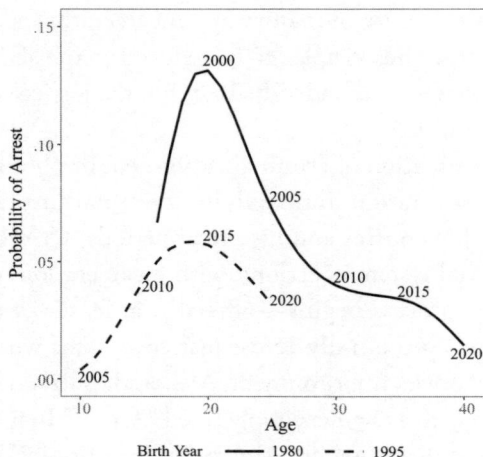

Figure 1.4. Changing Likelihood of Being Arrested. Likelihoods of being arrested vary by age and birth cohort.

isn't reached by the older cohort until age thirty-five. Crucially, I will show in a later chapter that neither the socio-demographic composition of these cohorts (such as race, income, family structure, or immigration status) nor the character-related composition of cohorts (such as impulsiveness or antisocial behavior) can explain these differences. Age and criminalization take on different meanings over time, and therefore so does the meaning of character. Perhaps counterintuitively, it may even be that in times of high incarceration or arrest, like the period experienced by the older cohort in Figure 1.4, the stigma that any single arrest carries for an individual's perceived character is less than in times when arrest is rarer, such as for the younger cohort. The signal that official criminality sends cannot be divorced from its changing sociohistorical context.

It is notable, as well, that the probability of arrest rises sharply during the teenage years, a time of life when neuroscientists claim the brain is maturing the fastest. If fifteen-year-olds are less mature or make more impulsive decisions than, say, twenty-year-olds, why do the latter show much higher rates of arrest, especially for the oldest cohort? Taken at face value, the maturing brain argument, which was given authority by the Supreme Court, sits uneasily with the data.[22] Consider, too, that declines in arrest after age twenty converge to similar levels at very different ages for the two cohorts. At the least, Figure 1.4 implies that the pace of brain maturing interacts with history, and that a supposedly stable trait like self-control cannot explain the changes.

Piecing together the story emerging from Figures 1.1 through 1.4 motivates the strategy of studying children growing up, coming of age, and becoming adults under changing conditions of crime, punishment, and inequality. More precisely, I study children at different ages for long periods of time—before, during, and after the peak ages of criminalization—and through rising and falling eras of aggressive policing and high incarceration. The children I study also lived through changing regimes of crime, gun violence, lead exposure, and cynicism toward the law. And their parents—from whom we similarly collected detailed data, including their own criminal behavior, substance abuse, mental health, and criminalization—came of age during their own defining moments of the urban crisis and the historic rise in violence in the 1960s and 1970s, followed by mass incarceration. As a result of this unprecedented breadth and depth of multigenerational and multi-cohort data, the design of the study which informs this book allows me to capture the consequences that the state and the environment impart within and across cohorts.

*   *   *

The intellectual history of the life course of both crime and punishment is important in its own right, but this literature is often disconnected. In Chapter 2, I therefore spend some time connecting the dots and articulating the ideas guiding this book, including how the classic theory of criminal labeling, originating in the early part of the twentieth century, can be repurposed and integrated with a life-course theory of how formal and informal social control in the contemporary era have been reshaped by social change. Chapter 3 describes how the longitudinal cohort study represented in Figure 1.3 was designed, from birth to adulthood, to permit examination of these and other hypotheses. Measuring what counts in the lives of individuals is crucial, so I detail the various measurement strategies that test and support the ideas of the book.

Part II presents the empirical backbone of the book. Here, I summarize and present data that bear on key life (and death) experiences, including arrest, violence, the carrying and use of guns, toxic environmental exposures, mortality, and hence more generally, adult well-being. Uniting these myriad and sometimes disparate experiences emphasizes the substantive influence of social context and societal change captured in both intra-cohort and inter-cohort variations. Put simply, this strategy allows me to focus on *when* we are and how that interacts with and affects *who* we are. I also dissect the mechanisms of social change that have transpired over the last quarter-century, highlighting organizational changes in law enforcement and leading hypotheses for the large-scale behavioral changes in crime.

Part III examines the broader implications of this book's findings for both theory and practice, particularly those policies that rely on predicting individual criminal behavior and theories that emphasize personal propensity. The final chapter, "Defining Character Up," shows how these findings offer an alternative framework for understanding human development and ultimately the proper role of character in American society.

CHAPTER 2

Becoming Criminal

The life-course paradigm remains a significant innovation in the study of crime, but to understand its enduring influence, we must connect it to an earlier breakthrough: labeling theory. Life-course research, with its focus on how lives unfold over time, has sparked new longitudinal studies and shifted scholarly attention—and later criminal justice reform—away from "static" snapshots of individuals toward a more dynamic, long-term view.

Rather than competing, the life-course paradigm and labeling theory complement each other, helping us understand complex phenomena like social change. Together, they add insight to the multi-cohort research design this book describes and expose fundamental flaws in how we think about character and criminality—especially when we fall into the character trap. To explain this connection, let me first outline labeling theory's origins.

Frank Tannenbaum took an unusual path to becoming a Columbia University history professor in the 1930s. Originally trained in economics, he spent years in Mexico studying rural education, writing about Latin American history and race relations, and advising Mexico's president. But his most formative experience came earlier: As a young radical in his twenties, Tannenbaum led the "Wobblies" labor union and organized a 1915 protest of unemployed workers demanding food and shelter from New York City churches. His arrest and year-long imprisonment on Blackwell's (now Roosevelt) Island—the harshest sentence among all protesters—left an indelible mark. Though he later abandoned radical politics, his firsthand experience with criminal labeling and harsh prison conditions never left his mind.[1]

We can see this influence in *Crime and Community*, which Tannenbaum published in 1938 and which went on to become the most cited work of his career. He drew attention with his concept of "the dramatization of evil" and by focusing on the importance of what he called "tagging"—the process by which individuals are officially defined, identified, and segregated for special treatment.[2] Many people commit deviant acts, he reasoned, but only some are arrested, and of those, relatively few are confined. Tannenbaum went on to argue that being officially tagged, or marked as a criminal, became a kind of a trap by stimulating the very traits of official concern: The "person becomes the thing he is described as being."[3]

In just a few sentences, Tannenbaum's conceptual intervention captured the essence of what later came to be known as "labeling theory" and a major part of today's narrative on mass incarceration—the notion that official labels themselves, which are at best imperfectly applied to actual criminal behavior, have the unintended consequence of reinforcing the very thing society means to stamp out. Developed, ironically, during a time of low incarceration, Tannenbaum's notion of tagging was an early conceptualization of the self-fulfilling prophecy, later popularized by the Columbia sociologist Robert Merton, whereby actions or predictions (here, an early criminal label encompasses both) cause criminality to become more pronounced over time. Crucial, in my view, is not just Tannenbaum's implicit claim about the effect of labeling on later behavior, but his insights on the centrality of the first tag. For without the initial tag, the process of criminalization is not set in motion. It follows, then, that investigating the causes of initial tagging is essential for making sense of the label and its consequences.[4]

It was not until Howard Becker published *Outsiders* in 1963, however, that the labeling theory of deviance broadly influenced both public opinion and policy. Becker became famous by transforming sociologists' ideas of what it means to be a deviant.[5] His now-classic intervention, also written during a time of relatively low violence and incarceration, upset the conventional apple cart by claiming that deviance was simply behavior that officials defined as deviant. Criminals were outsiders who broke society's rules.[6] Instead of taking for granted that an official record of crime indicates antisocial behavior, *Outsiders* put criminal definitions and rule enforcement under analytical scrutiny.

Although Becker's definition of deviance has been criticized as circular, his emphasis on labeling highlighted the amplification of officially marked behavior, consistent with Tannenbaum's dramatization of evil and an early form of the character trap. Becker also stressed the importance of studying stability and change in official processing, including the timing and stages of rule enforcement—what he called its "natural history."[7] By this, Becker meant to encourage a focus on the common processes and social order by which rules are enforced and deviant careers unfold, rather than on what was unique in each instance.

A rich flowering of research on the sociology of deviance and labeling theory ensued, all well before mass incarceration. Additional work in 1974 examined what John Hagan influentially called the "extra-legal" sources of official criminal entanglement, especially race and class discrimination in the criminal justice system.[8] Other scholars, including me, have broadened this vein of research to include intergenerational family and neighborhood disparities. Labeling theory played a critical role in the literature that has established the disproportionately high rates of incarceration among African Americans and the poor in the present era.[9] Surprisingly, this theory sometimes goes unacknowledged. For example, not once in Michelle Alexander's influential *The New Jim Crow* are classics like Becker's *Outsiders* or Tannenbaum's *Crime and Community* cited. Elizabeth Hinton's *From the War on Poverty to the War on Crime,* by contrast, directly engages the early contributions of Tannenbaum's "dramatization of evil" thesis.[10]

The key to understanding labeling theory's continued relevance is to connect its claims to a more recent but no less innovative development in the study of crime—the life-course paradigm, and especially its historical sensitivity. Although typically limited to single-cohort designs, life-course research on crime prioritizes longitudinal studies, which have provided researchers and reformers with the data necessary to analyze criminality and criminal labeling not as the result of isolated acts, but as threads within the larger, dynamic tapestry of life. Because Becker's and Tannenbaum's emphasis on the process and natural history of labeling is explicitly developmental in nature, it is worth spending some time on basic insights, general theoretical claims, and unanswered questions introduced by life-course theory. Each of these is scrutinized in later chapters, but a brief survey of the evolution of a research topic as complex as criminality is not only useful analytically, but also interesting in its own right.

To help make this case, I do not engage in a typical academic review of literature. Such reviews exist elsewhere.[11] Rather, I sketch the intellectual content of ideas in life-course inquiry and point out the strengths and weaknesses of labeling theory, as well as how those weaknesses can be overcome. Details on sources may be found in the notes. Telling the story of how these traditions come together yields fresh insights regarding the pathway to becoming a criminal in the last quarter-century.

TURNING POINTS IN THE LIFE COURSE

In American society, there has traditionally been a well-defined and privileged sequence of roles and social transitions—such as going to school, getting a job, and getting married—that are enacted at more-or-less expected ages throughout an individual's life. Imagine a person's trajectory through life, or a portion of it, focusing on long-term patterns of behavior at crucial transitions. Think, for example, of work careers that are punctuated by various age-graded events—first job, second job, promotion, and then perhaps a layoff or prolonged unemployment. Some careers unfold steadily or in a highly stable way as individuals age, whereas for others, work life is choppy and lacks consistency. In still others, transitional events lead to what life-course scholars call *turning points*—systematic changes in the trajectory of an individual's life. For example, being laid off unexpectedly from a steady job is a potential turning point that can bring on depression or marital conflict, possibly triggering other changes like an increase in substance abuse.

Crime might not be a normative pathway or a career in the same sense that lawful employment is, but it nonetheless appears to follow a distinctive trajectory across the life course. Recall Figure 1.4, which showed that the probability of arrest rapidly increases in adolescence and then declines more slowly but still rather continuously in adulthood, at least on average. This pattern is not unusual. Some scholars have argued that the distinctive shape of rising and then declining crime with age is so prevalent in existing research studies as to be "invariant" in nature.[12] Whether truly invariant or not, the age-crime curve, as it is commonly called, suggests that criminal behavior changes in important but predictable ways across a life.

In the late 1980s and early 1990s, my colleague John Laub and I proposed a life-course theory to help make sense of the intriguing relationship between age and crime. The life-course paradigm is united by an interdisciplinary analytic approach rather than a specific hypothesis, and its focus on developmental and social processes dictates longitudinal inquiry, typically emphasizing the long-term study of lives.[13] Adopting this general approach, Laub and I emphasized both stability and change in crime at different ages or life stages, and the turning points that shift people into and out of crime.[14] Going beyond the stable qualities of individuals traditionally associated with crime, such as personality or demographic makeup, we examined longer-term trajectories of crime in childhood, adolescence, and adulthood by analyzing longitudinal data among a thousand boys born in Boston in the late 1920s.[15] Although we did not pursue it at the time, already we were attending to factors influencing criminality that are sensitive to social change, such as marital status and military service. But because this was a longitudinal study of boys born within a few years of each other, the boys all aged through the same historical moments together, making it impossible for us to treat social change as a meaningful part of our analysis.

Rather, the idea we pursued was that crime was more likely to occur when an individual's ties or bonds to society were weakened, and that this relationship took different forms by age across the life course. We argued, for example, that informal social controls in childhood and adolescence, such as compassionate discipline and parental supervision of everyday activities, were strong predictors of lower rates of delinquency even among poor and otherwise highly disadvantaged boys.[16] Our emphasis was less on material deprivation, race (the boys were all white, although diverse in ethnicity), or deterrence by criminal justice institutions (like the police) than it was on inhibitions to crime governed by a person's ties to valued others, who in adolescence are typically family members. We referred to this general approach as the "age-graded theory of informal social control."

Extending this logic to later stages of life, we argued that salient life events and social ties in adulthood, such as a cohesive marriage, steady work, and military service, can stop or at least modulate criminal behavior even among those with troubled childhoods or who committed crimes earlier in life. We conceptualized these shifts as turning points along a life-course trajectory: Getting married, for example, can lead people to move neighborhoods, switch jobs, or change the number and type of friends with whom they associate. As one reflection of this, we discovered that marriage changed the drinking patterns of even the orneriest of men through a kind of supervision, analogous to the parental monitoring of adolescents, which promoted desisting from crime. As the wife of one man in our study blurted out during our interview, "It is not how many beers you have, it's who you drink with that matters." She prodded her husband to stay out of rowdy bars and let him know the costs of messing up: "It's them or me."[17] He was certainly no angel, but he was not robbing liquor stores like many of the other men in our study.

Our claim, in short, was that turning points *at all ages* have the power to modify patterns of criminal behavior in ways that cannot be explained by personal disposition or the individual differences in character that are commonly thought to emerge in childhood and that remain more-or-less constant, such as self-control. This in no way implies that childhood factors are unimportant—they are the foundation on which all else follows. But childhood is not destiny in the ways that many traditional and contemporary criminologists assert—especially those who believe that the small group of hardened chronic offenders who are responsible for most crime had their criminal propensities determined in childhood. At all ages, our research showed the importance of informal social controls for inhibiting crime.

The last few decades have witnessed an explosion of research on age, crime, and the life course. Some scholars have explicitly adopted the concept of career to explore crime (studying, for example, "criminal careers"), while others have invoked a developmental psychological framework, examining concentrations of crime among individuals of particular personality types.[18] David Farrington and Donald West's work with the Cambridge Study in Delinquent Development is an exemplar of the developmental approach, highlighting the emergence and long-term patterns of antisocial behavior in working-class London boys born in the 1950s.[19] Among others, important longitudinal studies on crime were also launched in Dunedin, New Zealand, in the 1970s, and in Pittsburgh, Denver, and Rochester in the 1980s.

In one of the most highly cited works in decades, Terrie Moffitt drew on her work with the Dunedin study to propose the influential concept of "life-course-persistent" offenders—individuals who have a continuously high level of committing crime at all ages, largely because of neuropsychological deficits. She also proposed "adolescent-limited offenders"—a relatively large, normative group who commit crimes during adolescence due primarily to peer influence, but who quickly desist and go on to lead conventional adult lives.[20] Dozens of other studies followed Moffitt to similarly dispute the invariant nature of the shape of the age-crime relationship, arguing that there are groups of offenders with distinct developmental profiles in crime. Still others have examined theories of turning points and desistance from crime in adulthood.[21]

This book will return to these themes repeatedly, offering new data bearing on them, but for now, what I want to emphasize is the common denominator across this body of work: a laser focus on the evolution of criminal behavior across significant phases of the age-differentiated life course. Prior scholarship, however, my own included, shares important shortcomings in uniting theories of the causes of crime with theories of official reactions to it, like arrest and imprisonment. Efforts to combine both have struggled to incorporate one of the deepest roots of the life-course way of thinking—the influence and mechanisms of societal change that confront different birth cohorts as they come of age.

Consider how different the world was for the Boston boys I studied from the world of today.[22] Older cohorts born in the early 1900s faced much shorter lifespans and were largely deceased by 2000, whereas twenty-five-year-olds in 1950 were living longer and aging into a more stable and protracted retirement. As for more recent cohorts, those turning fifty in 2000 and ensuing years live even longer. They also live in a climate of changing sexual norms, such as a surge in gay rights, that have transformed living arrangements, and in an era of changing retirement expectations (when "seventy is the new fifty"). We are also witnessing what developmental psychologists call *extended adolescence*—the stretching of a stage of life once confined to the teenage years to well past age twenty, with adult roles put off longer and longer.[23] Rates of marriage have been declining since the

1970s, while the median age at first marriage has been increasing, and those from lower educational backgrounds are notably less likely to marry at the same rate as in the past.

Work—and, along with it, implications for crime—have been equally transformed. In his books *The Truly Disadvantaged* and *When Work Disappears,* William Julius Wilson highlighted the changes that bore down on economically disadvantaged and racially segregated neighborhoods in US cities in the late twentieth century.[24] Deindustrialization and increasing demands for an educated workforce led to a loss of entry-level jobs for low-skilled workers. The decline of meaningful entry-level jobs for those without education influenced later cohorts of men most at risk for getting in trouble with the law.[25] More generally, insecurity in work is the new normal, especially in the so-called gig economy and what has been dubbed "The Great Resignation," with increasing numbers of workers quitting their jobs in the wake of the COVID-19 pandemic.

Military service has dramatically changed, too. Serving in World War II provided American men from economically disadvantaged backgrounds with unique opportunities to better their lives through on-the-job training and education supported by the GI Bill. Such opportunities were experienced by the delinquents in my Boston sample, as well, many of whom became carpenters or plumbers after their job training in the military. By contrast, there are now stricter standards for admission in an all-volunteer military. A high school diploma and a passing grade on the Armed Forces Vocational Aptitude Test are required, for example, as is the absence of a significant criminal record. At least in the United States, then, military service today is not the same pathway out of crime among the disadvantaged, and especially the criminalized population. For many, it is instead a closed door.

Taken together, these societal changes encapsulate the principle of cohort differences in coming of age. Improving our understanding of criminality requires us to find ways to study that change. The research described in this book provides just such a mechanism through its unique multicohort longitudinal design. History is full of startling changes to life milestones and outcomes that beg better explanations, which the approach this book introduces can inform.

Taking the historical observations noted above and putting them into a life-course narrative allows us to see that adolescents approaching the peak age of criminal behavior in 1950 transitioned to adulthood in a postwar boom, amid benefits from the GI Bill, relative social stability, high marriage and rates of childbearing, the widespread availability of work, and relative social stability. A stable conception of character is arguably easier to maintain in such a world, with a job, spouse, and family all reinforcing stable, predictable choices and routines. Just fifteen years later, the next crop of adolescents came of age in the 1960s, amid the turmoil of protests against the war in Vietnam and racial discrimination, the transformation of sexual norms, increasing drug use, and rapidly rising crime rates. Today's fifteen-year-olds are growing up in a technologically reconfigured landscape with weakened prospects for permanent employment and the continuing decline of marriage. Reinventing oneself is also more difficult: Nothing disappears from the internet, and computerized searches are widely used by employers—not to mention prospective partners—to investigate the past of job applicants and mates. These changes, which cannot be reduced to individual qualities, nevertheless shape individuals' ties to conventional institutions and relationships to criminality throughout the life course, from adolescent misbehavior all the way through to the social reintegration of former adult prisoners.

Conventional turning points, and the institutions supporting them, have thus been altered historically and culturally, shaping the course of individual criminality and the essence of character, which the philosopher John Rawls considered almost one and the same. Nontraditional or "deviant" turning points like arrest and incarceration also changed, producing even greater implications for understanding socially defined and rewarded aspects of character. It is here that the life course, social change, and labeling theory all come together to underscore the power of the multi-cohort approach.

PUNISHMENT'S TURN

The rate of incarceration was steady for almost fifty years, but it began a sharp increase circa 1975, ushering in the new era illustrated in Figure 1.1. The criminal justice system in this era altered the life course of Americans in unprecedented ways that probably would shock even Tannenbaum, were he alive. The fivefold growth in incarceration not only reshaped the life course of recent cohorts coming of age, but it also made going to prison an expected transition to adulthood for Black men with low education.[26] Even for whites and Hispanics—for nearly everyone—the rate of growth was unprecedented. The United States became a world leader in imprisoning its population, pure and simple. Seen through the lens of the life-course paradigm, this social change in criminalization imposed large cohort differences in aging, which in turn produced further social change that is still in progress, such as demands for criminal justice reform.

Although it came about twenty-five years after the spike began, the growth of incarceration eventually drew intense scholarly and public attention to the criminal justice system as a major intervention in the lives of ordinary citizens, especially African Americans. Some claim that America's incarceration binge helped reduce its crime problem, but the more frequent claim goes in the opposite direction. In the most definitive scholarly review, a panel convened by the National Academy of Sciences in 2014 concluded that while incarceration did help bring down the crime rate, at the same time it is associated with numerous adverse—and as a result, potentially offsetting—outcomes such as repeated criminality (recidivism), unemployment, poor mental health, and lower marriage prospects among former prisoners.[27] This is hardly surprising given the goals of punishment; it would be unusual, after all, to expect that incarceration after committing a crime would *increase* one's chances of getting a job, getting married, or bettering one's mental health. Punishment is meant to have negative consequences, and it does.

What came as a surprise was the reach of incarceration into numerous segments of society. The expanding definition of criminalization, and what scholars have termed "collateral consequences," created the spillover effects of incarceration beyond an individual's time in prison. It is one thing to expect criminals to pay their dues for crimes against society, but punishing more people, or punishing behavior more extensively than necessary for purposes of justice or crime control, is where the sheer volume of incarceration overshot its mark, yielding countervailing negative consequences—again, a kind of vicious cycle or trap. Moreover, whether to spouses, children, the community, or civil society, the consequences of incarceration stretch well beyond individual offenders. The extensive penetration of incarceration into American lives, particularly among the poor and minorities, is undisputable. In my own research, I confirmed the disproportionate burden that the African American community has borne, finding that the highest rate of incarceration in segregated Black communities in Chicago is some forty times higher than the highest rate of incarceration in segregated white communities.[28]

The preponderance of evidence of the stark reality of racial inequality makes it imperative that we shine a bright light on the antecedents of incarceration. A number of scholars, including historians, sociologists, legal analysts, and political scientists, have done so at the societal level, probing the increase in incarceration rates since the 1970s and, more generally, the rise of the punitive state.[29] The most famous of these is *The New Jim Crow*, where Michelle Alexander traces mass incarceration to the racially charged "war on drugs" and the locking up of low-level drug offenders from the inner city. Her widely influential argument has been dubbed "the standard story" on the rise in incarceration rates, with the drug war hypothesis at its core.[30] Other proposed causes include changes in sentencing decisions, such as the rise in longer prison terms for the same crime, and "three strikes" laws that swept up many low-level offenders.

Stylized or popular versions of the standard story, however, often deflect attention away from earlier layers of criminalization, missing or underappreciating the significance of sequence. Foremost, the logic of both labeling theory and the age-graded theory of the life course highlight the precursors to incarceration.[31] As the President's Commission on Law Enforcement and the Administration of Justice pointed out over a half-century ago, criminal justice is an interdependent system with incarceration at the end point of criminal processing.[32] In America, at least, for the most part you cannot be incarcerated without first being convicted and, before that, arrested.[33] This sequence in the criminal justice process means that for all intents and purposes, the police, not the courts, are the initial gatekeepers to the prison.[34]

Although incarceration may be uniquely severe, the experiences leading up to it are also punishments in themselves. There is a special case to be made that arrest itself has negative effects on the later lives of arrestees, for example in education, employment, and mental health, and there is growing evidence on the collateral consequences of aggressive policing on individuals and communities.[35] As Christopher Uggen has shown, even minor criminal records—not only the more severe—can be disruptive and stigmatizing.[36] The mark of a criminal record is lasting.[37] The rise in incarceration should therefore be understood as part of a broad expansion of the criminal justice system into the US population, especially among minorities and the poor.

In the extreme case, arrest can mark one for violence or even death. Most directly, hundreds of deaths each year are traced to the act of being arrested, over 60 percent of which occur at the hands of the police.[38] The death of George Floyd was a shocking example of the risks that police confrontations during arrest can produce, but it was only the most visible. A study in *Social Science and Medicine* found that 70 percent of Chicago's nonfatal gun violence victims came from just 6 percent of the city's population, all of whom who had been arrested before.[39] Police departments around the country are utilizing arrest records to predict who is going to become a future victim, and it is only a matter of time before health departments do as well.[40] There is additional evidence suggesting a gradient of mortality and criminalization—the more extensive the contact with the criminal justice system, the greater the risk of early death.[41]

As I noted earlier, however, it is not just prior arrest or a criminal record that matters. A prominent criticism of labeling theory and, in turn, the standard story on mass incarceration, can be summarized pithily: Criminal behavior matters. More concretely, the argument is that delinquency, criminal behavior, and antisocial tendencies are the essential predictors of who is officially labeled, particularly on a repeated basis. While I don't hold fast to this overall critique, and I am wary of character accounts rooted in individual differences, we must nevertheless account for the substantial variations in behavior correlated with criminalization that researchers have documented. At least for serious violence, there is also evidence that the crime-arrest link is at least as large as race or class effects on arrest.[42]

To be sure, we are all sinners, and it is likely that most of us have committed an officially defined crime at some point in our lives. I certainly have, and more than once. But to say that "all of us are criminal," as Alexander does, and which Tannenbaum and Becker implied before her, is a rhetorical move that masks tremendous heterogeneity across individuals and communities in the frequency and type of criminal behavior that often sets the wheels of criminal justice in motion.[43] Many of the behavioral precursors to persistent criminality also emerge early in the life course—before first incarceration and even first arrest. In this sense, the risks of going to prison, and other risks of criminalization, like arrest, are highly skewed among individuals and potentially have their origins in child or adolescent development.[44] Contemporary work in this area further neglects the role of exposure to violence in generating individual differences in criminal behavior, and the role of community violence in increased demands for crime control, resulting in largely separate literatures on the causes of violence and punishment.[45]

The splintering of research traditions and lack of attention to violence—and more broadly, what psychologists term antisocial behavior—confounds our understanding of the effects of criminal justice sanctions, like arrest and incarceration, on later outcomes. It is essential that we recover what is useful from these traditions and add to them to better understand and thereby address criminality. Being arrested or incarcerated is not a wholly random event, raising the question of whether the effects of criminal sanctions are stand-ins for other characteristics that existed prior to the sanction itself—for instance, criminal propensity or persistent marginalization that leads to criminal behavior. Prisoners—of all races—have committed more crimes over longer periods of time and come from much more disadvantaged childhood backgrounds than non-prisoners. Communities with high rates of violence and long histories of concentrated poverty are also the very same communities that generate high rates of arrest and incarceration—and into which ex-prisoners are being released in large numbers.[46]

Yet with few exceptions, the literature on mass incarceration has been reticent to seriously engage theories of criminal behavior, perhaps because it might be seen to undermine the cause of criminal justice reform by conceding the legitimacy of an arrest, offloading the moral burden from the police and the state to the one arrested.[47] Prior research is also highly uneven in its measurement of individual differences in antisocial behavior or personality.[48] I address these imbalances while integrating the insights of labeling theory, simultaneously examining behavior and punishment in the context of social change.

THE INTERGENERATIONAL LINK

Parental arrest or incarceration represents one of the earliest precursors to childhood and criminal justice involvement. Crime may be even more concentrated in families than individuals. David Farrington's influential studies of 1950s adolescents found that just 6 percent of families accounted for half of all criminal convictions.[49] More recently, Fox Butterfield's *In My Father's House* documents one Oregon family producing sixty imprisoned members across four generations.[50] This intergenerational pattern of criminalization exemplifies what Glen Elder Jr. called "linked lives"—or perhaps more aptly, linked fates.[51] Following labeling theory and the self-fulfilling prophecy concept dating to Tannenbaum, the official criminality of parents likely connects directly to their children also becoming marked and persistently delinquent.[52]

Sara Wakefield and Christopher Wildeman's *Children of the Prison Boom* made crucial contributions by demonstrating this linked-lives principle, examining mass incarceration's intergenerational impact on young children.[53] Growing paternal—and increasingly maternal—incarceration since 1975 has prompted researchers to examine families more closely, considering parenting practices, maternal employment, and divorce. Their evidence suggests recent-era parental incarceration generally harms children's mental, physical, and social development.

But what happens when these children reach adulthood? Only recently have children of the prison boom entered this phase. Understanding the true intergenerational cycle requires following these children through their peak risk period for arrest and imprisonment. Here, data remain limited—most longitudinal studies observe cohorts who came of age before mass incarceration's peak, aggressive policing's rise, and violence's dramatic decline.[54] Few studies account for children's antisocial and criminal behavior preceding criminalization.

Moreover, criminalized parents aren't randomly selected from the population. They possess many distinguishing characteristics beyond their criminal label, yet many studies, even from earlier eras, lack data to assess competing factors like preexisting parental or family differences.[55] Alcoholism, drug abuse, mental illness, family violence—these troubles often afflict both parents and children who encounter the criminal justice system, raising complex questions of cause and effect.[56] Testing parental criminality's influence on children demands rigorous study design, particularly strong measurement of parental criminal behavior across multiple birth cohorts. Until now, few studies have met this challenge.

SYNOPSIS

Institutional labeling through criminal legal processing represents a classic turning point in life trajectories. Early arrest acts as a unique snare, while repeated arrests mark a pathway of severe disadvantage and stigmatization—creating the "chronic offender." Official criminalization feeds the character trap, a self-reinforcing cycle of damage particularly difficult to escape when criminal records are public and personal responsibility is venerated.

Beyond legal marking, children face other forms of environmental inscription—lead exposure, guns, and violence—posing correlated and cumulative risks underexamined in the mass incarceration literature. These punishing and toxic environments often cluster and persist, as exemplified by Freddie Gray's life. While not all criminal acts receive state marking, decades of research demonstrate how violent or explosive antisocial behavior negatively affects life outcomes. Though the media may glorify aggression, those who attack others typically face social ostracism and retaliation. Enduring racial beliefs linking Blackness to inherent violence, criminal justice involvement, and moral worth further reinforce the character trap.

Historical turning points overlay these individual trajectories. Few would deny that history matters, but like the air we breathe, it typically serves as a background setting rather than an active force in life-course accounts of criminality. Despite rhetorical nods to historical context, individual disposition, family resources, and neighborhood environments dominate causal explanations of human behavior. These factors matter and have been the focus of much of my research career, but their interpretation shifts when viewed through social change's impact on life courses. I argue that both crime and criminalization's sources and consequences—and even our attitudes about legal validity, particularly what I have called legal cynicism—are fundamentally shaped by social transformations.[57]

Policy thinking about crime similarly evolves. Today's renewed emphasis on predicting criminal propensity may even exceed the "super-predator" era's focus. Indeed, the logic of selective incapacitation has returned transformed: Once championed by conservatives targeting "chronic criminals," prediction now attracts reformers across the political spectrum seeking to separate the "dangerous" from the deserving—a kind of selective ex-incapacitation. Such efforts' success depends entirely on classification systems' empirical validity. However, childhood origins, environmental marks, violence exposure, and criminal history—even if extensive—may not reliably predict future behavior in ways that serve justice effectively or morally. Character, justice, and behavioral prediction become problematic amid vast changes in crime, punishment, and inequality, necessitating

prospective study of long-term outcomes in historical context as we rei-
magine reform.

*   *   *

At this point you might wonder about the bugbear of causality, as this book
reports on no experiments. Establishing causality in social science presents
unique challenges—we cannot, and should not, randomly assign people
to experience arrest, imprisonment, toxic environments, or specific historical periods. But there is a silver lining. While we can analyze controlled
experiments for specific interventions like Head Start, we can consider
broader forces like age, birth cohort, and social change to be, for all intents and purposes, "exogenous"—assigned to people rather than chosen.
Though cohort composition may vary by demographic and crime-related
factors, these differences can be accounted for explicitly. With appropriate
multi-cohort data and reasonable assumptions, we can credibly estimate
how social change shapes lives. This approach thus allows us to examine
how individual development interacts with multiple social changes, moving
beyond the single-cause focus of interventions and static assumptions of
traditional single-cohort studies.

I follow this approach in studying the life course of multiple birth cohorts as a window on the experience of social change, uniting the longitudinal study of individuals—multiple biographies as it were—with the
changing social context of contemporary America over the last quarter-
century. Chapter 3 moves into the details of measuring what counts and
when, and describes how, through the integration of original data, the
power of social change can be revealed.

CHAPTER 3

Measuring What Matters and When

Why do we know so little about how birth timing—being born just a few years earlier or later—can alter life trajectories of crime, criminal justice involvement, and general well-being? It is because properly studying such a vast question requires decades of observations across multiple birth cohorts, combining detailed population, neighborhood, and individual data from multiple sources. We now have such a resource, allowing us to disentangle differences between birth cohorts and isolate how major social changes shape lives across a number of domains. But understanding these analyses requires first understanding how the data came together—a story that reveals both their promise and limitations.

Darnell Jackson and Andre Lewis, introduced earlier, joined hundreds of others from their birth cohorts in an ambitious collaborative study initiated in the 1990s: the Project on Human Development in Chicago Neighborhoods (PHDCN). As its title suggests, this project united individual development with neighborhood context. How these two boys—just two among over a thousand children whose lives I examine—came to join this long-term study is a story of both unique research design and considerable luck and perseverance. My 2012 book, *Great American City: Chicago and the Enduring Neighborhood Effect,* explored one piece of this puzzle, focusing almost exclusively on neighborhood-level analysis.

This book examines the longitudinal, life-course study of these children, including follow-ups through 2024. While readers might be tempted to skip details on the research architecture, remember: The devil is in the details. Like a building, a study's worth depends on its design and raw materials. This chapter therefore provides a comprehensive yet accessible overview, with technical details available in the endnotes and other sources.[1] In the spirit of accessibility, many results are also presented here in clear visualizations.

When the PHDCN planning phase launched in the early 1990s, no one on the large team, myself included, could have predicted the momentous social changes ahead, or our ability to follow subjects for over twenty-five years. Social science funding, especially today, rarely values promises of important findings nearly a generation after a study begins. Even in the headier funding days of the 1990s, the original PHDCN lacked the resources to begin collecting the full sweep of data that would make the analyses reported in this book possible. This chapter reveals how a broad, large-scale study of children became narrower in sample but deeper in insight over time.

THE ORIGINAL STUDY

The original PHDCN study has evolved over the years to include multiple follow-up studies and many additional data sources; as already noted, I refer to the overall, three-decade study as the PHDCN+. Because only a subset of the data from the original PHDCN study makes it all the way through to the analysis presented here, it is important to describe that study in its entirety to clarify how elements of its structure dictated what we can and cannot analyze today.

The major goal of the original PHDCN was to study the development of individuals, varying in age from infancy to eighteen years old, residing in a wide range of representative Chicago neighborhoods. The study ran over the course of about six years, from the mid-1990s to the early 2000s, but it was not until recently that enough time had elapsed to enable a developmental or life-course phase of study, allowing the questions that I raise to be addressed with long-term data. While we may have begun in the mid-

1990s, the fact is that it takes time for children to come of age and for adolescents to achieve middle adulthood. The six years of the original PHDCN could capture only a small chunk of each life. It is only now, after more than twenty-five years of accumulating information that builds on that original effort, that anything meaningful can be said about the long-term courses that these children's lives took in differing times of social change.

Sheila, for example, a participant from the youngest cohort in our study, was only five years old at the end of the original PHDCN, too young to have experienced much of life outside her local environment, much less with criminal justice authorities. Even in older cohorts, the endpoint of the PHDCN was still too early to gather information on individuals' experiences in early and mid-adulthood. Danny, for instance, who was in a much older cohort than Sheila, had not yet reached age twenty-one by 2001; he was still in the phase referred to by contemporary scholars as "extended adolescence," which is said to reach into the mid-twenties and maybe longer. As the *New York Times* put it, the "long road to adulthood is growing even longer."[2] To understand Sheila's and Danny's lives from childhood, through adolescence, and into adulthood, we needed to follow them for decades. Researchers and funders rarely stick around that long.

The original goal of the PHDCN was to enroll over six thousand children who were representative of the population, spanning from birth up to the legal age of adulthood. To accomplish this ambitious target, the project hired a research team of about 120 members who were trained to find and enroll children and their families, conduct interviews with them, and follow up with them over time. We also hired a survey research firm to help us determine the best way to ensure a representative sample at the outset. Many studies of development have been based on select samples, such as people with criminal records or living in concentrated poverty. These are interesting populations for some purposes, but for the PHDCN, we did not want to restrict the variation in childhood experiences. Doing so would have biased the goals of the project and eliminated questions of paramount interest. One can't understand the path to becoming a criminal by studying only those so defined, or by studying only the poor and down-trodden, which research tells us are overrepresented in crime statistics.

The design of the original longitudinal study was based on a two-stage procedure, beginning with neighborhoods then zeroing in on individuals.

We began with a representative sample of 80 of the 343 Chicago neighborhoods in the mid-1990s, chosen to represent the wide variability, by race and class composition, that existed—covering areas of low, medium, and high income, and with majority Black, white, Hispanic, and heterogeneous populations. Both Sheila and Andre, for example, came from low-income Black neighborhoods. But within every part of Chicago, even on its South Side—so often depicted negatively and uniformly in the media—the neighborhoods vary widely in their demographic composition. We collected data from neighborhoods that were high-income Black, middle-class Black, mixed-income and racially heterogeneous, and so on. These neighborhoods represented not just Chicago, but neighborhood types found across American cities and suburbs.

Mirroring our selection of neighborhoods for the initial sampling frame, our aim in stage two was to select children who were representative of the entire population. To capture the full age range, we enrolled a cohort of children at birth, a cohort of eighteen-year-olds, and five more cohorts spaced at three-year intervals in between. A survey organization, along with our research team, went door to door in the eighty neighborhoods around the city, creating lists of the residents in each housing unit and the ages of any children. Like the census, the idea was to document the full underlying population, which meant contacting over thirty-five thousand households and gathering information on their occupants. We selected dwelling units systematically, starting from a random point within enumerated blocks and screening all households, seeking children of eligible age. From this information, children falling within the seven approximate age cohorts (zero [or birth], three, six, nine, twelve, fifteen, and eighteen) were sampled from randomly selected households in each of the eighty neighborhoods. For the prospective birth cohort, pregnant women were enrolled if their due dates fell within the data collection window.

Because of these procedures, the PHDCN sample, which consisted of just over 6,200 children at the outset ("wave 1"), was broadly representative of children born or living in a wide range of Chicago neighborhoods at the time. Starting in late 1994 and running through early 1997, the children, along with their primary caregivers, were visited for extensive in-home interviews and assessments. The process took place over three years due to the large number of people interviewed and the complexity of carrying out lengthy in-person interviews, many of which ran for hours. We talked with caretakers for some time, and children aged nine and above were also interviewed in depth.

Then, at roughly 2.5-year intervals, the PHDCN research team collected two more waves of data (wave 2 was concentrated in 1997–1999, and wave 3 in 1999–2001). Although all of the children were living in Chicago during wave 1 and most stayed in Illinois or nearby states (Indiana or Wisconsin), participants in our study were followed no matter where they moved, fanning the study out well beyond Chicago. Some moved to the east or southeast coast (such as New Jersey, Virginia, or Florida), others moved south (Texas, Mississippi, or Tennessee) or west (California or Colorado), and a few moved as far as Puerto Rico and Israel. Fortunately, the participation at wave 1 and our retention through wave 3 were comparatively high for a contemporary urban sample, 75 percent and 78 percent, respectively. This high rate of participation gives us confidence in the continuing representativeness of the sample, though we can also account for any biases based on the kinds of individuals lost in waves 2 and 3, as I will later describe.

The data collected on the PHDCN children and families were rich in content and detail, including but also expanding beyond the standard characteristics typically accounted for in household surveys or longitudinal studies. More details on specific measures, which were guided by theory and based on the prevailing standards at the time, will be provided in chapters to come, and more technical content in the notes. But to give some flavor of the scope of the data collection, our research team conducted interviews and assessments with parents and adult caretakers, which allow me to assess important characteristics of interest. Relevant to testing the impact of social change along with its competing hypotheses, parent-reported factors examined include:

- Race / ethnicity
- Immigrant status
- Social class (based on income, poverty assistance, education)
- Family structure (including cohabitation), household size, and composition
- Parental employment histories
- Family domestic violence and marital relations (such as conflict among partners)

- Exposure of the parents and their children to violence
- Parental substance and alcohol abuse
- Mental illness and depression; physical health
- Academic and intellectual ability
- Criminal records of parents, siblings, aunts, uncles, cousins, grand-parents, and more
- Family member troubles with social institutions (as in employment and school settings)
- Aggression and self-control of the child

These and select other measures comprise the major theoretical domains that I capitalize on in waves 1 through 3, meaning that I can assess key predictors of life outcomes. We also comprehensively interviewed the children themselves from age nine and above, covering the same factors asked of parents where relevant, in addition to topics germane to growing up that the children and adolescents reported, such as gun carrying, gun use, delinquency, contacts with the police, and exposure to violence.

These measures are used in theoretically motivated ways to assess the core hypotheses on cohort inequality that I set out. But my goal is not to assess the effects of each and every one of these early-life factors—that would be madness. Instead, the idea is to account for the "gold standard" measures relevant to a focus on character, criminality, and life-course development. Telling the story of the character trap requires more than just, for example, the confirmation of criminal records and a few data points to index background features like parental employment, educational status, and income. A more complete picture demands information that is less often collected, like behavioral reports of temperament and self-control, or substance abuse and criminality among extended family members. The original PHDCN provides the early window necessary to assess the individual and family conditions of children before their transitions to adolescence and adulthood.

The PHDCN team also collected detailed neighborhood measures at the beginning and end of the survey period, at the bookends as it were, in 1995 and 2002. A dense amount of data was collected from each neighborhood, including independent surveys of residents, videotaped observations of city streets, and interviews with community leaders.[3] These different strategies allowed us to capture features like public disorder, social cohesion, and organizational strength. These data are combined with more traditional measures from the census, such as concentrated poverty, racial composition, and residential stability, in addition to merged records on crime and justice, such as neighborhood crime rates, policing intensity, and incarceration.

Results from the first three waves of the PHDCN and the community data are found in articles I or my colleagues have published, in addition to many articles written independently by others.[4] We made the data public, and I am grateful that those data have been widely used. But now we can go beyond our original aims. To report how the younger cohorts of these children turned out over the long run during times of major social change, supplemented by new forms of data, I had to conduct a study with multiple waves of interviews and administrative records over twenty-five-plus years—all linked together in these pages. Except for confidential records, replication data for core analyses are now public, completing the cycle of data collection by returning our efforts to the wider community as a common good.

PHDCN+: THE LONG-TERM FOLLOW-UPS

The PHDCN might have remained closed forever after 2002 had we not found a new research avenue to justify the first of the follow-up studies comprising the PHDCN+. In 2011, Robert Mare, a leading sociologist and demographer at UCLA, and I were appointed to a study group on housing and mixed-income neighborhoods funded by the MacArthur Foundation. We had never worked together before, but found common ground in our belief that, in a period of rapidly rising inequality, it was important to understand the loss of middle-income neighborhoods in US cities and the conditions under which individuals were able to achieve residence in stable, mixed-income neighborhoods, as opposed to being stuck in concentrated poverty or, by contrast, far removed from the rest of the pack in segregated, affluent enclaves.

After that study group ended, Rob became increasingly intrigued by the processes shaping individual decisions to move or stay put. How, he wondered, did the processes of residential mobility contribute to neighborhood change, to citywide inequality, and to the viability of mixed-income neighborhoods? Given my long history of studying neighborhoods, not least as part of the original PHDCN, I was a natural convert. But what really piqued my interest was the potential to situate this line of inquiry within a larger life-course framework, which would require a longitudinal study design. After many long conversations, we agreed that tracing people's residential trajectories over time was critical, and that we should seek to understand neighborhood mobility in a representative sample of urban dwellers.

To do this, we conspired to capitalize on the PHDCN's preexisting longitudinal design and a related study that Rob had been involved with, called the "Los Angeles Family and Neighborhood Survey." This well-regarded study was modeled in major aspects after the PHDCN and had begun about five years after it, in 2000.[5] I realized that this was a unique chance not just to study mobility and neighborhood change, but if carefully planned, to revisit the children of the PHDCN and lay the groundwork for a major life-course study of social change, as well. Finally, I had begun to conceive of the research program that would eventually inform the multi-cohort longitudinal approach of this book. Although daunted by the prospects of initiating new data collection in two very different and complex cities, we wrote a proposal to do just that, a project designed to assess long-term change at both the individual and neighborhood levels, and much more.

The funding stars aligned. In 2011, we launched what at the time we called the "Mixed Income Project" to reflect the original motivation of our MacArthur study group and new funding from the foundation. Over the course of three years of planning and execution, we had the good fortune to carry out the new data collection effort, locating and re-interviewing randomly sampled participants who took part in the third wave of PHDCN interviews and the second wave of the Los Angeles Family and Neighborhood Survey, with a common protocol for adult respondents. Over a thousand respondents were located and interviewed from each study location in 2012 and 2013. Tragically, Rob was struck with cancer in late 2014, and while he pushed on with his life and work as much as his energies allowed, he never got to carry out the hoped-for analyses before his death. But his unique insights on designing the research helped make the Chicago and Los Angeles studies much stronger, adding to his scholarly legacy.

Since the original PHDCN contained three waves of data collection, the Mixed-Income Project became the vehicle for what would be the fourth wave, carried out in 2012 and 2013. For this wave, we narrowed the sample from the original PHDCN base of over six thousand individuals by selecting only four of the original seven cohorts—the infant cohort and the ages nine, twelve, and fifteen cohorts. Within each of these four cohorts, we then selected a 60 percent random sample of the approximately 2,800 respondents last contacted at wave 3 in the early 2000s. Our rationale for focusing on these cohorts was to maximize variation in life-course experiences and exposure to social change at different ages. We also prioritized the infant cohort—a rarity in the social sciences—by targeting a larger sample of the original infants, who were adolescents in 2012.

To find respondents in these cohorts, we hired a Chicago survey research firm to set up a field operation and execute a multi-method tracking effort using electronic, phone-based, and in-person methods, including old-fashioned knocking on doors and talking to neighbors.[6] Despite the long time that had elapsed since the last contact at wave 3—over a decade—and the difficulty of reaching people in an era of caller ID and ever fewer home phones, our collective research effort located and collected data on 1,057 members of the third wave of the study, a response rate of 67 percent of eligible cases in the birth cohort and 63 percent in the older cohorts. As in the first wave of the study, our rate of locating and interviewing participants compared well with other urban studies and especially survey mailings, which today are considered lucky if they achieve a 10 to 15 percent response rate. Moreover, our knowledge of the study members from earlier interviews allowed us to know in detail, and accordingly adjust where appropriate, the characteristics associated with those respondents we were unable to locate. In short, the study is not perfect, but it is representative.

Ranging between ages twenty-five and thirty-one at wave 4, in the final tally we found 227 respondents in the nine-year-old cohort, 235 in the twelve-year-old cohort, and 217 in the fifteen-year-old cohort. There were 378 children in the birth cohort, who were nearly seventeen years old at wave 4. As with Chicago, the sample was also diverse economically and by race / ethnicity. For example, almost 20 percent of wave 4 respondents were white or European American, 37 percent Black, 40 percent Latino, 2 percent Asian, and the rest a mix of other races including Native American.

Almost 60 percent of the interviews were carried out in person, a waning practice in contemporary surveys. Phone interviews were used if preferred by respondents or if they were easier to implement. Members of the three older cohorts (the nine-, twelve-, and fifteen-year-old cohorts) had become adults by wave 4, so we developed a survey protocol to collect extensive information on the respondent and his or her household. Parallel to waves 1–3, we assessed multiple domains including family structure, income, education, household composition, job history, physical and mental health, financial assets, neighborhood perceptions, and residential histories.[7] The caretakers of the infant cohort members were also asked a battery of items measuring the behavior and circumstances of the child as an adolescent, including aggression, impulsivity, school performance, trouble with the law, and health.[8] Combined with parent reports on children's temperament and similar behaviors from the other cohorts in earlier waves, this data set means that I can examine key elements of societally defined character, like self-control and antisocial propensity, across all cohorts.

PHDCN+ WAVE 5

The vision I began to realize in wave 4—that of a longitudinal study capable of revealing the subtle impacts of social change—would require years more waiting for the younger cohorts to pass far enough into adulthood. Beyond patience, getting to wave 5 would again require new collaborators, and new funding. David Kirk, a professor at Oxford University in England until he moved to the University of Pennsylvania in 2024, was a graduate student at the University of Chicago in the early 2000s and worked on the original PHDCN as a research assistant. He went on to write a groundbreaking thesis using the PHDCN data that would later turn into a number of influential publications. While we kept in touch and published together on the deleterious effects of arrest on the educational attainment of the PHDCN children in the earlier waves, Dave moved on while maintaining his interest in life-course studies. Among other important later works, he collected original data and published a fascinating account of the effects of Hurricane Katrina on the reentry of released prisoners into society.[9]

At a 2015 criminology conference in Washington, DC, Dave and I met to catch up on our lives and discuss his latest research over smoked bourbon cocktails. We also talked about the PHDCN in the context of all that had happened since the original data collection, and the importance of keeping it going. That was a revealing conversation to me, and I began to think about intergenerational continuity of the study. At the time I was nearing sixty and, while I was not at all ready to retire, the legacy of the PHDCN loomed large in my mind. The very youngest study members were rounding twenty, almost but not quite old enough for us to measure how they would arrive at adulthood. The PHDCN needed new stewards. Dave was an obvious choice in the next generation of scholars to bring aboard.[10]

A few years later, we began a long conversation that resulted in a major grant proposal that was funded by the National Collaborative on Gun Violence Research, with Dave as a co-principal investigator. With this support, we launched an effort in early 2021 to begin wave 5. First, we had to locate and survey as many of the wave 4 respondents as possible, expanding the study to a quarter-century since its inception. In our design of wave 4, we had intentionally narrowed the original PHDCN sample by randomly subsampling respondents from four of the seven cohorts who took part in wave 3. In wave 5, however, we attempted to contact every study member who had responded in wave 4, maintaining continuity for our core, longitudinal sample from 1995 all the way through 2021.

Charting a complex follow-up during the pandemic and its many challenges, and with Dave ensconced in England, was a crazy endeavor, but we pressed ahead. At this point, we came up with the label of PHDCN+ to describe the extension of the original PHDCN study, which consisted of waves 4 and 5 plus the (soon to be described) collection of additional administrative data over the last ten years.

From May through October of 2021, the National Opinion Research Center at the University of Chicago carried out the fifth wave of the PHDCN+ data collection. The survey administration included an extensive effort to locate the 1,057 wave 4 respondents. Whereas prior waves of the PHDCN were conducted in-person or over the telephone, to keep up with the times we added a web survey mode, with English and Spanish versions available. The survey was not in the field during the height of COVID-19 related lockdowns, but the web mode proved important for securing respondents' participation in the immediate aftermath.[11] Of the 1,040 individuals from wave 4 who remained alive and were eligible as of 2021, 682 completed the survey in one form or another, for a response rate of nearly 66 percent.[12] While the participation was again high for a contemporary urban sample, differential response rates over time leave open the possibility that nonrandom loss to follow-up could affect results. Although

there are conflicting views on whether to account for attrition and features of the survey design with various weighting procedures, weighted
and unweighted results typically converge.[13]

The final respondents at wave 5 range between ages twenty-four and
forty-one, with 135 respondents in the nine-year-old cohort, 165 in the
twelve-year-old cohort, and 165 in the fifteen-year-old cohort. There are
217 children in the infant cohort who were on average twenty-six years old
at wave 5. Like all waves of the study, wave 5 is diverse by race / ethnicity,
with 21 percent white, 32 percent Black, 42 percent Hispanic, and the remaining 5 percent Asian or other. Interestingly, 51 percent of sample
members who completed wave 5 lived in the city of Chicago in 2021, with
another 28 percent outside of the city limits but still within the state of
Illinois. Forty-two percent of the wave 5 respondents lived in the city of
Chicago at each survey wave, and the rest were divided into those who
left Chicago and had not returned, and those who had moved in and out
of Chicago across the study periods.

With a bloc of individual life courses in four cohorts across a quarter-
century, at last we had the heart of the dataset necessary to investigate the
differential impact of social change by birth cohort. The PHDCN+ design can be visually represented as in Figure 1.3, back in Chapter 1: five
waves of data collection spanning twenty-six years, with the four age cohorts ranging from twenty-six years old to forty-one years old in 2021.
While this trove of fine-grained interview and survey data over many years
is illuminating on its own, I wanted to go further, incorporating other
sources of information on the same study participants, adding nuance and
confidence to our knowledge of their lives, personalities, and health, as well
as the particulars of their recorded interactions with the criminal justice
system.

CRIMINAL HISTORIES

A distinguishing feature of the work presented here is its independent collection and analysis of over twenty years' worth of criminal history records of the more than one thousand individuals of the PHDCN+—
detailing everything from arrest to incarceration. These data satisfy my
theoretical goal of studying official criminalization over the life course.
Many population-based studies rely only on self-reports of official contact

instead of defining criminalization based on official contact histories that can be reliably placed in time. It is not just that people often have faltering memories and cannot place past events accurately in time over the course of multiple decades. If a police officer stopped you on the street and restricted your activity, you might consider that to be an arrest even if it did not result in a record. In fact, an earlier analysis of the PHDCN study found that a sizable percentage of adolescents—almost a quarter of them— reported an arrest that did not exist officially. Perhaps more worrisome, nearly half the adolescents who did have an official arrest record failed to report that they had been arrested.[14]

What is needed, then, is a dynamic flow of data that captures the timing of all events of criminal justice sanctioning across many years of interest. Our data collection already provides us with both caretaker accounts and self-reported behavior, depending on the wave. But to supply the official records, I carried out rolling stages of data collection from an official criminal history repository. The main data source is the Criminal History Record Information (CHRI) reported to the state of Illinois and housed by the Illinois State Police. Under a joint agreement with the Illinois Criminal Justice Information Authority (ICJIA), all wave 4 respondents (cohorts zero, nine, twelve, and fifteen) were first matched by name (including aliases) and date of birth with all criminal records for the state of Illinois in August of 2015. At that time, the birth cohort members were almost twenty years old on average and the fifteen-year-old cohort members were in their early thirties. The official criminal histories cover both the city of Chicago (from the Chicago Police Department) and all jurisdictions (amounting to about 1,200) outside the city, including detailed information, by date, on arrests, charges, disposition, and sentences.[15] The initial search netted records on 354 of the 1,057 cohort participants and over 2,200 unique charges. As of 2015, nearly a third of the sample had official criminal records.

Criminal history databases are created for administrative purposes and not just research, however. Sometimes it takes time for the disposition of a given criminal case to be resolved or recorded digitally. Given the backlog as the ICJIA upgraded and updated their system after our initial search, we might have undercounted arrests or sentences. In other words, our one-time-only search might have resulted in an incomplete picture—and moreover, our study members, especially in the birth and age-nine cohorts, were accumulating criminal activity after 2015. To circumvent these issues, we repeated the search process three more times, in 2017, 2019, and 2021. The records were integrated with the 2015 search and an updated sequence was created, yielding a final twenty-five-year record of official criminal histories.

These data, like all data, still have limitations. They are based only on Illinois criminal records—but note that the proportion of our sample that still lived in Illinois at wave 4 was near 90 percent, while others had lived in Illinois for many years just up to wave 4, and still others had moved out in earlier waves but moved back to the state after wave 4 (some of whom were in fact arrested). To avoid the undercounting of criminal sanctions for those at risk of arrest in the state, I generally consider criminal records to be "missing" only among cohort members who moved out of Illinois at wave 2 and never returned for waves 3 and 4; fortunately, this is less than 2 percent of the sample. Also fortunately, the results do not change if I use less restrictive or more restrictive definitions, such as focusing only on those who lived in Illinois their entire lives.[16]

Overall, then, there is no reason to believe that missing juvenile records amount to more than a handful—and felony arrests, especially those that result in confinement, are the least likely to be missing from the criminal records.[17] Most important, for purposes of studying the process of criminalization, if an official record does not exist for someone in the main databases used by state agencies, the police, and prospective employers, then for all intents and purposes they do not bear the mark of a criminal record.

DEATH RECORDS

In addition to criminal history, we also gathered official records from the National Death Index maintained by the US Centers for Disease Control and Prevention (CDC). A daunting but essential final "outcome" of the life course is, of course, death. Collecting accurate data on deaths from survey reports is nearly impossible, and requesting death information from caretakers or family members is not preferred, assuming they can even be contacted. Thus, we leveraged this comprehensive nationwide data source of death records, searching from the beginning of the study (1995) through the end of 2024. We searched death records on the main subset of our sample: cohorts that were aged zero, nine, twelve, and fifteen, meaning that the ages of these cohorts at the most recent iteration of searching ranged from twenty-nine to forty-four at the beginning of 2025. We can search this geographically comprehensive sample because death records are national in scope and do not require that we know where our participants in the United States, who constitute virtually everyone, live. As a result, we were not limited to the participants who stuck with the study all the way to wave 5 in 2021.

The National Death Index was not without complications; because people move, get married, use aliases, and even simply mistype their information, it has duplicate and incorrect records. Some individuals were clear matches with the index records, but many had to be independently and manually reviewed, checking information on the death records or external sources, such as online obituaries, against our records.

Through such efforts, we ascertained that more than 100 of the 3,571 individuals within the four selected cohorts, more than 3 percent, were deceased as of the end of 2024. From the National Death Index, we also collected the cause of death for each deceased individual. Of particular note to this study were the firearm homicides (accounting for twenty-seven deaths) and firearm suicides (three deaths). More analysis will be shared in pages to come of the link between childhood developmental context and later-life, sometimes fatal, experiences with gun violence. The National Death Index data informed this analysis through the collection of data on fatal experiences, including those involving firearms.

ENVIRONMENTAL INEQUALITY

There is one additional stream of data augmenting my PHDCN, PHDCN+, and official criminal and death record research. Recall from the Introduction and Chapter 1 that one reason for reconceptualizing the idea of character is because of how the environment independently shapes our various propensities and properties of self-control. The pathways by which environmental toxins literally get into the bodies and minds of children are unequal, and as they shape children's development differently, potentially over long periods of the life course, the result is what I will later discuss as *toxic inequality.*

In particular, I report on exposure to a major toxin, lead, at both the neighborhood level and in the blood levels of the individuals in my study. I also report on air pollution and its link to important life outcomes. To measure neighborhood-level lead toxicity, I extend prior work with Alix Winter examining lead-test results from the Chicago Department of Public Health (CDPH). Fortuitously, unique records from blood assays dated back to 1995, the origin year of the PHDCN. We first gathered all tests by the CDPH for lead exposure in children ages one through five and matched them to Chicago neighborhoods, starting in 1995 and for every year until 2013. By aggregating individual test results geographically, we were able to assess links between lead exposure and neighborhood indicators such as racial segregation and concentrated poverty. The CDPH data we examined included an average of seventy-five thousand lead tests per year.[18] In light of the Center for Disease Control's recommendation at the time that blood-lead levels of more than 5 micrograms per deciliter (μg/dL) indicated a need for further monitoring, we calculated the percentage of children in each block group and census tract with blood-lead levels greater than 6 μg/dL and the percentage of children with blood-lead levels greater than 10 μg/dL.

Despite the richness of these neighborhood lead measures, our second and major innovation was to obtain the individual blood-lead levels of much of our infant cohort from the mid-1990s. Working with the CDPH, we matched identifiable blood test results starting in 1995 to our birth cohort members who were studied at wave 4. Of the 378 eligible birth cohort members, 254 were successfully matched with blood-lead test results. To account for any selectivity in measurement, I adjust for the CDPH's lead testing coverage rate in each child's neighborhood, along with personal characteristics.[19] Lead's harmful effects have been detected even at very low levels, and the CDC maintains that there is no safe level of exposure. Therefore, instead of trying to discern a "safe" level of exposure, as many previous studies have done, I have available the full range of each tested child's average blood-lead level.[20]

Additional ecological data on environmental toxins were gathered from the EPA's archival records and historical research on the location of industrial plants. These include the Toxics Release Inventory (which measures the amount of waste released into the environment) and details on the locations of leaking underground storage tanks, brownfield locations, and sites of industrial smelters both historical and contemporary. As the title of a recent book on environmental inequality notes, many of these are "sites unseen"—often "relic sites" where past manufacturing put toxic contaminants into the soil or groundwater—which are dangerous for children, yet often unrecognized or weakly regulated even though toxins deposited by smelters are known to decay slowly, if at all.[21]

Later, in Chapter 7, this focus on environmental inequality will be extended to the entire United States, and I will explain how I approached toxic inequality from another angle. That work, undertaken with my former graduate student Robert Manduca, now a faculty member at the University of Michigan, merged national census tract-level estimates of child mobility over the life course with measures of ambient air pollution and lead exposure risk levels. We examined three main outcomes: individual income rank in 2014–2015, when subjects had reached ages thirty-one to thirty-seven; incarceration of the boys, as the expected fraction on April 1, 2010; and teen childbearing among the girls, as the expected fraction on the same date.[22]

Knitting together these various data sources allows both a Chicago-specific and a national look at how exposure to air pollution and lead, which are environmentally and politically determined, shape the long-term developmental outcomes that are used to infer character. This is a case, as Chapter 7 elaborates, of when the biological is in fact social.

WHERE ARE THEY NOW?

While we pulled criminal records only from the state of Illinois, we were still able to include valuable data about the life outcomes of study members who moved to other parts of the country. The movement of people through time and space is central to understanding the evolution of their lives, requiring detailed knowledge of where people live at all times. Wherever our study members moved, we followed them.

The data we collected at each wave of the PHDCN+ provided us with addresses that allowed us to link individuals to their census tracts, no matter where they were in the United States. These codes were then used to integrate census data from 1990 and 2000 (interpolated by year) and the later American Community Surveys (ACS) up to 2020, permitting measures of neighborhood context (such as concentrated poverty and racial composition) every year from 1995 (and even earlier in the case of older cohorts) through the late 2010s or early 2020s. This approach affords a view of, among other things, the trajectory of upward or downward socioeconomic

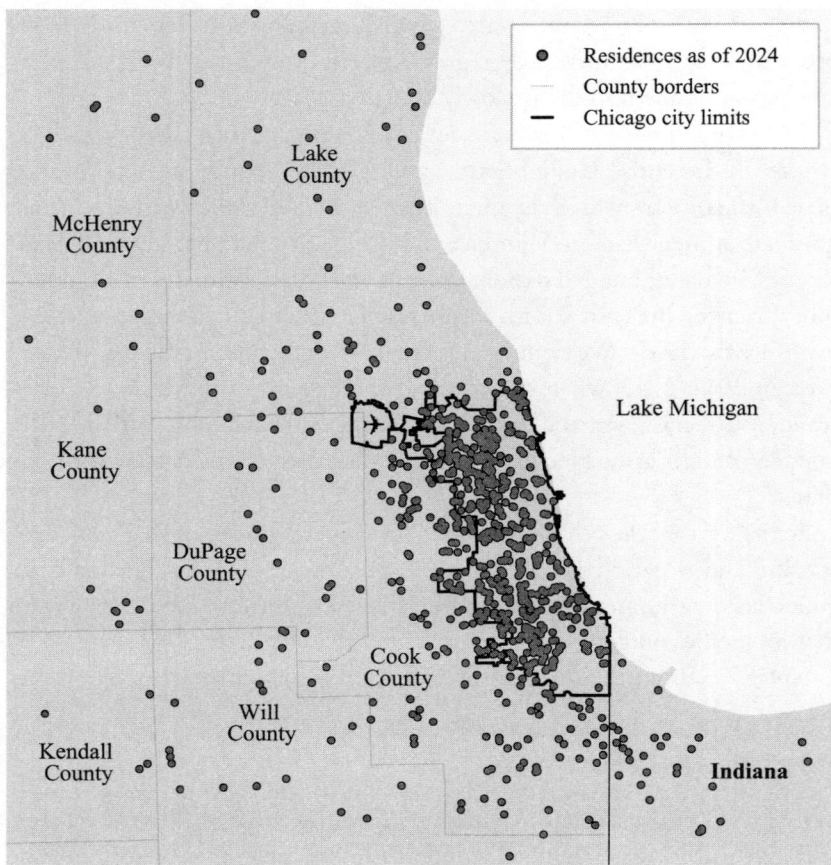

Figure 3.1. Study Member Locations as of 2024, Greater Chicago.

neighborhood mobility from adolescence to early adulthood across all cohorts.

Figure 3.1, displaying the distribution of PHDCN+ respondents in the Chicago area as of 2024, shows a spreading-out of respondents from the original eighty neighborhoods, especially to the north, west, and southwest sides of Chicago and into the western and southern suburbs of Cook County. Figure 3.2 shows the distribution across the entire country.[23] Although most people remain in Illinois or nearby, such as various cities and towns in Indiana, there is representation both far and near, with clusters in cities like Milwaukee, Detroit, Phoenix, New York, Los Angeles, Atlanta,

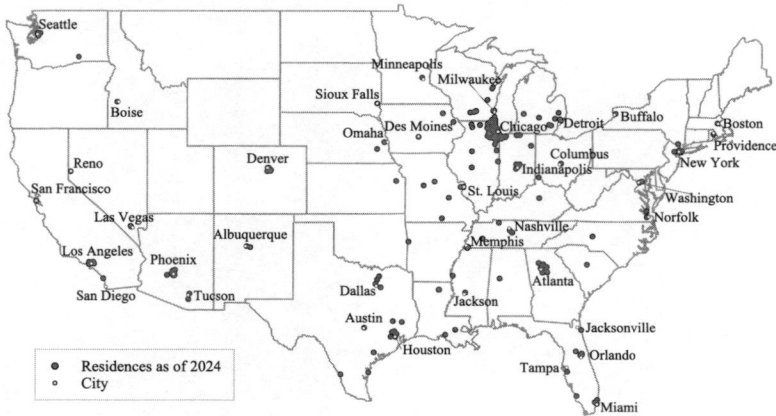

Figure 3.2. Study Member Locations as of 2024, United States.

Dallas, and Houston. The reach of the PHDCN+ thus extends across the entire country and the flow of movement matches known patterns of movement, such as the distinct pattern of return migration to the South.

* * *

To study the lives of former or current Chicagoans across more than a quarter-century, from 1995 through 2024, is to examine a unique slice of American history. At the outset of this study, it was never guaranteed that the work could be maintained for so long or would go on to integrate numerous other disparate yet crucial streams of information. True to the study's focus on social change, none of the major upheavals since its inception were anticipated—and many, with the pandemic being only the most notable example, significantly disrupted our data collection.

Yet despite the challenges that society presented—as it does for everyone—the effort has proved more than worthwhile. The combination of the cohort sequential design of our longitudinal study (portrayed in Figure 1.3) and the multiple stages of data collection described in this chapter provides a unique vantage point. From here, we can examine how crime, criminalization, toxic exposures, and other life outcomes unfold amid transformative social change. It is time now to turn to these children's lives—and their experiences coming of age in different historical moments of the last quarter-century.

PART II

REVEALING THE POWER OF CHANGE

CHAPTER 4

The Arrested Years

Why does crime increase steeply in adolescence and then see a less steep but nearly continuous decline throughout adulthood? Or, as exasperated parents often ask: Why are teenagers so damn unruly? These questions have animated decades of research and soul searching, but they may well be the wrong questions.

In an influential 1980s article, criminologists Travis Hirschi and Michael Gottfredson sparked controversy by arguing that the effect of age on crime transcends social and historical conditions.[1] They demonstrated that across time and place, young people on the cusp of adulthood break the law more than those younger or older. Though they left unresolved why age so strongly relates to crime, they showed that traditional explanations—lack of financial resources, delinquent peer influences, or even biological factors like high testosterone—could not fully account for this pattern of spike and decline, known simply as the "age effect." In their later and even more influential work, they argued that attention should focus instead on low self-control, which emerges early in life and directly causes crime at all ages.[2]

These provocative arguments implied that the age effect would persist regardless of attempted responses by parents or societal interventions. A surge of cross-disciplinary studies examined Hirschi and Gottfredson's claims, testing whether age's effect on crime was truly universal and whether early individual differences, especially in self-control, predicted crime across ages. The debate spilled beyond academia into public discourse, spanning sociology, criminology, psychology, economics, and law.

Yet the lively debates about age, crime, and the life course—and consequently much empirical research, including my own earlier work—sidestepped an important question. Longitudinal research testing the age-crime relationship has largely held history and social change at bay. Over a hundred published studies have examined individual age-crime trajectories, attempting to identify different offender groups underlying the aggregate age-crime curve, such as "life-course-persistent" or "late-onset" offenders.[3] Other longitudinal research has tested whether age effects are direct or mediated by social factors like employment, antisocial peer exposure, marriage, and poverty.[4]

Social change remains largely absent from life-course research, however, with many studies reading as if they could describe any cohort of children aging through any historical period. This poses a major problem for the age-crime debate if, in fact, just *being* a teenager matters less than *when* one is a teenager. As Stephen Raudenbush notes, "What is lost is the notion of development as an ongoing interplay between individual action and social intervention."[5] Social change represents the ultimate intervention, an argument consistent with life-course scholars' recognition that it can alter trajectories of human development. My longitudinal study with John Laub, focused on Boston men in the mid-twentieth century, approached this idea by highlighting turning points in relation to historical events like the New Deal, World War II, the Korean War, and the GI Bill.[6]

But recognizing social-historical change's role differs from studying how it distinguishes various cohorts' life courses. My Boston study, like nearly all crime-based research in the life-course tradition, focused primarily on individual transitions and turning points, such as marriage, and didn't empirically examine how social change interacted with aging to shape life-course patterns. Nor could it have: The Boston study, like most work in this tradition, examined individuals born within just a few years of each other. Moreover, it predated the major social changes in crime and justice motivating this book—rising incarceration, proactive policing, and the large crime declines since the 1990s.

Studying how the age-graded life course is affected by its historical period requires a theoretical strategy with demanding data requirements. While social science now has many long-term longitudinal studies, they typically use single-cohort designs, especially in studies of crime. In such designs, subjects were born around the same time, and therefore age effects and historical effects move in parallel and cannot be disentangled. Even when studies include multiple cohorts, historical context doesn't vary meaningfully if cohorts are born in years too close together or during less eventful periods.[7]

To address these challenges, this chapter advances the ideas introduced in Chapters 1 and 2, applying them to our longitudinal data. Building on work with Roland Neil, I study how shared historical circumstances, rather than individual or family circumstance, shape different birth cohorts' experiences with arrest—that crucial first step toward being defined as criminal. This examination of arrest covers some of recent history's largest social changes—the rise of mass incarceration and proactive policing on one hand, and the "great American crime decline" on the other. I consider the long-term consequences of arrest over the life course and test competing hypotheses about cohort variation in arrest trajectories during this period.[8]

THE CRITICAL YEARS

In his classic work on generations, Karl Mannheim argued that the ages between about seventeen and twenty-five constituted the life stage at which social changes in the larger society made their most potent and lasting mark; Howard Schuman and colleagues would later call these the "critical years."[9] But studies of crime that follow multiple birth cohorts to compare how social change stratifies their life experiences are rare, whether relating to the critical years or before (childhood) or later (mid-adulthood). Rarer still are prospective studies with the rich measurement needed to assess whether the diverging life outcomes of cohorts (notably in the critical age period of seventeen to twenty-five) arise because they face different social worlds as they come of age or because they are made up of different kinds of people—or both. Essentially, by having enough data about enough of the life course of different cohorts, we can adjust for the ways in which cohorts differ—for example, in demography and childhood poverty. If, after accounting for all of these compositional and early-life differences, two cohorts still show widely divergent outcomes, we can plausibly attribute that divergence to the forces of social change.

Relatively few long-term studies in the United States compare the crime patterns of multiple cohorts, and fewer still highlight differences by birth cohort in the socio-historical contexts through which those individuals come of age. One study followed up the classic Philadelphia birth cohort of 1945 with another born in 1958. While briefly acknowledging the role of changing social contexts, the authors argued that criminal justice practices were mostly unchanging as the cohorts aged, and they found small differences in various metrics of criminal careers across the cohorts.[10] Another study compared two cohorts of males born in Pittsburgh in the late 1970s and early 1980s, showing that the older cohort was more violent at a given age after controlling for several cohort characteristics.[11] Neither study was focused on isolating social change from its competitor explanations, however, nor did they focus on the transformations of the last quarter-century or so.

By contrast, the latest phase of the Project on Human Development in Chicago Neighborhoods (PHDCN+) offers a unique strategy allowing contemporary historical change to be captured and its influence on the life course to be studied. As a 2003 article noted, the PHDCN multi-cohort data present an unusual opportunity "since successive cohorts will reach specific ages (such as age twelve) in different years and their life experiences can be compared."[12] Using the first waves of PHDCN data, Raudenbush started to do just this, but with only five years of available data for the older cohorts. Examining crime across a substantial portion of the life course or stages of historical importance with PHDCN data was impossible then. But with the data we collected on PHDCN+ respondents to 2021, a good deal of the life course can be portrayed through different periods of the transformation of crime and punishment over the past quarter-century for cohorts whose birth is separated by up to seventeen years.

It has been hypothesized that the shifting metrics in crime over the last quarter-century or so can be attributed to a number of compositional or early-life characteristics, such as cohorts' different racial structures, childhood exposures to violence, levels of access to legal abortion, early family problems, exposures to lead toxicity, and (from the crack generation) numbers of latent "super-predators"—all leading to changing propensities to commit crime.[13] Although some of the features that vary by cohort, like childhood exposure to violence in the neighborhood, are in part the result of social changes, what these factors all have in common is that the PHDCN participants experienced them before they reached the prime teenage years for arrest. It follows that if these compositional or early-life experience factors vary systematically by cohort, then they may create selective cohort differences that potentially account for arrest differentials later in life.

The argument assessed here is whether cohort variations in arrest over the adolescent and adult life course arise from social changes in the larger environment that go beyond demographic composition, stable individual traits, and differences in early-life family (and even neighborhood) experiences. These overarching social changes, discussed in detail in Chapter 6, could include widespread shifts in police behavior, drug use, economic and environmental conditions, and technology usage, among others. Of course, both hypotheses may be in operation, and as noted earlier, I take for granted, as research has long revealed, that individual and early childhood experiences are important. It is useful to label the strong versions of each position to help clarify the stakes—we can call these the *cohort compositional* and the *cohort social change* arguments.

WHY ARREST IS CRITICAL

The large body of work on mass incarceration reviewed in Chapter 2, along with evidence of cohort differences in incarceration, might make the reader wonder anew: Why the focus on arrest? If one's incarceration is a powerful and negative turning point along the life course, it may seem like incarceration itself should be the focus rather than arrest. For this and other reasons, many scholars have centered their research on incarceration.

The work of sociologist Bruce Western, for example, was notable in its demonstration of large differences between birth cohorts in imprisonment by race and class. He showed that the rapid growth in incarceration not only reshaped the life course of certain cohorts but also made going to prison an expected transition to adulthood for Black men with low education.[14] Western and his colleagues' work inspired a body of research examining how an individual's incarceration influences later outcomes in life such as employment, health, and criminality—often called "collateral consequences."[15] Even if we take these findings as a given, as I largely do, this

body of work focused largely on individuals born in the 1950s and 1960s—
the cohorts of the parents of the children I study. My intention is not to
demote the consequences of imprisonment, but to supply the critical, earlier
piece of the picture that researchers have thus far largely set aside, and to
update the picture to the 2020s.

Arrest is the first step in the punitive process of confinement, and as
the age-crime debate revealed, it peaks in the late teens or early twenties—
before the average age of those admitted to prison for the first time, which
is in the mid-twenties.[16] Among the PHDCN+ subjects with records of
arrest, for example, the average age of first incarceration is in the mid-
twenties, though juvenile detention can happen earlier. For prisoners in
the United States as a whole, more than 90 percent are age twenty-five or
older. Pathways to incarceration thus start earlier in the life course than
commonly studied, and for criminal behavior, often earlier still. Arrest also
reaches a much wider swath of the population than incarceration in early
adolescence.

These facts have important implications for the literature on mass incarceration, including the well-documented racial inequalities in the risk
of imprisonment. Consistent with this prior research, there are large racial
disparities in incarceration among the approximately one thousand participants of the PHDCN+ study for whom we have official records through
2020. The left panel of Figure 4.1 shows that the probability of incarceration among Black individuals in the data, at nearly 10 percent, is more than
double that of whites or Hispanics, both of which are below 5 percent.
This panel includes the entire sample and asks: What percentage of each
racial category became incarcerated at least once?

But to address questions about the connection between arrest and incarceration, we need to know how closely the two are correlated, and if
that correlation is consistent across racial groups. We can do this by comparing the average likelihood of arrest in a group to its average likelihood
of incarceration. In two groups of the same size, for example, if one group
has ten arrests and one imprisonment, and another has twenty arrests and
two imprisonments, then we can say that, adjusting for arrests, the two
groups are equal. A member of each group is, on average, equally like to
be imprisoned given an arrest.

The right panel of Figure 4.1 reveals that adjusting for the number of
arrests removes racial differences in the probability of incarceration; be-

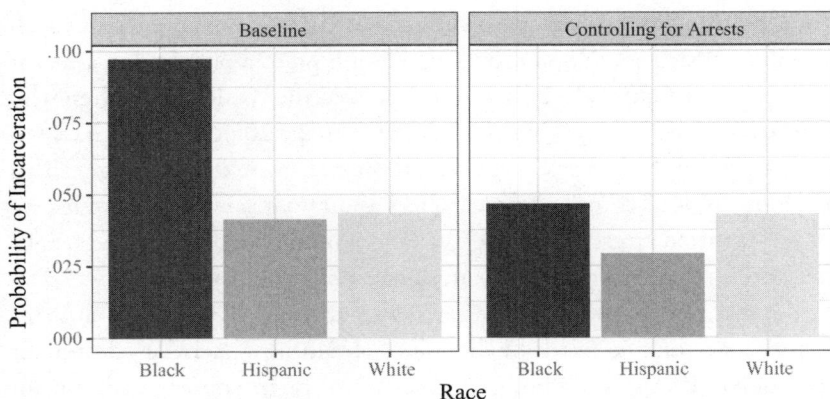

Figure 4.1. Probabilities of Incarceration, by Race. After controlling for the number of prior arrests, the probabilities of incarceration of Blacks and non-Blacks converge.

tween Black and white individuals, the chances of incarceration for those with the average number of arrests in the sample are now nearly indistinguishable (and not significantly different), at just under 5 percent. Latinos show a slightly lower probability of being incarcerated than either Black or white individuals, though this difference, too, is within the margin of error. In the data underlying Figure 4.1, the number of prior arrests is also the strongest predictor of being incarcerated at all levels of arrest frequency for all racial groups. The important point, then, is that, conditional on arrests, there are no significant or meaningful differences between Black and white individuals in incarceration.[17]

To be clear, these results do not imply there is no racial bias in arrest. What they do reveal is that racial disparities in incarceration in these data are fundamentally linked to racial disparities in prior arrests. It follows that, if there is bias in arrests, including by cohort, it will be reflected in later stages of criminal processing such as incarceration. Chapter 5 will examine how racial disparities in arrest are explained by individual, family, and social contextual factors, and whether the underpinnings of racial disparities in arrest change over historical time. For now, however, we can expect that if one cohort is arrested more often, its members—of all races—will also be imprisoned more often.

Arrest not only predates incarceration, but it is also a kind of punishment in itself, with considerable evidence, including in the PHDCN+

study, pointing to the deleterious influence of arrest on later outcomes such as being arrested again and dropping out of high school.[18] And in a recent study, Garrett Baker, Dave Kirk, and I showed that Chicago children who were arrested before age nineteen were on average 20 percent less likely to graduate from a four-year college than those not arrested by that age.[19] This relationship persists for college enrollees and remains even after adjusting for self-reported arrests and a wide variety of individual, family, and neighborhood factors, including measures of academic ability.

Notably, Figure 4.2 shows that being arrested is linked to a 15 to 30 percent reduction in the likelihood of obtaining a bachelor's degree for both older (1980s) and younger (mid-1990s) birth cohorts and, within them, all groups of participants defined by race, gender, parental education, and neighborhood economic status. While there are some modest variations across groups, none are significant or substantively large. Given this broad and consistent pattern, we concluded that arrest during adoles-

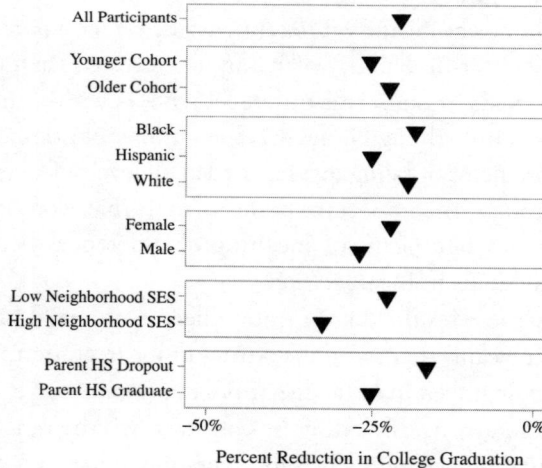

Percent Reduction in College Graduation

Figure 4.2. Links between Teenage Arrest and College Graduation. Being arrested as a teenager is linked to a substantially reduced likelihood of graduating from a four-year college in both the 1987 and 1996 birth cohorts, and for all race, sex, and socioeconomic groups, adjusting for early-life differences and academic ability. *Source:* Reformatted from Garrett Baker, David S. Kirk, and Robert J. Sampson, "The Great Leveler? Juvenile Arrest, College Attainment, and the Future of American Inequality," *Sociology of Education* (2025), figures 2 and 3, https://doi.org/10.1177/00380407251338844.

cence may be the "great leveler" in the sense that it spares no demographic, racial, or socioeconomic group in exerting its educational penalty. Put another way, in terms of their respective differences from a zero relationship, each subgroup's associations are significant, consistently large in magnitude, and in the same direction.[20] This consistency of arrest's reach has broad consequences in our increasingly schooled society, where receiving a college education is perhaps the most salient determinant of well-being throughout life.

In many different ways, then, the evidence supports my focus on the course of becoming officially arrested in different times, especially given the large-scale changes in punishment and violence over the last half-century. It seems obvious in retrospect, but as Tannenbaum and Becker emphasized, official deviance does not exist absent a record—typically, a *public label*. Police stops, for example, are much in the news and they are important for many reasons, but they do not result in the designation of official criminality, which for Becker was the crucial definition of a "master status," whereby the official identification becomes the controlling one.[21] Given that, as we've seen, a more-arrested cohort is also expected to be a more-imprisoned cohort, the fact that little is known about the competing reasons for cohort variability in arrest over the life course is a major problem—not least because the negative consequences of a criminal record, even for low-level arrests, are broad and enduring.[22] Another overlooked fact is that predictive tools used in the criminal justice system and beyond largely rely on official indicators of criminalization, with arrest history most prominent among them. The age at first arrest is also a factor in contemporary predictive risk assessments for sentencing and bail decisions.

Motivated by these facts and challenges, the remainder of this chapter flips the usual script by treating age-based trajectories of arrest and the cumulative risk of official criminalization by age as the objects of interest, rather than the collateral consequences of arrest. My specific aim is to examine how social changes alter the age-graded course of arrest, and to test the cohort social change argument against the major alternative explanation—the cohort compositional argument, which views variations in arrest, and by implication later incarceration, as stemming from cohort differences in demographic makeup, early-life experiences, or criminal propensity (which is in turn the product of a host of family and individual troubles).

ASSESSING EARLY-LIFE COHORT DIFFERENCES

Even with long-term data, testing the cohort compositional argument requires exacting measures of each cohort's distinctive composition and character, reflecting the circumstances of its unique origination. The rich measurement of individuals and the contexts of their childhood development makes the PHDCN nearly ideal for meeting this challenge; it makes it possible to account for a wide-ranging group of important concepts and isolate how historical change influences trajectories of arrest. In effect, I look at each of the compositional and early-life factors recognized to influence criminality and adjust for them, just as arrests were adjusted for in the preceding section. Once the influence of these factors has been removed from the picture, the divergences between cohorts that remain will reveal the impact of social change.

Chapter 3 described the PHDCN design, which is used to measure six sets of differences among individuals based on prior research. Here I provide a brief description of each domain, proceeding from the individual to their family and then to their early-life neighborhood context. Then I show how many of these factors vary by cohort.

Demographics: I include three basic factors that have well-established links to crime and criminalization: sex, race/ethnicity, and immigrant generational status. While sex composition has been relatively constant over the study period, Hispanic and immigrant populations have been growing and remaking the composition of cities like Chicago. Immigrants have been linked to lower crime rates at the community and individual levels and could thus be another differentiator of cohorts.[23]

Personal Behavioral Troubles and Propensity: Early-life behavioral problems may set in motion a cycle of events that perpetuate persistent behavioral problems. They may also signal stable individual tendencies to criminality. As we have seen, criminologists Gottfredson and Hirschi proposed that low self-control is the major individual-level cause of crime, a capacity that is presumed stable from childhood or early adolescence onward. Other scholars, such as James Heckman in his focus on character and psychologist Angela Duckworth in her focus on grit, similarly propose self-control as a major construct in assessing life outcomes.

Accordingly, I control for low self-control (or impulsivity), along with antisocial behavior and anxiety/depression, using the Child Behavior

Checklist.[24] This is a well-known and validated instrument for identifying childhood emotional and behavioral problems based on parental interviews. If there were a super-predator or crime-prone generation, these measures of early predispositions and behavioral tendencies to delinquency would likely flag it. Self-reports of delinquency or low self-control are a possible alternative, but my theoretical focus requires that all early-life cohort characteristics predate crime and arrests, meaning childhood or early adolescence, when self-reports are less common or unavailable across all cohorts. There is also evidence that the validity of self-reports varies by age among juveniles.[25] For these reasons, parental reports of childhood behavior are highly desirable, and as the literature has consistently shown, there is considerable evidence that differences between individuals' antisocial behavior and low self-control in childhood are relatively persistent over time. Furthermore, although data limitations preclude the application of the Child Behavior Checklist in the same exact way across cohorts, the low self-control and antisocial behavior measures nonetheless similarly predict arrest in the full sample and within each cohort, consistent with past research.

Family Structure and Socioeconomic Status: Early-life characteristics related to family structure and socioeconomic status, while not destiny, are well established as important sources of criminality across the life course, whether for developmental or sociological reasons. I measure parental age at the time of participant's birth, whether parents were employed, on welfare, their educational attainment, relationship status, household size, household income, the family's residential stability, and homeownership.

Family Troubles: Basic family structure does not give a wholly satisfactory picture of early-life family context, especially when the goal is to measure factors that may ultimately prove to be criminogenic, or at least criminalizing. Accordingly, I examine an array of problems besetting families that have been shown to affect children's subsequent life-course patterns of crime and the impacts of which may vary by cohort. I measure the extent to which family members have been in trouble with the police or other core institutions, arrested or incarcerated, treated for substance abuse or emotional problems, or had trouble with alcohol or drug problems. Additionally, I measure whether the participants' parents have experienced exposure to violence, trouble with the police, arrest, and depression. Many of these criminally relevant parent- and family-level factors differ across cohorts during a period that saw the rise of mass incarceration, the fall in violence, and the rise and fall of the crack epidemic.

Neighborhood Socioeconomic Context and Composition: Early-life development occurs not just within a family but within a larger neighborhood context. Put simply, where people are born and grow up matters for their subsequent life course. Yet, neighborhoods are not static entities but are themselves subject to change over time, and Chicago, like many contemporary American cities, has changed in recent decades. People are also not static—they often move neighborhoods of residence. The implication is that neighborhood exposure—for example, one cohort being more exposed to high poverty in their neighborhood than another cohort—may constitute a cohort difference in early life exposure that materializes as differences in lifetime patterns of arrest. Accordingly, I adjust for socioeconomic and demographic neighborhood characteristics measured in respondents' early lives and before the onset of first arrest. Because children were followed no matter where they moved, our team was able to create measures from the US Census of the percentage of residents in poverty, foreign born, Black, Hispanic, unemployed, and college educated, as well as the percentage of housing units that were owner occupied and the percentage of female-headed households with children. These variables, all of which were measured at age nine for every cohort, constitute elements of neighborhoods that consistently predict crime, violence, and arrest.

Neighborhood Crime, Criminal Justice, and Toxic Environment: Finally, I consider early-life neighborhood crime, criminal justice, and environmental factors as separate domains because these are distinctive features of neighborhoods that varied greatly across the childhoods of the cohorts. Crime began its swift decline in Chicago in the mid-1990s, for example, just as the younger cohorts were born. I focus on violence, given the detrimental development consequences of exposure to violence for children. Similarly, while the ascent of incarceration was already underway when the oldest cohort was born, incarceration rates continued to climb throughout the 1990s, making childhood exposure to neighborhood incarceration also vary by cohort. Given the geographical concentration of incarceration in Chicago, these changes are particularly pronounced for a subset of neighborhoods, as I showed in *Great American City*. To tap such neighborhood differences, I include neighborhood incarceration rates (admissions per

100,000) and violent crime rates per 100,000 for three types of crimes—homicide, robbery, and weapons offenses—that were available for the city of Chicago from the early 1990s to the early 2000s. Each measure taps the neighborhoods where children were living when they were between about five to twelve years old.[26] While I cannot measure it at exactly similar ages, I also adjust for neighborhood differences in policing intensity in childhood, a composite measure based on the ratio of Chicago Police Department arrests to offenses in neighborhoods that were available in the late 1990s.

Similarly, I adjust for several environmental risk factors, including lead levels measured in the blood of neighborhoods' children by the Chicago Department of Public Health. Lead exposure has been linked to crime and children's exposure to it has declined markedly in recent decades, as further documented in later chapters. I also adjust for signs of physical disorder (such as graffiti or vacant buildings) and social disorder (such as drinking or fighting in public) that may trigger police responses, as well as the density of alcohol stores and gated buildings, determined through videotaped systematic observations. From surveys with residents, I adjust for the social cohesion and informal social controls in a neighborhood, what previously I have called "collective efficacy," and which has been shown to predict crime.[27]

Before heading into my analysis, I want to reiterate that my goal here is to first determine the extent of variance in compositional and early-life conditions between cohorts, then see how well that variance explains divergence in official criminalization between cohorts over the life course. Figure 4.3 demonstrates that non-trivial differences do in fact exist between the mid-1990s cohort and those born before then. For example, those born in the mid-1990s were systematically advantaged in their exposure to potentially criminogenic early-life conditions compared to the older cohorts born in the early to mid-1980s. The younger cohort's parents were 57 percent less likely to be arrested and almost 70 percent more likely to have a university degree, and their early-life neighborhoods exposed them to considerably less poverty, lead in the environment, violence, and concentrated incarceration. Depending on the offense type, neighborhood violence rates in childhood were anywhere from 83 percent (homicide) to over 200 percent (weapon offenses) higher among the older cohorts. These are large

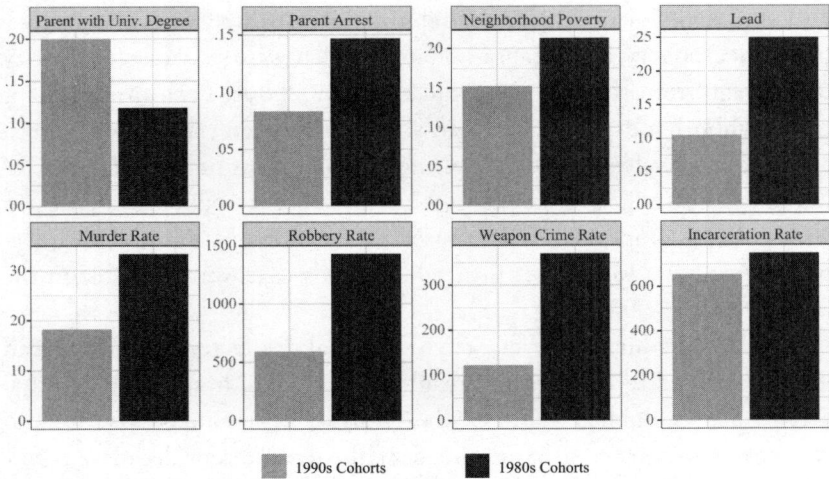

Figure 4.3. Cohort Comparisons of Early-Life Disadvantages. *Top row:* The first and second panels show the proportion of participants whose parents obtained a college degree and had been arrested, respectively. The third and fourth panels show the average poverty rate and the proportion of children with unsafe blood-lead levels in participants' neighborhoods, respectively. *Bottom row:* Rates per 100,000 people in participants' neighborhoods. *Source:* Reformatted from Roland Neil and Robert J. Sampson, "The Birth Lottery of History: Arrest over the Life Course of Multiple Cohorts Coming of Age, 1995–2018," *American Journal of Sociology* 126, no. 5 (2021): 1127–1178, figure 2.

differences, large enough that it seems plausible that, on their own, these compositional and early-life circumstances may explain divergences in arrest and other outcomes between cohorts.

COHORT DIVERGENCE IN ARREST TRAJECTORIES

What we need now is a way to quantify arrest along the life course for each cohort, using respondents' official arrest histories from 1995 through 2020. I focus on an easily understood metric in answering the question—what is the probability of being arrested at each age over the life course during this period? With the multiple cohort design, we can determine how the relationship between age and arrest varies as a function of historical period.[28]

Figure 4.4(a) presents visual results of the arrest trajectories for three birth cohorts that capture the range of historical time examined—those born in 1980 (representing the cohort aged 15 at the beginning of the study), those born in 1985, and those born in 1995 (the infant cohort).[29] This panel does not adjust for any early-life or compositional differences between the three cohorts. The specific years in which the cohorts reached various ages are denoted to clarify the historical periods through which they each aged. The multi-cohort design permits us to see the distinctive and persistent differences in arrest trajectories that separate the mid-1990s cohort and those born in the 1980s. For example, people born in 1995 had just over a .05 probability of arrest when they were twenty years old, in 2015, compared to the 1980 birth cohort, whose arrest probability in 2000 at the same age was more than twice as high. Arrest rates among the 1980s cohorts, by contrast, are more similar. The main distinction, then, and it is a substantial one at roughly 100 percent, is between the older and younger cohorts.[30]

Now we can ask the critical question. How much of the difference between older and younger cohorts can be attributed to the cohort compositional argument (illustrated in Figure 4.3), and how much to the social change argument? It is clearly possible that the observed inter-cohort differentiation in arrest trajectories reflects the influence of individual, family, and neighborhood factors that are determined at birth or during childhood rather than aging through a changing social world during late adolescence

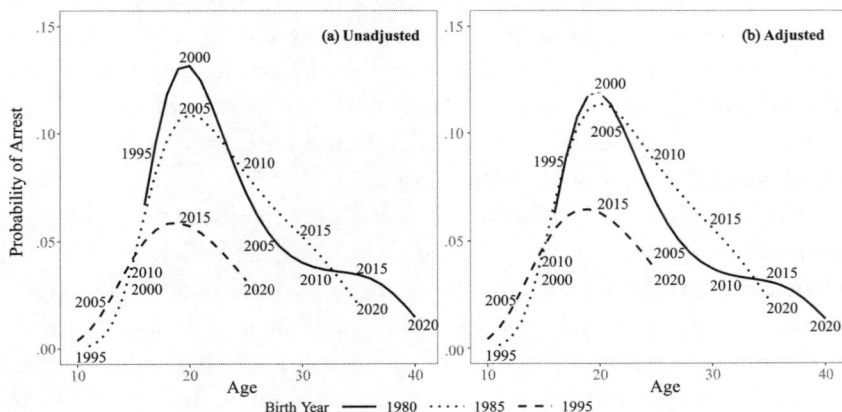

Figure 4.4. Diverging Life-Course Patterns of Arrest for Three Birth Cohorts. Before and after adjusting for compositional and early-life differences, older cohorts are more likely to be arrested across most of the age range.

and early adulthood when we observe peak difference in the chances of arrest. To assess these competing explanations of the results, I control for the five sets of differences in composition and early-life experiences described earlier (the sixth category on neighborhood crime and toxicity will be revisited later in the chapter): demographics; respondents' low self-control, aggression, and anxiety/depression levels; family structure and status; family problems with the law and substance use; and early-life neighborhood social structure and processes. These new results are visualized in Figure 4.4(b).

Strikingly, in comparing panels (a) and (b), we see that there is no material difference in the general pattern. This is the case despite the general importance of the factors that I adjust for in predicting crime and criminal justice, and despite variability in many of these factors across birth cohorts. The logical implication is that cohort differences in arrest trajectories are not confounded by the characteristics of the subjects, their families, or their early-life neighborhoods, but rather are due to the strongly divergent historical periods through which the cohorts aged as adolescents and beyond.

At this point, you may have noticed that the social change argument is being illustrated by removing all the factors that it does not include, namely the compositional and early-life influences we looked at above, and ascribing what differences remain to social change. Chapter 6 will take a different approach by teasing out the often-countervailing mechanisms of social change such as policing behavior, police size, drug enforcement and use, violent behavior, economic conditions, lead exposure, and technology. But for now, it is important to notice that existing theories of criminalization built on compositional and early-life factors are insufficient to explain the divergences in arrest between cohorts.

The next feature to notice in Figure 4.4(b) is the sheer power or size, even after adjusting for early-life differences, of the influence of social change, which can be visualized by looking at the differences in the height of the curves. Figure 4.4(b) reveals that a rapid increase in arrest during early adolescence is visible across cohorts; this is the age-crime spike that researchers have confirmed for a wide variety of times and places. What we can now isolate using the multi-cohort study design is that while the spike as such is given across cohorts, simultaneously there is clear evidence of large historical variation in later arrest trajectories despite cohort controls. Different cohorts can have spikes of highly divergent shapes, and those shapes matter immensely for life outcomes. Around the age of sixteen is where a notable divergence begins, with the probability of arrest for the 1980s birth cohorts rising and then reaching a peak at just under .12 when the 1980 cohort was twenty. By contrast, the 1995 cohort has an age-arrest trajectory that increases at a less steep rate, reaching a peak probability of arrest just over .06 at age nineteen, before quickly returning to the levels of earlier adolescence. The extent of arrest at peak ages of offending therefore differs by a factor of nearly two between younger and older birth cohorts.[31]

Figure 4.4(b) also reveals that the 1995 cohort can be expected to be arrested in their early twenties at a rate that the older cohorts did not experience until they were in their thirties. For instance, at the age of fifteen both the 1985 and 1995 birth cohorts had an arrest probability around .045. Yet the 1985 cohort did not experience this same probability again until it was thirty-one, in sharp contrast to the 1995 cohort who did so at the age of twenty-three. Put simply, there is an eight-year gap between the older cohorts and the youngest cohorts in the time it takes for arrest to lower to a given point. These large differences in the level and age-graded pattern of arrest over the life course seem to have been brought about by the differing socio-historical contexts through which individuals came of age.

One might reasonably argue that the key difference in the makeup of the cohorts lies in their early exposure to local crime, violence, lead, disorder, policing, and incarceration within their neighborhood, and that these differences drive the overall disparities in cohort arrests. Crime and punishment were changing over the period in which various cohorts were children, and we have seen large differences between the 1980s and 1990s birth cohorts in neighborhood crime and criminal justice-related variables, along with exposure to lead toxicity (Figure 4.3), which was declining rapidly in the 1990s and 2000s. One might also reasonably argue that those children who stayed in Chicago were most at risk for arrest. Chicago generally had higher rates of crime and disorder than surrounding areas, and prior work on the PHDCN showed that those who moved out of the city reported lower rates of violence.[32] Does controlling these early neighborhood differences or residential location in Chicago change the story?

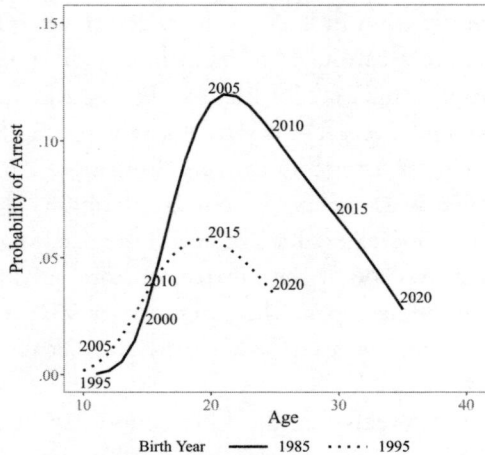

Figure 4.5. Persistent Cohort Divergences with Additional Adjustments. Cohort divergences persist among those living in Chicago until age seventeen, additionally adjusting for their childhood neighborhood crime and toxic environments.

Not according to the results presented in Figure 4.5, which is limited to study members who lived in Chicago up until age seventeen (about 71 percent of the sample). This figure accounts for exposure to toxic environments, crime, and criminal justice factors along with the same factors as Figure 4.4(b).[33] For simplicity and a conservative test, I focus on the 1985 and 1995 cohorts, where there is similarity in age coverage up to the mid-twenties and where only ten years separates historical experiences coming of age. Yet Figure 4.5 shows that the 1985 birth cohort of Chicagoans still had arrest probabilities in late adolescence and early adulthood that are approximately twice the size of those of the mid-1990s cohort who lived in the city over the same ages. Further analysis reveals that a similar pattern holds for other 1980s cohorts. And while arrest rates are expectedly somewhat lower for non-Chicagoans, the same cohort pattern holds when we examine their trajectories.[34]

In short, the data reveal that cohort differences in childhood exposure to local crime and toxic conditions within their neighborhoods, while important, do not explain why some cohorts went on to be arrested later at such persistently higher levels. Nor does selectivity in residential mobility—Chicagoans and non-Chicagoans alike are subject to the birth lottery of history.

Cumulative Cohort Risks by Age

So far I have looked at the probability of arrest across the life course, which captures multiple arrests that individuals accrued at different ages. A different question is the extent to which different groups are ever arrested, and the life stages during which first arrests tend to happen. Especially in adolescence, the first moment of official criminalization becomes, for many, a turning point leading to a kind of downward spiral that includes further contacts with the criminal justice system and other problems later in life. I am thus motivated to also ask, how large is the group at risk of adverse life chances that flow from arrest?

To answer this question, we can borrow from life-history methods widely used in demography to examine, at all ages for which we have data, what percentage of a cohort has ever been arrested. We would expect this percentage to see the greatest jumps at the ages where the most individuals are being arrested for the first time, and for it to level off at ages where few to no individuals encounter their first arrest. Because I am interested in arrest at early ages, I focused this analysis on the youngest (mid-1990s) and slightly older 1987 (age nine) cohorts, for which we have the most complete data on arrests prior to age seventeen. Analogous to Figure 4.4, I not only examined the raw, cumulative prevalence of first arrest by cohort, but also the prevalence of first arrest by cohort after adjusting for all the compositional and early-life characteristics used in previous analyses.

The differences between cohorts are pronounced. Arrest profiles, whether looking at raw arrest data or arrest data that accounts for early-life characteristics, begin to diverge quite early at about age thirteen and then continue to diverge so that by about age twenty, approximately 30 percent of the older cohort members had been arrested, compared to less than 20 percent among the younger cohort. Even after controlling for a wide range of individual, family, and neighborhood characteristics, these differences continue to grow so that just five years later, at age twenty-four, over 40 percent of the older cohort had been arrested, compared to just over 20 percent of the younger cohort. The age at which one is first arrested and the cumulative prevalence of arrest over their life course are therefore direct functions of when one reaches adolescence in historical time.

Persistently Bad? "Chronic Offenders" Revisited

Now that we've established substantial divergence in arrests between cohorts, we can drill down into those arrests and see if that inter-cohort divergence holds true for particular subgroups of officially-defined offenders. Essentially, we want to know if social change operates on the whole cohort equally, or if certain subgroups are more impacted. The publication of Marvin Wolfgang and colleagues' *Delinquency in a Birth Cohort* animated nearly fifty years' worth of research on repeated criminal activity and especially on what they called "chronic offenders" who were processed time and again by the criminal justice system.[35] The basic claim in this research turn was that there are subgroups of offenders with distinct trajectories of crime that are masked in averages like the age-arrest probabilities that I have shown so far. Chronic or life-course-persistent offenders in particular are thought to be qualitatively different than intermittent or adolescent-type offenders, or those who refrain from crime altogether.

Based on research with Roland Neil and Daniel Nagin published in the *Proceedings of the National Academy of Sciences,* I examine two questions about so-called offender groups that are typically set aside.[36] First, are there distinct trajectories of such groups, defined by arrests, and if so, do they vary by cohort? Second, we need to apply the same control test for those subgroups we performed above for entire cohorts, seeing if cohort differences in arrest-group membership are explained by the cohort compositional argument; that is, if they reflect the fact that cohorts differ demographically or in their level of exposure to early-life risk factors. If we get the same result as above, we will be able to say that a particular subgroup, for example, the highest-rate group, is as susceptible to social change as the group at large. Establishing whether cohort differences in subgroups reflect the dynamic influence of social environment across the life course, what I've been calling social change, is crucial for our understanding of crime more broadly in terms of theory, policy, and, ultimately, our conception of individual character.

Answering my first question, the results in Figure 4.6(a) are consistent with past research in revealing three basic trajectory groups. At the bottom is the Low group that categorizes those with few or no arrests over the life course, which in effect means they are "innocents" with respect to criminal legal contact. In the second or Medium group are those with higher

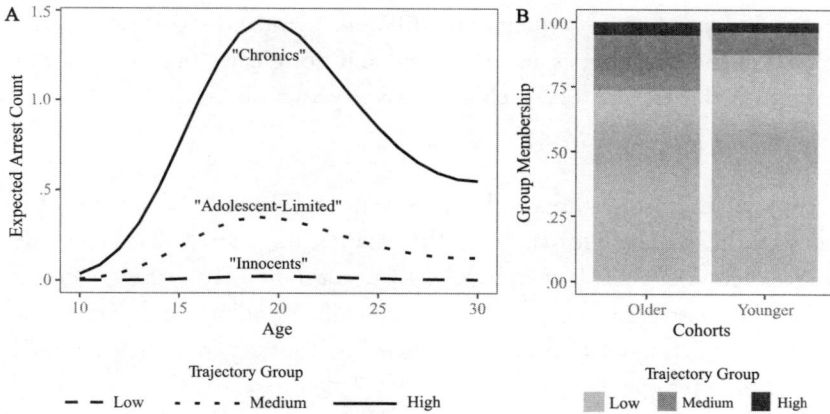

Figure 4.6. Cohort Differences in Arrest Trajectories. Younger cohorts are more likely to be in the low-arrest trajectory group and less likely to be in medium- or high-arrest trajectory groups. *Source:* Reformatted from Roland Neil, Robert J. Sampson, and Daniel S. Nagin, "Social Change and Cohort Differences in Group-Based Arrest Trajectories over the Last Quarter-Century," *Proceedings of the National Academy of Sciences* 118, no. 31 (2021), figure 1.

arrest rates that peak in adolescence and then decline to nearly the level of innocents, a pattern similar to what Terrie Moffitt called "adolescent-limited" offenders.[37] The top or High group contains the persistent or chronic offenders that have so fascinated students of crime. Whatever we wish to call each group is less important than the answer to my second question, whether each group is as impacted by social change as the entire cohort. The result in Figure 4.6(b) shows that controlling for the wide-ranging set of demographic characteristics and early-life risk factors employed earlier, the older cohorts sorted into the medium / adolescent-limited and high-rate chronic categories at rates that vastly exceed those of the younger cohort.

One way to quantify the divergence between cohorts is to determine the odds of a randomly chosen member of each cohort falling into one subgroup rather than another. In this case, a member of the older cohorts had odds of ending up in the Medium arrest trajectory group compared to the Low group over five times higher than a member of the younger cohorts. The odds of membership in the High "chronic" group as opposed to the "innocents" was over 2.5 times higher for the older compared to the younger cohorts, and both differences were statistically significant. Not only does cohort membership predict how individuals sort into these three trajectory groups independent of demographic differences and early risk factors, the impact of social change is also comparable if not greater in size to that of several notable risk factors, such as of poverty and self-control.

*   *   *

Teenagers and young adults will always be in trouble with the law. But this fact's implications are misleading. This chapter has shown that *when* one is a teenager matters at least as much as—if not more than—the age-crime spike itself, with some teenagers facing radically different consequences for identical behavior solely because of their birth lottery, not their parents' actions or inactions.

That might be a relief to parents, but I am concerned with societal implications. The evidence reveals stark cohort inequalities in arrest probability by age, membership in traditional criminological groupings like "chronic" and "adolescent-limited" offenders, and cumulative arrest prevalence. Chicago's older birth cohorts, compared to those born just a decade later, faced up to double the likelihood of arrest—both during peak adolescent delinquency and later when adult arrest rates typically decline. These differences don't stem from factors emphasized by scholars and popular discourse—antisocial disposition, lack of grit or self-control, race, family background, economic status, or childhood neighborhood poverty. Instead, they arise from the distinct socio-historical environments each cohort encountered while coming of age.

CHAPTER 5

Race, Class, and Grit Meet the Mark of Time

Every birth cohort includes a mix of people from diverse racial and social class backgrounds. So far, in the interest of isolating the impact of social change, I've adjusted for the variations in these factors. Now it's time to examine these differences more closely, so that we can develop a more nuanced understanding of who is most affected by social change, and how. As will become clear, this direct analysis of race and class builds on surprising findings from multi-cohort studies in other fields.

Take health, for example. A long-term study in China found that the association of socioeconomic status with positive health trajectories, usually taken for granted, actually depends on the historical context through which different birth cohorts age. Unexpectedly, among recent cohorts, it is less true that being in the upper-income class brings greater assurance of leading a healthy life.[1] This weakening of an advantage enjoyed by older cohorts does not align with how we usually think about the durable or even increasing advantages of possessing economic resources. Or consider the divergent race- and class-specific trends for the intergenerational economic mobility of US children born between 1978 and 1992. Research shows that among Black children in families at all income levels there have been improvements in children rising above their parents' station in life—but among low-income whites there have been declines.[2]

While long-term, multi-cohort studies of crime and legal system involvement are relatively rare, we have compelling reasons to examine how the birth lottery of history intersects with race and class in shaping arrest patterns from the late twentieth century to today. Are disparities growing or shrinking for disadvantaged groups? Have racial gaps in arrest rates changed across recent birth cohorts? Have the factors explaining racial disparities shifted? Having a vast multi-cohort dataset enables the investigation of these crucial questions about how race and class interact with social change.

Cohort differences in the experience of historical transformations at critical ages may also depend on individual developmental characteristics that are less structural in nature, like people's varying temperaments and levels of self-control. Stick-to-itiveness, or what has popularly been called *grit,* is a valued trait in our society.[3] The natural question that follows from the logic of this book is whether grit can outmaneuver social change. Some scholars claim it can, even though existing evidence is typically ahistorical or limited to comparisons within a single cohort. But individual self-control or perseverance might be valuable in any cohort, even if its relative impact changes between cohorts—just as we saw in Chapter 4 that the adolescent age-crime spike exists in every PHDCN+ cohort but its velocity and magnitude can vary dramatically between cohorts, with major life consequences for the unlucky. Assessing this possibility requires looking at variations both within birth cohorts and between them to determine the extent to which the meaning of individual characteristics, such as self-control, are shaped by social change.

Accordingly, the content of this chapter will continue to unite life-course development and social change by assessing how trajectories of arrest by age vary among the PHDCN+ cohorts of children, isolating a few of the compositional and early-life factors that were previously controlled for. Chapter 4 showed that these factors cannot explain much of the variation in arrest patterns between older and younger cohorts, whereas social change does. Here, the objective is not to account for why that inter-cohort variation exists, which Chapter 6 disentangles, but to understand it in greater detail by testing the general hypothesis that not all groups experienced social changes like the crime drop and the rise and fall of aggressive policing in the same way. I focus on three of the most influential factors in the study of crime and criminal justice contact: socioeconomic disadvantage, race, and self-control.[4]

THE DISADVANTAGE GRADIENT

What has been called the *socioeconomic gradient* is a well-known phenomenon—for virtually every aspect of health and well-being in American life and beyond, those in higher socioeconomic positions tend to do better, and those lower on the ladder, worse.[5] Simply put, socioeconomic status and its correlated advantages provide protection from the slings and arrows of life. But is this true for every major snare in life—including arrest by the police? The strength of the socioeconomic gradient has led many scholars to assume its durability with respect to historical change, but as the research mentioned above from China suggests, this may be a faulty assumption. And what about the disadvantaged end of the gradient? The wealthy or educated might be stably buffered from hard times, at least relatively speaking, but the poor, especially poor people of color, might be uniquely vulnerable during periods of rapid change.

Empirically, cohort data on socioeconomic status and criminal legal involvement are contradictory and slim overall. Those born between 1965 and 1969 who were poor and lacked a high school diploma were locked up at a far higher rate than poor high-school dropouts born in earlier decades, for example, especially among Black individuals.[6] In this case, the relationships among education, race, and incarceration seemed to change, getting worse with regard to racial and class inequality in the middle to latter part of the twentieth century. But these are aggregate statistics that do not account for other cohort compositional differences or individual trajectories, making it impossible to say whether those trends are the result of social change in the same way that shifting arrest patterns between the PHDCN+ cohorts were influenced by social forces. And besides, the 1960s reflect an older cohort and thereby a different historical context from the standpoint of this book.

Consider also that at least in national trends, white imprisonment rates have been increasing in recent decades, especially among women, while the rate of incarceration for Black individuals has been declining, quite rapidly.[7] Increasing "deaths of despair" such as suicide or drug overdoses, especially among low-educated whites, indicate worsening inequality over

time.[8] These changing and sometimes contradictory race and class differences across cohorts in incarceration and other dimensions of well-being
further motivate a life-course inquiry into arrest, which is a trigger for a
host of collateral consequences including incarceration and lower educational attainment. In this chapter, I thus explore whether socioeconomic
and race differences in trajectories of arrest have narrowed, expanded, or
remained the same across the era of crime declines and the moderation of
incarceration since about 2010.

There are good theoretical reasons to take up this inquiry as well. Classic
theories of crime such as strain, social disorganization, and social control
all point to the importance of socioeconomic disadvantage in both motivating and regulating crime.[9] Several influential scholars in the strain theory
tradition, for example, highlight the impact on crime and criminal legal
involvement of contentious peer encounters and conflictual interactions
with the police among disadvantaged groups. Notably, Elijah Anderson
argued that the escalation of friction in what is called the "code of the
streets" is exacerbated in poor, racially segregated neighborhoods, and, I
would argue, in times of aggressive law enforcement tactics such as broken-
windows policing.[10] Research on economic deindustrialization and the
growth of urban violence also points to the vulnerability of socioeconom-
ically disadvantaged adolescents, especially minorities, who came of age
during the height of the drug wars and extreme violence of the late 1980s
and early 1990s in Chicago, as in other cities.[11] Breaking down and comparing PHDCN+ cohorts by socioeconomic status and race will not only
show who is and is not vulnerable, but how that vulnerability changes
across time.

A revealing ethnography by the sociologist Randol Contreras tells such
a story of how macrosocial changes intersect with individual disadvantage
in very personal terms. He grew up at the tail end of the crack epidemic in
the South Bronx, experiencing a very different iteration of the drug trade
than his older neighbors.[12] Contreras documents how he and his friends
became teenagers just at the time when crack was fading away and the
profits from crime were plummeting. Yet, they had grown up watching
their older peers get rich and naively entered the drug trade themselves,
only to find that it had quickly dried up, leaving them with few other options once they had committed to the drug life. Contreras and his peers
traveled down a road of sometimes desperate crime, chasing dreams of get-

ting rich like the flashy guys just a few years older than them. But large social changes—especially in policing and incarceration, forms of urban revitalization, and falling violence—rendered that world almost extinct, altering the South Bronx and cities across the land, including Chicago.

The drug trade of yesteryear might have disappeared and along with it dreams of getting rich, but of course those dreams were always illusory. The drug trade was violent, and its participants faced heightened risks of mortality and incarceration, which Contreras described in painful detail. The influence of social change is often paradoxical like this, bringing improvements in some areas and increased risks in others. In this case, despite obvious hardships, we have reason to believe that the disadvantaged members of birth cohorts who came of age more recently will face substantially improved prospects because of changing social mechanisms like the crime drop and the slow recovery of the South Bronx from the heyday of urban despair. By luck of the birth lottery, the youth of Contreras's cohort may have missed out on the gangster life they imagined, but at the same time, they, and especially subsequent cohorts, fared better in avoiding the snares of arrest, incarceration, and mortality over the life course relative to disadvantaged individuals who were born before them but who were otherwise similar in all other respects. Contreras himself is today a tenured professor, an achievement that would have been even more difficult had he been born only a few years earlier.

A different way to state this idea is that the consequences of poverty have been altered over time, due in important ways to changes in crime and criminal justice contexts. The penalty for being poor, contrary to what is often portrayed as an age of inexorably rising inequality, might have actually decreased in recent decades, at least for some groups. But the increase in deaths of despair among those at lower education levels, for example, complicates the narrative of improvement in life chances among those in the lower socioeconomic brackets. If social change really has provided greater protections for the disadvantaged, at least where arrest is concerned, then we will expect to see larger disparities between higher and lower socioeconomic status brackets in the older PHDCN+ cohorts, and less disparity within the younger cohort.

Looking at socioeconomic status also requires looking at race, which as we know are interrelated. It is thus important to assess if the socioeconomic gradient of arrest has changed over time in ways that impact racial groups differently, especially Black individuals, who experience on average the greatest concentration of disadvantage. This analysis will also indicate if racial disparities in arrest among white, Black, and Hispanic people have changed between cohorts, and what might explain those disparities. There is surprisingly little research that has examined whether the racial disparities in criminal legal involvement over the life course have changed during mass incarceration and the crime drop, or whether their determinants have changed. If, for example, poor minorities or wealthy whites are relatively advantaged today compared to their counterparts of an earlier era, or alternatively, are worse off, at least with respect to criminalization's early stages, then we need to revise our thinking on how social and racial inequality relates to contemporary social change.

THE SELF-CONTROL GRADIENT

Low self-control has been posited as *the* individual-level cause of crime at all ages, and considerable research has established low self-control is a strong predictor not just of criminal behavior but also a wide range of adult outcomes.[13] The title of a paper in a leading journal, the *Proceedings of the National Academy of Sciences,* stated the thesis clearly: "A gradient of childhood self-control predicts health, wealth, and public safety."[14] In popular terms, the grit inherent in high self-control seems to be the elixir for challenging situations.[15] Based on this logic, low self-control should predict arrest at all ages and times.

The criminologist Per-Olof Wikström has drawn attention to the interplay of self-control with the environments in which individuals are embedded, in his case micro-environments like conflictual situations or neighborhood disadvantage.[16] Here I shift the focus further upward by examining how low self-control leads to differing chances of arrest depending on the historically varying macroenvironments in which aging occurs. Given the historical shifts that I demonstrated in Chapter 4, I expect that both high and low self-control individuals in older birth cohorts, even if they possess the same socioeconomic resources and are otherwise identical to those individuals from younger cohorts, are nonetheless uniquely disadvantaged. They were exposed to higher rates of criminal justice interactions and potentially violent encounters, especially disputatious encounters and interpersonal provocations from peers (such as threats and insults) during the vulnerable stages of growing up and coming of age. Adolescence is hard enough in the best of times, rife with fraught interactions among peers and with authority figures that are always at risk of escalation. But the chances that impulsive outbursts and everyday interactions of low self-control youth with school officials and the police will result in formal discipline or arrest are likely to be enhanced in times of heightened punitive school policies and "zero tolerance" policing.

Theoretically then, there is reason to hypothesize that the conversion of given tendencies to crime and disputatious encounters into a criminal record is dependent on historical context. In this interpretation, whether low self-control or a hot temper leads to arrest is shaped by macrosocial changes that go well beyond individual-level and even many family or social class explanations, in turn altering our understanding of what the gradient of low self-control portends for the future life course. The historical trends in policing and violent crime suggest that even high self-control adolescents of the older cohort faced greater challenges than their low self-control counterparts from later cohorts. If social change between those cohorts were drastic enough, individuals with the highest self-control in the older cohorts might even have faced the same odds of arrest as the lowest self-control group in the younger cohort. If high self-control in one year is worth the same as low self-control ten years later, then we will need to revise some of our core assumptions about individual character and its bearing on the life course.

RACE AND CLASS INEQUALITY

In Chapter 4, I demonstrated the stark divergence in arrest patterns between the older and younger PHDCN+ cohorts. But that analysis did not identify whether any particular groups are more impacted by social change than others. By breaking the cohorts down by class and race, I can now show what groups are most vulnerable to or insulated from the shifting tides of social change. I first examine how the arrest trajectories vary between older and younger cohorts based on socioeconomic status, controlling for all other variables. I base this analysis on a broad-based index of socioeconomic advantage (or, at the other end, disadvantage) that combines household income, parental education, parental work status, and whether parents received public assistance (or TANF).[17] This index was interacted with the age and period effects examined in Chapter 4 while including all the same control variables such as individual, family, and neighborhood characteristics, allowing the age-arrest relationship to vary as a function of historical period (as indicated by cohort) and (dis)advantage.

The results are shown in Figure 5.1. To simplify the visual presentation, I collapse the 1980s cohorts into one category because of the similarity of their arrest patterns in Chapter 4 and to increase the sample sizes when splitting the results by disadvantage.[18] We can see that the youngest (mid-1990s) cohort is similar to the 1980s cohorts until around the age of fifteen, after which it diverges on a flatter, less criminal trajectory. However, we can see also that there are large differences in the extent of this divergence according to how privileged individuals' backgrounds were, such that just five years later, at the age of twenty, the gap in arrests between cohorts is quite large among those from disadvantaged backgrounds. Panel (a) reveals, for example, that the 1995 birth cohort had just over a .05 probability of arrest at age twenty compared to over .13 for the older 1980s cohorts, which translates into more than double the rate of arrest, net of all other factors. Differences from the ages of eighteen to twenty and after age twenty between the disadvantaged 1995 birth cohort and the 1980s birth cohorts that are plotted in panel (a) are notable, as well.

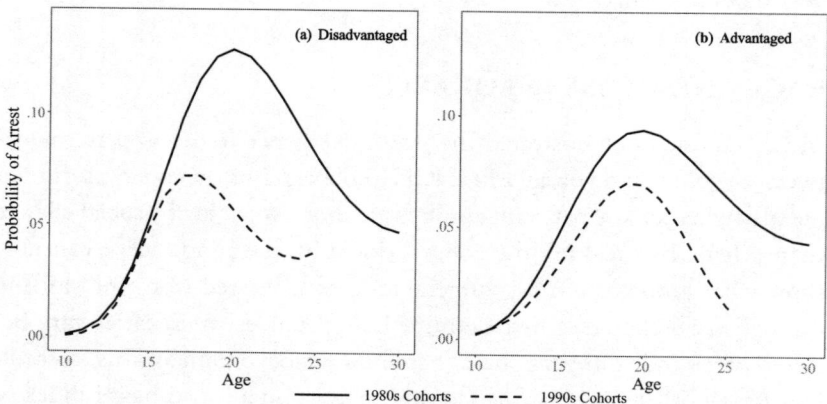

Figure 5.1. Arrest Gaps between Birth Cohorts and Advantage Levels. Arrest gaps between birth cohorts are wider for disadvantaged than for advantaged individuals.

By contrast, the cohort gap is more compressed among advantaged individuals—the 1980s birth cohorts had just over a .09 probability of arrest at age twenty, not that much higher (and not significantly different) than the approximately .07 probability of their otherwise similar advantaged counterparts born in 1995.[19] Another way to state these patterns is that the penalty of disadvantage weakened over time, such that for the younger cohort the traditional relationship between socioeconomic status and arrest is minimal. One can trace almost a straight line at peak arrest from the disadvantaged younger cohort on the left to the advantaged younger cohort on the right.

That there are larger inter-cohort differences for disadvantaged individuals than advantaged individuals means that disadvantaged individuals are important in driving the overall inter-cohort differences reported in the last chapter. In other words, social changes in crime and punishment in the last quarter-century have most acutely affected the disadvantaged. A related, yet distinct implication, as evidenced by the fact that the arrest curves vary within the left panel, is that coming from a given background of disadvantage does not carry static implications for subsequent life-course patterns of criminalization, as is often assumed. Rather, the relationship between disadvantage and arrest is changing, and in this case, improving for the poor.

Another way of parsing the data, like I did in Chapter 4, is to look at the cumulative proportion of individuals who have ever been arrested against their age, now broken down by cohort birth year and by levels of disadvantage. This strategy allows me to ask how large the gaps are in overall arrest likelihood between advantaged and disadvantaged individuals coming of age through different time periods. I pay particular attention to the early life stages during which first arrests tend to happen, the teenage years and early adulthood.

Figure 5.2 graphs the cumulative prevalence of arrest for the economically advantaged and disadvantaged, here defined by the top and bottom fourths of the overall socioeconomic status distribution, respectively.[20] The results, though based on a different metric and using different definitions of (dis)advantage, are pronounced in much the same way as Figure 5.1. Those born into advantaged families in the mid-to-late 1980s have similar patterns as those born in the 1990s, both advantaged and disadvantaged. Indeed, the three cumulative prevalence curves are nearly indistinguishable at all

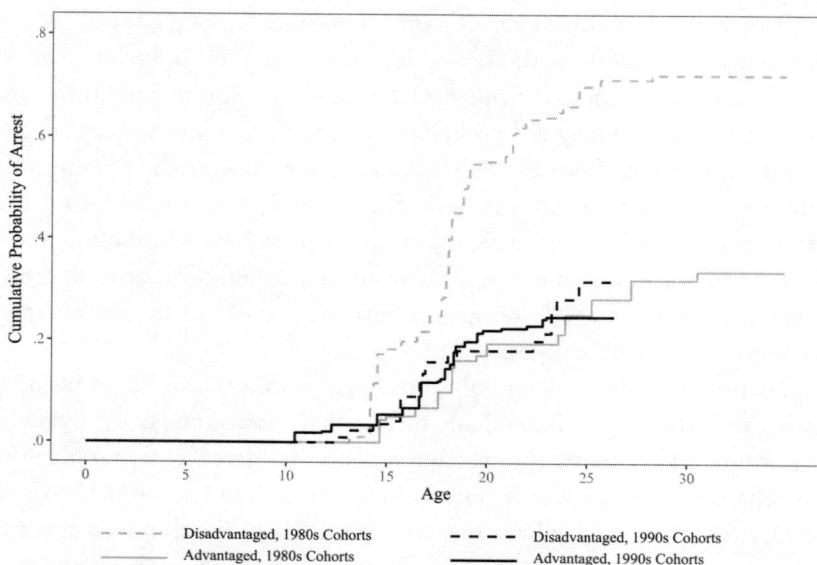

Figure 5.2. Cumulative Arrest Prevalences of Cohorts and Advantage Levels. Cumulative arrest prevalence is highest for the disadvantaged in mid-1980s birth cohorts compared to the advantaged in the same cohort and to both advantaged and disadvantaged individuals in the mid-1990s birth cohorts.

ages for which data exists on each group. About 25 to 30 percent of these groups were arrested by about age twenty-five.

In contrast, some 70 percent of individuals born in the mid-1980s to disadvantaged families were arrested by the same age. Yet unexpectedly, if we are to believe the theories positing that early childhood is destiny, arrest prevalence was similar for this group compared to the others up to early adolescence, before quickly diverging around the age of fourteen. Compared to their advantaged contemporaries, this divergence continues to grow until the mid-twenties and then plateaus. As a result, while advantaged individuals exhibit no material variability in the prevalence of arrest across cohorts, and modest variability in their trajectories of arrest in Figure 5.1, disadvantaged individuals of different cohorts have different trajectories and cumulative prevalence of criminalization as a result of the changing historical contexts through which they've aged. Social change is most visible in its impact on those with the fewest resources.

Racial and Ethnic Disparities

A similar but more nuanced conclusion emerges when we look at interactions with race / ethnicity. The prevalence of arrests has dropped most for African Americans over time, even though arrest is still more prevalent among more recent Black cohorts than white and Hispanic cohorts. Because of the relatively small sample size of whites who are poor, combined with their relatively low arrest levels, I lack the statistical power to do a precise test of disadvantage differences among whites. But the disadvantage results are not explained by racial and ethnic differences—repeating the analysis for only Blacks and Hispanics reveals that the disadvantaged individuals from more recent cohorts had the largest reductions in arrests compared to similar members of older cohorts.

This basic pattern can be seen visually by displaying the simple proportion arrested for Black and Hispanic individuals at the prime ages for arrest, as shown in Figure 5.3. Disadvantaged individuals, or those of lower socioeconomic status, have seen large reductions in arrests in more recent cohorts compared to similar members of older cohorts. For example, in the older cohorts, 60 percent of Black disadvantaged members were arrested in their late teens and early twenties, compared to 26 percent of younger cohort members who were Black and disadvantaged. The corresponding figures for Hispanics are 38 percent and 21 percent, respectively. Moreover, Figure 5.3 reveals small differences in arrest between disadvantaged and advantaged members of the younger cohorts for both Hispanics and Blacks. Moreover, even though the white group presents statistical challenges, they also experienced decreases in arrests among the disadvantaged compared across cohorts. These are not the results we would expect if the disadvantage findings were driven by racial / ethnic differences alone. Although the vulnerability of low socioeconomic status cuts across race, the fact that socioeconomic disadvantage is strongly concentrated among the Black population of Chicago (and elsewhere in the United States) means that the weakening of its relationship with arrest has benefited this population the most.[21]

When it comes to arrest, therefore, the disadvantage penalty has attenuated the most in recent decades among the group that has historically borne the brunt of discrimination, racial segregation of resources, and mass

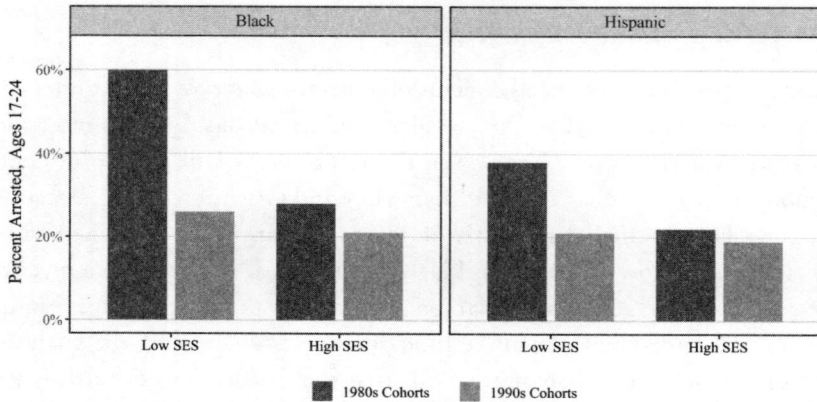

Figure 5.3. Prevalence of Arrest by Race, Cohort, and Socioeconomic Status. Prevalences of arrest by race, cohort, and socioeconomic (SES) status demonstrate a wide gap between birth cohorts for disadvantaged Black individuals.

incarceration—Black Americans. That result hardly calls for a victory lap, but it is good news nevertheless given the history of racial inequality in America and in highly segregated cities like Chicago. Although the magnitude is not as great as for Blacks, the marked decrease in arrest among poor Latinos in the younger cohort is similarly good news and deserving of further study, especially relative to poor whites.

The Social Foundations of Racial Disparities

To better understand racial disparities in arrest rates, we also need to examine competing explanations of their origins. While low socioeconomic status and more generally disadvantage increases arrest risk regardless of race, suggesting that disadvantage might explain racial differences in arrest rates, we must ask whether this relationship holds true across different birth cohorts. Does social change alter what drives racial disparities in arrests? To answer this question, Roland Neil and I analyzed the PHDCN+ data, comparing arrest trajectories by race between two groups: a younger cohort born in the mid-1990s and older cohorts born in the early to mid-1980s.

Our specific aim was to see if childhood inequalities in individual, family, and neighborhood disadvantage (the compositional and early-life factors of Chapter 4) were able to explain disparities in arrest similarly across racial and ethnic groups, and if so, whether this pattern held over time in successive cohorts despite the large social changes that took place from the mid-1990s to 2020. We found this explanation was correct: Large racial disparities in arrests from ages ten up to forty arise from racial inequalities in exposure to cumulative childhood advantages and disadvantages rather than race-specific effects. In other words, we argued that an individual's constellation of compositional and early-life factors affected them similarly, no matter which racial group they occupied; the cause of the racial disparities in arrest was therefore the uneven distribution of these advantages and disadvantages across racial groups.

These results are summarized visually in Figure 5.4. The top row represents baseline differences, similar to the baseline model of Figure 4.4 in the last chapter, but with race pulled out as the variable of interest. The first thing we see is that, as expected, Black individuals have arrest rates much higher than whites—more than double, in fact. Hispanic individuals sit in between, though their average probability of arrest is not that much higher than whites. As also expected based on earlier findings in this

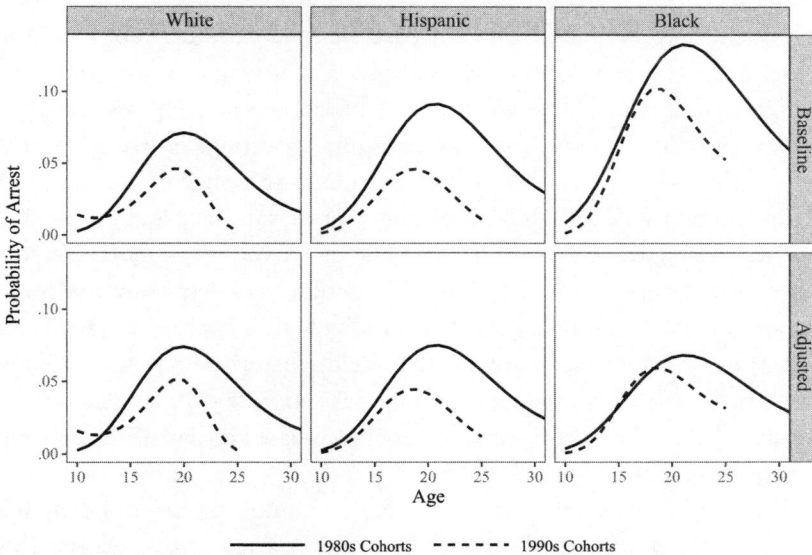

Figure 5.4. Explaining Racial Disparities in Arrest, by Cohort. When early-life factors are held constant, the probability of arrest converges across races.

chapter, the younger cohorts face lower arrest levels than older cohorts, especially for Hispanics, whose arrest levels are about half as high as their older cohort same-race peers were at the same ages. Black arrests vary less by cohort but are still lower for the younger cohort.

One way to begin probing the obvious disparities is to examine for each cohort how arrests would look if everyone faced the same early-life conditions as whites. Essentially, this will control for compositional and early-life factors (excluding race), showing what arrest patterns would be if advantages and disadvantages were evenly distributed across racial groups. Although there are few extremely disadvantaged whites, there are enough Black and Hispanic individuals who grew up in conditions overlapping with whites to support cross-racial group comparisons of arrest disparities. Specifically, we can assign Black and Hispanic individuals the same distribution of individual, family, and neighborhood conditions as whites in childhood and adolescence and then observe arrest trajectories.

As seen in the second row of graphs, once we make these adjustments for compositional and early-life factors, we see that they account for most of the social foundations of inequality; in other words, racial and ethnic differences largely disappear. The older cohort curves are almost identical to one another in each of the three panels, while the younger cohort curves are much more similar than in the baseline model, though not quite the same. It is rather remarkable, for example, that among older cohort members, Hispanic, Black, and white people have essentially equivalent arrest rates at peak ages when they share the same conditions growing up. It is not race per se, then, or even direct racial bias in police encounters, but social inequality in early-life conditions that explain race and ethnic disparities in later arrest.[22] A similar story holds for younger cohorts but to a somewhat lesser extent. For example, younger cohorts converge more toward the older cohorts among Black individuals compared to Hispanics and whites.[23] Moreover, similar results hold when this analysis is broken down further by different types of offenses, not just drug arrests, which are often held to be the principal target of race-based disparities in policing during mass incarceration.

The main conclusion we can draw is that compositional and early-life characteristics durably predict racial disparities in arrest across cohorts. This result implies that early-life structural factors, which themselves are historically shaped by long-term contexts of racial inequality in America, trigger processes of cumulative advantages and disadvantages that produce racial disparities in arrests over the life course and that persist across different points in contemporary history. Looking now at the differences in arrest patterns between birth cohorts using the adjusted model, we see that the older cohort curves are still generally higher and wider than the younger cohorts. Since we control for compositional and early-life risk factors, the persistent differences between cohorts mean that knowing early-life risk factors for an individual is not enough to predict their arrest trajectory. We also need to know when they were born.

SELF-CONTROL AND SOCIETY

It is certainly surprising that the vulnerability of lower socioeconomic status can change dramatically over only ten years. But none of us choose the circumstances of our birth, making socioeconomic status external to us in ways that our personality traits are not. An investigation into self-control and arrest against the background of social change calls into question some of our most cherished assumptions about the value of internal grit in the face of adversity.

As described in Chapter 4, the child behavior assessment protocol from parental interviews is a standard and reliable procedure for assessing characteristics such as low self-control, aggressiveness, and anxiety / depression. Here I focus on low self-control for the theoretical reasons noted earlier and because of its key role in contemporary research as a metric tapping early predispositions and behavioral tendencies to delinquency.

A limitation of the PHDCN+ data is that I cannot measure self-control at the exact same ages for all cohorts, but I can come close on average and rely on the fact that levels of self-control between individuals are quite stable over short periods of time. Roland Neil and I collaborated on this topic as well, showing that self-control measured at an average age of eleven to twelve strongly predicted arrest for both the youngest birth cohort and the next oldest cohort born circa 1987 where we had the closest age-alignment of measures.[24] Here, I broaden that analysis to include later years of data and thus ages of arrest, and in this case using adolescent self-control measured at an average age of fifteen to seventeen, just before the peak ages

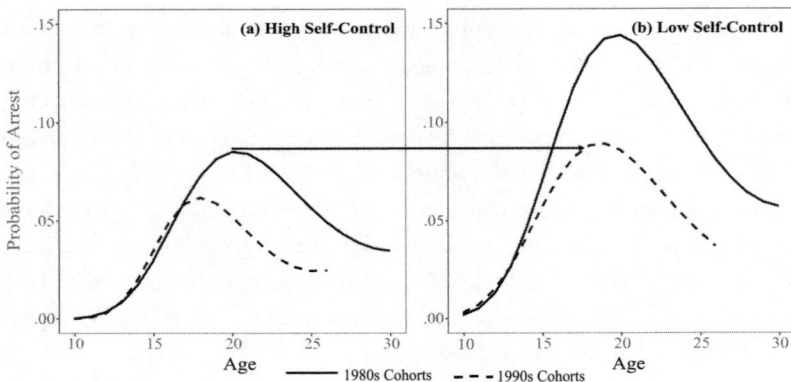

Figure 5.5. Cohort Comparison of Self-Control Levels and Arrest Rates. High self-control individuals in older birth cohorts have arrest rates at age twenty similar to those of low self-control individuals in younger birth cohorts. *Source:* Reformatted from Robert J. Sampson and L. Ash Smith, "Rethinking Criminal Propensity and Character: Cohort Inequalities and the Power of Social Change," *Crime and Justice* 50 (2021): 13–76, figure 2.

of arrest and in the period of adolescence where conflictual encounters have more serious consequences. As parents know, impulsive acts by a teen at say, age seventeen, pack more peril than the same acts at earlier ages.

Figure 5.5(a) presents the results for those with high adolescent self-control, defined as those individuals one standard deviation above the mean. The arrest trajectories of the different cohorts begin to diverge at the age of fourteen and grow to a maximum difference at about age twenty-two. Whereas the differences in these curves before the age of nineteen are insignificant, those from the age of nineteen onward are significant. Figure 5.5(b) plots the analogous arrest trajectories among those with low adolescent self-control, defined as those one standard deviation below the mean on the self-control measure. Consistent with considerable prior research, and thereby validating the measure, arrest trajectories for those with low self-control are generally higher. That is, compared to their high self-control contemporaries, arrest is more likely among those with low self-control at all ages after early adolescence. The proponents of self-control as a key concept in criminalization are clearly on to something.

Looked at differently, however, we nonetheless see that the relationship between low self-control and arrest exhibits substantively meaningful historical patterns. For example, whereas the probability of arrest at age twenty was almost .14 for those born in the mid-to-late 1980s with low self-control, individuals who were otherwise the same but born in the mid-1990s had an arrest probability of .08. The differences between the curves from the ages of twenty to twenty-three are statistically significant and substantively large. This is most clearly illustrated by the fact that the arrest trajectories of *low* self-control individuals born in the mid-1990s are virtually identical to those of *high* self-control individuals born in the mid-to-late 1980s, seen in panels (b) and (a) of Figure 5.5, respectively, and as represented by the left-to-right arrow. That the arrest trajectories are lower for the 1990s cohort in both panels of Figure 5.5 indicates that individuals of all levels of self-control contribute to the inter-cohort variation in arrest patterns.

I can drill down on this intriguing pattern even further by matching almost exactly, down to just a few months' difference, our measure of self-control to the age of seventeen, right before the point of maximum arrest probability. I do this by examining three birth cohort groups, infancy (mid-1990s), 1984, and 1981, for whom I can use the different timings of measurement by interview wave to center on self-control at age seventeen. Furthermore, to assess the robustness of earlier results, I limit the items to concrete behavioral indicators of the participant within the past six months of the interview that can be directly compared on a simple scale—hyperactivity (can't sit still), impulsive and acts without thinking, and inability to concentrate or pay attention.[25] Like Figure 5.5, the high self-control kids of the 1980s cohorts had a similar probability of arrest (.27) from ages seventeen to twenty-four as the 1990s cohort members with low self-control (.32). Comparing only the 1984 and 1995 cohorts, where the arrest data are maximally aligned by age in terms of both criminal histories and self-control, the oldest cohort members with high self-control actually had a slightly higher probability of arrest at ages seventeen to twenty-four (.34) than the youngest low-self-control members (.32). For just juvenile arrests—seventeen and under—the high self-control members of the 1987 cohort and the low self-control members of the 1995 cohort had virtually identical arrest probabilities, at .10 and .09, respectively. These simple patterns substantiate and extend those seen in Figure 5.5.

Finally, we can consider cohort differences in the cumulative probabilities of arrest for individuals classified by cohort and whether they qualified as low or high in self-control. Like the disadvantage analysis in Figure 5.2, I focus on the mid-1990s cohort and the mid-to-late 1980s cohorts to use those groups for which we have the most complete arrest data in the teenage years. The results yield the same pattern as Figure 5.5 in a somewhat different form. Among those with high self-control, 37 percent of the older cohort had been arrested by their early twenties, compared to just under 32 percent of the younger cohort. But these are small differences compared to those for individuals with low self-control: Whereas 30 percent of such individuals in the younger cohort were arrested by the time they turned twenty-three, over half (54 percent) of the older cohort had been arrested.

Among the older cohort, then, differences in self-control translate into large differences in the prevalence of criminalization; among the younger cohort, they do not. Again, as was the case with the age-arrest trajectories in Figure 5.5, low self-control individuals are about as well-off as high self-control individuals born one decade earlier in terms of the prevalence of arrest.

REINTERPRETING "RISK FACTORS"

The results are clear when it comes to inequality by socioeconomic status: The disadvantaged members of younger cohorts have benefited the most from social change, whereas the returns to advantage are declining. Those from advantaged socioeconomic backgrounds have seen modest (at most) inter-cohort variation in arrest over the life course, whereas those from disadvantaged backgrounds have seen large improvements in avoiding arrest. In fact, 70 percent of individuals born in the mid-1980s to disadvantaged families had been arrested by their mid-twenties, compared to about a quarter of the disadvantaged members of the younger cohort from the mid-1990s. The implication is that those from disadvantaged backgrounds drive inter-cohort variation in the age-crime relationship. This varying disadvantage penalty holds within each racial group, as well. This means that, for example, Black individuals with higher socioeconomic status showed similar arrest patterns between cohorts while their lower status peers experienced a marked improvement over time. In this sense, race is not confounding the socioeconomic status patterns.

We also saw that social change produces large cohort differences in being arrested. Nonetheless, the major structural sources of racial disparities in arrests, especially between Black and white individuals, do not vary meaningfully by cohort, showing that they are reproduced over time. In other words, the unequal distribution of compositional and early-life factors like poverty and violence persists between cohorts, even when social change makes them less predictive of arrest. Further inspection reveals that arrest disparities between Hispanics and whites do not exist among the more recent birth cohorts, mainly because Hispanics are more likely to come from immigrant families, whose members tend to have low rates of contact with the criminal justice system.[26] Together, these findings imply that even though racial inequalities in arrests can be reshaped by patterns of social change, the structural drivers of these inequalities are persistent over several decades in the contemporary era.

Other implications and hypotheses bear on a dominant concept in modern studies of crime, and human development in general: self-control. Although there is some evidence that low self-control individuals have been more important in creating inter-cohort differentiation in arrest than high self-control individuals, individuals of all levels of self-control have contributed to these inter-cohort differences. In this case, the impact of low self-control on crime theorized by Michael Gottfredson and Travis Hirschi, and on human capital development more generally by scholars such as James Heckman, is supported within all cohorts. I have no quarrel with their overall arguments, but my results demand a new look and interpretation.

Viewing the problem differently, I asked another question: What if individuals who share similar profiles of criminal tendencies or low self-control have enormously varied outcomes as a function of when they reach the vulnerable ages associated with crime? The answer is telling: Reductions in the chances of arrest have been so large that they have made the low self-control individuals of one cohort nearly indistinguishable from the high self-control individuals of a cohort born just one decade earlier. The role of self-control therefore depends in a substantial way on age-graded historical context, such that knowing self-control levels alone is not particularly informative about the magnitude of future arrest trajectories.

*　*　*

This chapter reveals a crucial but often overlooked insight: We cannot fully understand socioeconomic opportunities or criminal propensities, even those considered most interior to the individual, without considering cohort differences. Instead of focusing solely on individual virtues or flaws

within a particular cohort, we must examine the broader social environment in which people come of age.

By analyzing the life course in this way, we can see that supposedly stable
individual traits like self-control are more context-dependent than
commonly believed. Socioeconomic disadvantage, central to sociological
theories of crime, proves even more historically contingent. Individual
differences and social inequality interact with historical timing. The magnitude of societal changes is striking: Disadvantaged individuals with low
self-control from recent cohorts show outcomes similar to advantaged,
high-self-control individuals born just a decade earlier. This finding challenges our assumptions about inequality and crime prediction, forcing us
to rethink how social inequality itself evolves—topics addressed in the
book's final section.

Importantly, this evidence suggests that conditions aren't necessarily de-
teriorating, even in an age of extremes. Individual capacities and resources
may work differently than we assume, and historical timing shapes outcomes in unexpected ways.

CHAPTER 6

Disentangling Mechanisms of Change

The large cohort differences in arrest that I have established are not attributable to standard individual, family, and neighborhood risk factors in childhood (such as poverty, family structure, and temperament) measured before the onset of official police arrests. That these usual suspects—compositional and early-life factors—can't account for what we have seen raises a key question: What changed for those transitioning into adulthood in the late twentieth and early twenty-first century? Put differently, what mechanisms of societal change drove the birth lottery of arrest?

Earlier chapters introduced several clues, noting, for example, how the bulk of social change's impact is visible through the improving arrest outcomes for individuals of low socioeconomic status—an effect that cuts across racial lines. But history does not follow a neat playbook. Narratives of linear progress or decline over the long durée have always been popular—especially predictions that "the world is going to hell"—but at least over the twenty-five years that we tracked the lives of the PHDCN+'s children, history was pockmarked with all sorts of zig-zagging and countervailing changes. As we saw in Chapter 1, crime exploded in the 1960s and 1970s and stayed at high levels until the mid-1990s, when it began a remarkable and unexpected decline. This period also saw the fast rise of incarceration followed by a decline, along with the rise and then fall of novel policing practices that abruptly shifted the status quo, such as the notable broken-windows form of policing that encouraged the aggressive crackdown on disorder, drugs, and minor offenses.[1]

Another common strategy in thinking about social change is to focus on large discrete events like the Great Recession, the COVID-19 pandemic, or the George Floyd murder—all of which can be placed rather neatly in time. To be sure, these were major events, but as we shall see, they are not neatly aligned with the directional changes that were predicted at the time, such as crime rising with recession or declining with fewer people on the streets during COVID-19. Adding to the challenge is the reality that multiple factors can and do change simultaneously, making it even harder to identify any single cause. No one has established with any confidence what caused the large decline in crime in recent decades, for example, and few if any predicted or neatly explained the spike in homicide in 2016 and again in 2020. But explaining macrolevel trends or events like these is not my goal; I seek instead to explain cohort differences in the experience of arrest.

In this chapter, I therefore take a different approach by disentangling the multiple changes that took place in Chicago and elsewhere in the country as the different birth cohorts that I study grew up, came of age, and transitioned to adulthood from the 1980s to the early 2020s. I begin by highlighting patterns of law enforcement and criminal behavior, examining trends in policing tactics and intensity as well as the underlying prevalence of arrestable offenses relative to crimes. This focus is motivated by a desire to investigate the crime and criminal justice practices closest to the arrest process. But neither law enforcement nor criminal behavior occurs in a vacuum, so I also consider a broad range of theoretically plausible forces that bear on crime and its control, including changing landscapes of technology, economic conditions, gentrification and urban change, youth supervision, community organizations, and lead exposure.

Sorting out changes in all these factors is challenging, not least because the period in which the PHDCN+ cohorts came of age is short by conventional metrics—about twenty-five years—whereas historians are used to thinking in longer terms, typically across centuries. In *The Better Angels of Our Nature: Why Violence Has Declined*, Steven Pinker even ranged across millennia in his focus on what he argues was a long-term turn to peace.[2] By contrast, this chapter zeroes in on a radically shorter period to scrutinize the whipsawing in some trends and nearly linear progress in others. I proceed logically, assessing the relative contributions of key factors and ruling out potential rival explanations. Chapters 4 and 5 demonstrated the power of social change. This chapter will reveal which forces best account for that change, explaining the mystery behind the birth lottery of arrest.

DRUG-WAR POLICING AND MASS INCARCERATION

The "war on drugs" is at the center of much of the criminological and popular literature, epitomized by Michelle Alexander's argument in *The New Jim Crow* that increasing drug enforcement, especially of African Americans, was the primary driver of mass incarceration.[3] Indeed, virtually all accounts of mass incarceration highlight the drug war of the 1980s as a central explanation of why imprisonment skyrocketed when it did and for whom.[4] Because the police are the front end of the criminal justice system, I will call this influential account of incarceration, or in effect mass criminalization, the drug-war policing hypothesis.

Despite its influence, the implications of Alexander's argument for my findings are unclear, as every child in the Chicago study came of age after incarceration's ascent. In particular, while the literature on mass incarceration emphasizes the rise of the punitive state and increasing criminalization, which was true through the 1980s and early 1990s, times have changed quite dramatically. Chapter 4 revealed that arrests dropped substantially between the older and younger PHDCN+ cohorts. More broadly, as we will see in this chapter, policing tactics on drugs pivoted in the 1990s and 2000s in ways unpredicted by and inconsistent with the drug war narrative. Also going against the grain of dominant narratives on mass incarceration, rates of imprisonment have declined nationally by a substantial amount, as have racial inequalities in incarceration.[5]

However, the drug-war policing hypothesis could still be relevant to the downward arrest trends I've observed. If increased drug enforcement drove arrests up for cohorts preceding those in the PHDCN+, ushering in the era of mass incarceration, it stands to reason that decreasing drug enforcement might explain the arrest gap between the 1980s and 1990s cohorts. One test of this drug-war policing hypothesis is to separate out arrest trajectories according to whether they contain a drug charge and reexamine cohort inequalities. I do this in Figure 6.1, which shows a continued

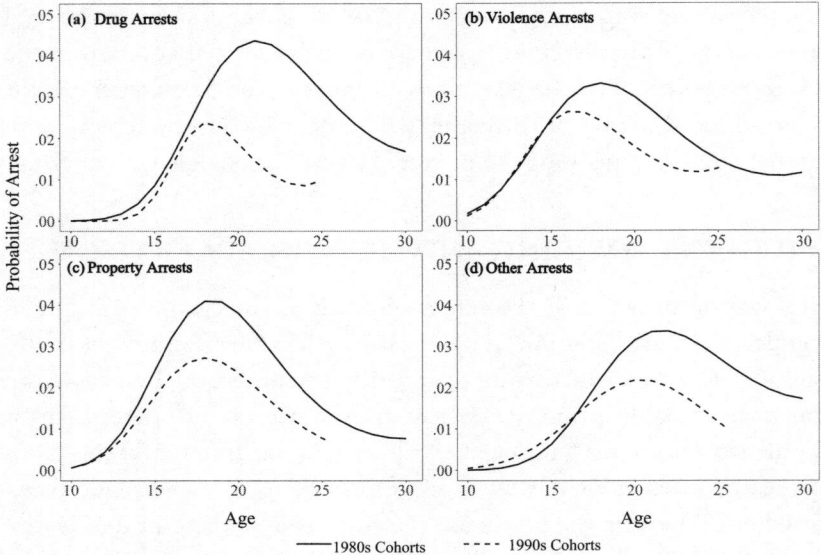

Figure 6.1. Life-Course Patterns of Arrests by Type of Crime. Life-course patterns of drug arrests are similar to non-drug arrests for younger and older cohorts, adjusting for compositional and early-life differences.

difference between the younger and older cohorts in the probability of being arrested by age for both drug and non-drug crimes. Consistent with the drug-war hypothesis, the difference is greatest for drug crimes, with arrests more than 100 percent higher for the older cohorts around age twenty compared to the younger cohorts. Yet *non-drug* arrests are much higher for the older cohorts as well, though with less of a differential at the peak ages of arrest circa ages eighteen to twenty.

In short, the key finding in Figure 6.1 is that the probability of being arrested is significantly higher for the two older cohorts than the younger, mid-1990s cohorts prior to about age twenty-five, especially for drug offenses. Logically, the fact that the cohort pattern holds for all offense types (including violence and property arrests) means that changing drug enforcement alone cannot explain the gap in arrests in these peak ages, though it is certainly an important part of the explanation.[6]

To confirm and extend this analysis, I re-estimated the group-based trajectory models from Chapter 4 that distinguished "chronic" arrestees from adolescent-limited and low-rate arrest groups, eliminating arrests for drugs but otherwise using the same strategy. By eliminating drug arrests from consideration, we can determine whether the war on drugs is responsible for the larger proportions of both chronic and adolescent-limited arrestees in the older cohort. The same basic pattern of cohort differentiation in Figure 4.6(b) holds, which again means that drug arrests are not the sole explanation of cohort differences. Further, there was no significant interaction between race and cohort in the prediction of arrest group membership—in other words, Black, Hispanic, and white individuals who were born in later cohorts all had a decreased likelihood of being in the chronic group compared to earlier cohorts. This result indicates that while African Americans were uniquely exposed to the war on drugs, cohort differences in arrest patterns were similar for all racial groups, whether low-rate arrestees or the "chronic offenders" that policymakers and the public so liked to focus on. Applying the logic of a detective, we must conclude that changes in drug enforcement, from the first to the second decade of the 2000s, represent a relevant but incomplete explanation of cohort changes in criminalization.

So far, I've discussed arrest rates as if enforcement is what matters most, implying that we can assume that fewer arrests indicate less enforcement. But this isn't necessarily true. There's another critical component to the drug-war policing hypothesis that needs to be addressed: the underlying prevalence of drug use. If drug use decreased in lockstep with drug arrests, then it wouldn't be less enforcement that lowered arrests, but simply that fewer people were committing arrestable drug offenses in the first place. To assess this aspect of the drug-war policing hypothesis, I switch strategies by comparing trends in drug use against arrest numbers. To track drug use, I present two samples, one a national sample of high school seniors and the other a sample of Chicago adolescents. For drug arrests, I show the numbers recorded by the Chicago Police Department.[7] This strategy shifts the level of analysis from the PHDCN+ longitudinal data to macro-level trends. I focus on marijuana because it is by far the most commonly used drug by young people, and implicated in more arrests by the police than any other drug. It is also, many assert, a drug around which law enforcement policy has long been racially targeted, with the effect of over-criminalizing communities of color.[8]

Figure 6.2 plots standardized changes in the percentages of Chicago high schoolers and high school seniors across the nation who had used

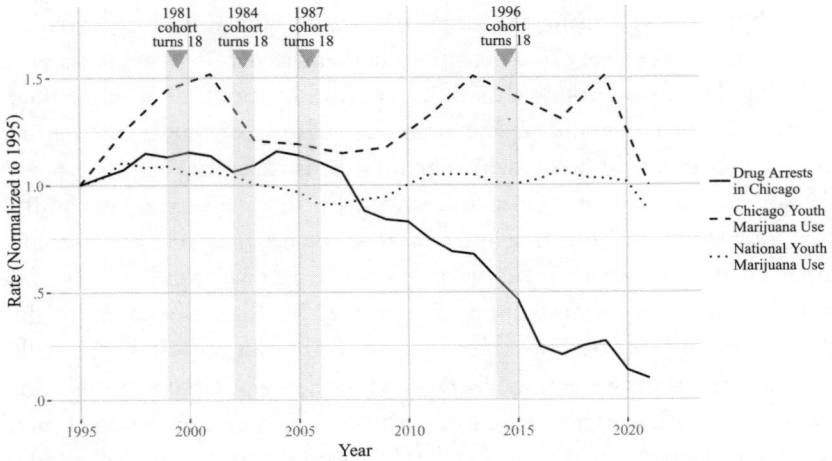

Figure 6.2. Patterns of Drug Use and Drug Arrests. Drug use patterns do not align with drug arrests.

marijuana in the past year over the period of the PHDCN+ study, with vertical columns showing when each birth cohort turned eighteen.[9] Drug arrests are similarly plotted. Changes in all three lines are normalized to 1995 levels so that we can directly compare changing patterns.[10] The figure reveals that for the most part, marijuana use remained relatively stable for many years, in both Chicago and the rest of the country. Chicago teens follow a more up-and-down pattern than their national peers after 1995, but there is no linear increase or decrease that lasts. Marijuana use nationally and in Chicago in 2021 was basically at the same point it was in 1995, a rather remarkable stability.

By contrast, and inconsistent with the idea of a persistent drug war over the course of the past quarter-century, drug arrests by the Chicago Police Department (CPD) were mostly steady for about a dozen years, from 1995 to 2007, after which they declined dramatically and consistently. For example, by 2020 drug arrests had dropped more than 75 percent from levels in 1995 through about 2005. All three older cohorts from the 1980s (indexed by birth years 1981, 1984, and 1987) endured the brunt of aggressive drug policing compared to the luckier mid-1990s cohort, who turned eighteen experiencing a social context with half as many arrests as their age peers a scant ten years or so earlier.[11]

These data are imperfect, to be sure. Measuring the changing prevalence of drug use over time is an inexact science, and not all PHDCN+ children lived in Chicago for their entire lives. But about half did, and in addition, Illinois drug arrests dropped quickly at around the same time. Considering that the use of marijuana and other drugs was mostly stable in the long run, taken as a whole, the data trends implicate sharply declining law enforcement around drugs—and not levels of use—as the key explanation of the cohort divergences in the drug arrest patterns in Figure 6.1. As we saw earlier, however, the drug-war policing hypothesis can only account for some of the cohort divergence in arrests. That fact motivates me to now turn to alternative explanations, in the hope of accounting for the rest of that divergence.

"BROKEN WINDOWS" POLICING

While drug enforcement patterns have garnered considerable attention in the literature on criminalization, they are not the only aspects of policing that have varied in recent decades. Disorderly conduct arrests by the police are known to be even more discretionary than drug arrests. In fact, aggressive styles of policing are rooted in the idea of ratcheting up the discretionary policing of visible disorder offenses such as panhandling, scrawling graffiti, or drinking in public—aptly named "order maintenance" in the field-altering essay on broken windows by the late James Q. Wilson and George Kelling.[12] Their essay was an intellectual and policy sensation, leading police departments to increase arrests for perceived disorder in public spaces, on the idea that one broken window (or act of social disorder) leads to another, signaling to would-be offenders that the neighborhood makes for easy prey. Although not the same policy as "zero tolerance," no arrest is too minor according to this theory of order, what I will call the broken-windows policing hypothesis.

The switch to a proactive style of broken-windows policing was made famous in New York City under Mayor Rudy Giuliani in the 1990s and the regime of Chief William Bratton and later Raymond Kelly of the New York Police Department (NYPD). Disorder-based policing there, along with the drug war, has been widely criticized for its role in mass incarceration. Notably, scholars have argued that the order maintenance approach to policing that emerged in the 1990s in New York City and that expanded

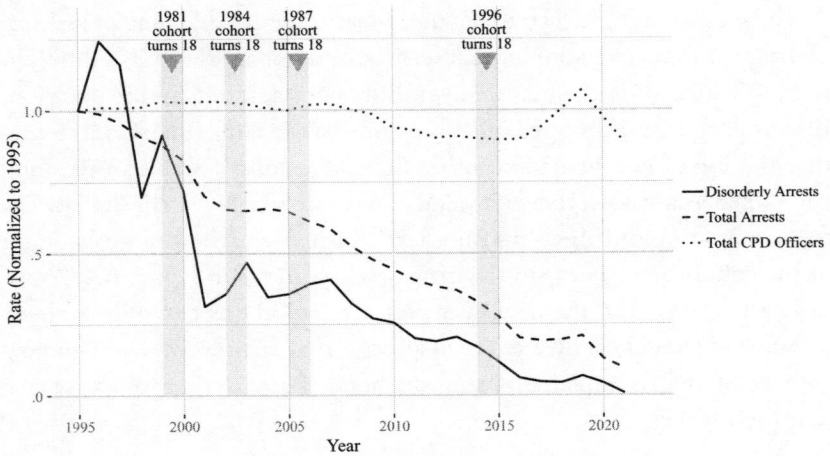

Figure 6.3. Disorder, Total Arrests, and Police Size. Disorder and total arrests decline while police size stays constant.

widely around the country "exacerbated police–citizen encounters in low-income neighborhoods," which in turn "entangle[d] people in the tentacles of the criminal justice system . . . under the banner of broken windows, order maintenance, or quality-of-life policing."[13]

Figure 6.3 assesses this hypothesis in the context of Chicago by showing trends in the size of the Chicago police force alongside disorder arrests and, for comparison, the total number of arrests in Chicago over the decades when the different birth cohorts were coming of age. This strategy allows us to see how much disorder arrests diverge from overall patterns and from the sheer size of the police force. In other words, if the size of the police force is constant during a period where arrests drop, we can say that arrest intensity is lower, or that each officer is, on average, responsible for fewer arrests.

The trends paint a clear picture. Since 1995—a year in which disorder arrests made up over 22 percent of all CPD arrests—they proceeded to fall by nearly 100 percent. This rather astonishing decline, which coincides with the ramping up of broken-windows policing in New York City, exceeds the magnitude of the decline in drug arrests we saw in Figure 6.2. The total number of arrests declined substantially as well, though the drop was not quite as large as for disorder arrests. All these changes occurred while the size of the police force remained relatively constant.

For the broken-windows policing hypothesis to contribute meaningfully to the cohort gap in arrests, however, disorder arrests not only need to drop between cohorts, but they also need to make up a substantial percentage of total arrests for the older cohorts. In the era of mass incarceration and a presumed culture of aggressive control in the era of broken-windows policing, such a dramatic and stable decline in arrests is unanticipated, and it is unlikely to be the product of a decline in actual disorderly conduct, meaning that changing policing styles are the cause of declining arrests. Reflecting this powerful aggregate trend, not one 1990s birth cohort member was arrested for disorderly conduct between the ages of eighteen and twenty-two—compared to the 1980s cohorts, for which they made up 3.5 percent of arrests at these ages. Yet, because disorder arrests made up only 3.5 percent of the total number of arrests for older cohorts, the broken-windows policing hypothesis cannot be an important explanation of the overall cohort arrest gap, even though the overall decline in disorder arrests still reflects a large change in the CPD's enforcement practices in an unanticipated direction.

The drops in disorder arrests overall and arrest intensity per officer do not conform to how we usually think about broken-windows policing, which is often portrayed as an extensive and prolonged presence over the full period of mass incarceration, but especially since the 1990s. Although the 1980s witnessed a higher number of disorder arrests, well before broken-windows policing was invented, most of the PHDCN+ children, including two of the 1980s cohorts, benefited from a distinctly less proactive stance on the part of the CPD toward disorder starting at the turn of the twenty-first century. Today, barely anyone is arrested for disorder in Chicago.

The fact that broken-windows policing arrests fell substantially between cohorts but explain so little of the arrest gap makes sense when we think more carefully about the differing times at which the Chicago cohorts reached peak offending ages. In contrast with disorder arrests, drug arrests contributed meaningfully to the cohort arrest gap and, critically, did not begin falling until 2004 (as shown in Figure 6.2), at which point disorder arrests had already fallen by over 70 percent since 1996. It follows that most of the decline in disorder arrests happened before any PHDCN+ respondents were older than their early teens, whereas most of the decline in drug arrests happened between the peak arrest years for the 1980s and 1990s cohorts.

Remarkably, then, both drug and disorderly conduct arrests were declining dramatically from the mid-1990s on—at least in Chicago, a fact at odds with prevailing assumptions about mass criminalization in recent decades. As a result, while policing obviously matters, neither the standard drug-war hypothesis nor the broken-windows policing hypothesis is sufficient to explain the distinct patterns of cohort differentiation in criminalization.

STOP AND FRISK

Tallying arrests for disorderly conduct is not, however, the only way to measure high-level changes in policing styles. While arrests (and as we will see, crime) were in free fall in most of the country, so-called "stop, question, and frisk" policies that also derived from the broken-windows theory emerged, going beyond what even Kelling and Wilson originally proposed. By stopping and frisking large numbers of what the police deemed suspicious people on the street, the idea was that guns or contraband would be found, and that "bad guys" with outstanding warrants would be arrested. Although unproven, stop and frisk was touted as necessary to keep cities safe. Strangely, this strategy became most popular in the rather tranquil mid-2000s, led by New York City in the wake of Chief William Bratton's tenure, with the most intense period of stops occurring during 2006 to 2011.[14] In New York, at least, stop and frisk was ruled unconstitutional in 2013, so its reign was relatively short.

An important literature has examined stop and frisk in both New York and Chicago, mainly focused on its disproportionate impact on minorities.[15] Stops were hardly random, of course—the police claimed that they were merely stopping suspicious people in high crime neighborhoods, but the proportion of stops resulting in drug or gun seizures was extremely low and the burden imposed on African American communities was extreme.

Moreover, there is little evidence that stop and frisk blunted much, if any, crime. Arrests had begun falling years before stop and frisk policies arrived in Chicago, and, as we will see, they continued to fall after those policies were withdrawn. Therefore, stop and frisk does not appear to have played a role in the cohort arrest gap. But as a high-level change in policing style, it is nevertheless worth considering how stop and frisk policies changed between our Chicago birth cohorts. True to its second city reputation, Chicago lagged behind New York City and implemented stop and frisk at its most intense level about five years after its peak use in New York City and, it turns out, in a very bumpy way overall. Unfortunately, but perhaps unsurprisingly given the troubled history of the Chicago police, the department did not provide reliable data on stop and frisks that we can compare across the full time series like we have for arrests.

The key facts are nonetheless clear. We start getting data on stop and frisks by the CPD in 2004. In January of that year and in January of 2005, stops hovered around twenty thousand, after which they increased two-fold to over forty thousand in January of 2007 under then Superintendent Philip Cline. Variations over the year were up and down. The next chief, Jody Weis, was reportedly not a big fan of stop and frisks, and they abruptly declined back to about twenty thousand by the end of 2011. But the next chief, Garry McCarthy, most certainly was a big fan. McCarthy was recruited to Chicago from Newark, where he was the chief of police, but most of his career was spent with the NYPD under Bratton, where he was a deputy commissioner for operations and director of the department's famous CompStat management (an influential policing data tool used by police officers and public policymakers). Greatly influenced by his former NYPD boss, McCarthy championed number crunching and especially putting "cops on the dots" of crime, to use the words of police insiders. Accordingly, he ramped up the stops from the Weis downturn by pressuring patrol officers and demanding increased numbers. Sure enough, by January of 2013, monthly stops increased more than 100 percent to over seventy thousand. They dipped sharply the rest of the year but then rebounded to over sixty-five thousand in January of 2014 and again in 2015.

McCarthy was also police superintendent when Laquan McDonald was murdered by a Chicago police officer in 2014, and during the following thirteen months in which the CPD did not release the body camera video. Notably, the highly publicized video of the killing of McDonald was released in late 2015, coming on the heels of widespread national protests after Michael Brown's killing by a police officer in Ferguson, Missouri, in 2014. The McDonald tape was held back at the highest level in City Hall for over a year, leading to intense public protests once it was released, eventually bringing down Mayor Rahm Emanuel, who had recruited McCarthy as his chief of police—and whom he promptly fired in the heat of the controversy.[16] I will have more to say about the protests around police killings, but for now, the short summary of stop and frisk in Chicago is that this was a story of large ups and downs, with the most intense and invasive regime of police stops centered on the three-year period from 2013 to 2015, even as arrests remained low and continued their decline. Almost immediately after the release of the McDonald tape, stop and frisk by the CPD collapsed as a strategy and the numbers stayed low (below 2004 levels) past 2015.

The implications for our birth cohorts are a bit murky, but as far as we can tell from the available data, the older cohorts escaped the wrath of the CPD's stop and frisk campaign in their teens and early adulthood. Ironically, however, the cohort that was most privileged in terms of its comparatively low rate of being arrested, the mid-1990s cohort, turned eighteen at the peak of stop and frisks in 2014. The somewhat paradoxical result is that members of the youngest cohort were at the lowest risk for arrest and a permanent mark of criminality when coming of age but were, at least for those living in Chicago in 2014, far more likely to be stopped and frisked by the CPD. In this sense, broken-windows policing survived, but in a restricted time frame and for a specific kind of policing strategy. This result, combined with plummeting disorder and drug arrests at the peak of stop and frisk, reminds us that even within a category, such as policing, social change is far from linear. It does not necessarily progress in a certain direction, and it can turn on a dime, again and again.

CRIMINAL BEHAVIOR

We've already seen that, from one cohort to another, drug arrests fell despite stability in the underlying measures of drug use. A similar kind of analysis—comparing arrests to underlying crime rates—is possible for non-drug crimes, although it is a bit more complex. Unfortunately, there is no pure measure of criminal offending, and there are almost as many proposed causes of criminal behavior as there are academic criminologists. But while it is true that offenses reported to the police are an imperfect measure of criminal behavior, it matters that the reports originate almost exclusively from citizens themselves and not the police. Considerable research has also established a close similarity in trends of violent crimes reported to the police and crimes reported to survey interviews in national victimization studies over the decades covering the PHDCN+ study.[17] It is fair, then, to use the term *criminal behavior* as shorthand for reported offenses, which we can directly assess against patterns of arrest, and answer the simple but basic question: Are falling arrest rates for non-drug crimes due to falling rates of underlying criminal behavior? This possible explanation for the co-hort arrest gap could be termed the *reduced crime hypothesis.*

The answer is that non-drug arrests like those for violent crimes and property crimes do, in fact, track very closely with underlying crime rates as measured by citizen reports. Figure 6.4 shows normalized trends in re-ports for violent offenses graphed alongside arrests for violence from 1990 onward, a period in which the incidence of homicide, the most precisely measured of all crimes, peaked in the early 1990s and then plummeted.[18] Figure 6.5 follows with the same trend lines and times, but for property crimes. The important result is that both arrests and citizen reports declined dramatically over time, especially after 1993.[19]

In both graphs the declines in arrests and in crime measured by reported offenses are substantial, but note that the relationship between those lines is not quite the same. In Figure 6.4, focused on violent crime, the line for arrests and the line for reported offenses stick closer together than they do in Figure 6.5, focused on property crime. In the case of the latter, the two lines begin to meaningfully diverge around 2003 and remain apart through the end of the data in 2020, with reported offenses declining to a quarter of the 1990 offense rate, but arrests dropping more steeply to less than

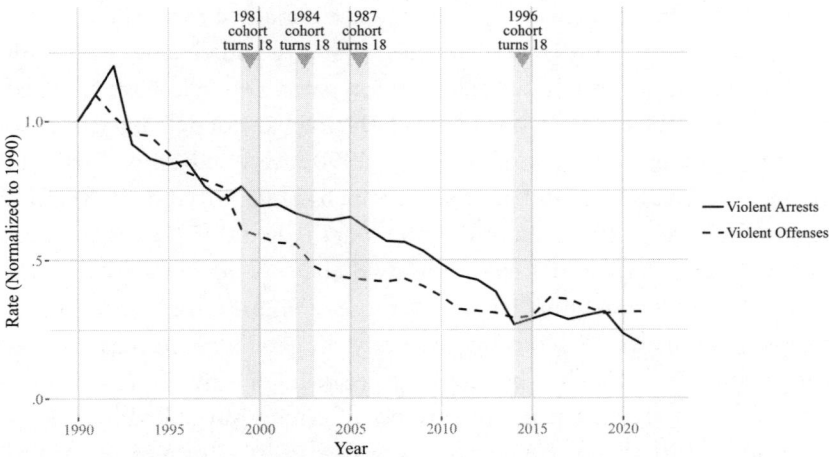

Figure 6.4. Violent Offense and Arrest Trends. The trend over the course of thirty years is a decline in both violent offenses and arrests.

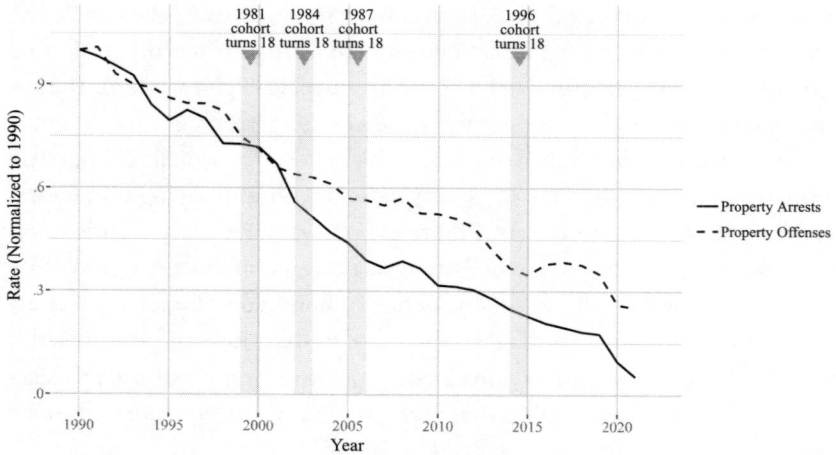

Figure 6.5. Property Offense and Arrest Trends. The trend over the course of thirty years is a decline in both property offenses and arrests.

10 percent of the 1990 arrest rate. This divergence in one graph and not the other means that during that eighteen-year period—at the end of which, all cohorts would have been at least twenty-one years old—the ratio of arrests per reported offense, a common proxy for police enforcement intensity, dropped for property crime while remaining roughly stable for violent crime. In other words, after 2005, it became less likely that a property offense would result in an arrest. For violent crime, however, this measure of policing intensity appears to have remained more stable.

To evaluate these differences between property and violent crime with more precision, we can examine how arrest patterns would have changed in two hypothetical worlds: one in which the intensity of policing (the ratio of arrests to reported offenses) stayed at 1990 levels and crime varied in the way it actually did, and another in which crime stayed at 1990 levels but policing intensity varied in the way it actually did.[20] Rather than relying on the inexact visual reasoning used above, where we saw the two lines in Figure 6.5 roughly diverge and those in Figure 6.4 roughly remain together, this analysis will precisely quantify the gaps between the two lines using a simple model of how arrests are generated: For a given type of crime, the number of arrests equals the number of crimes multiplied by the average probability that a crime will result in an arrest. This measure of police arrest intensity quantifies the chance that police will make an arrest for a given crime. Figures 6.6 and 6.7 display the hypothetical scenarios

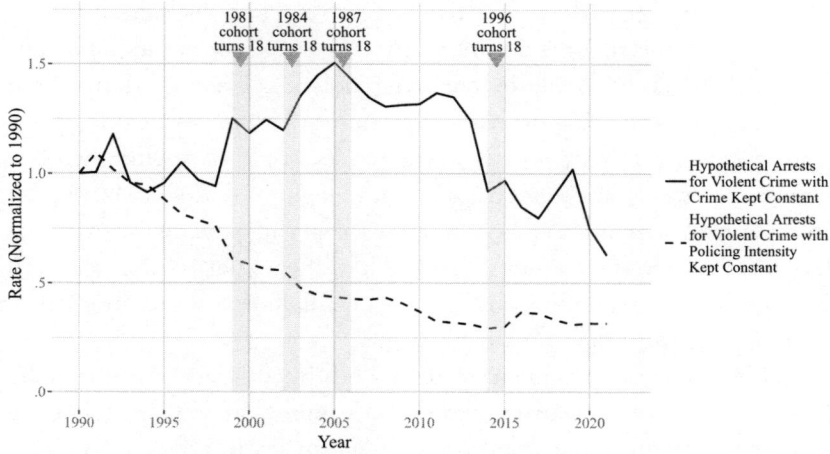

Figure 6.6. Violent Arrest Patterns in Two Hypothetical Worlds. In these two hypothetical worlds, violent arrest patterns diverge.

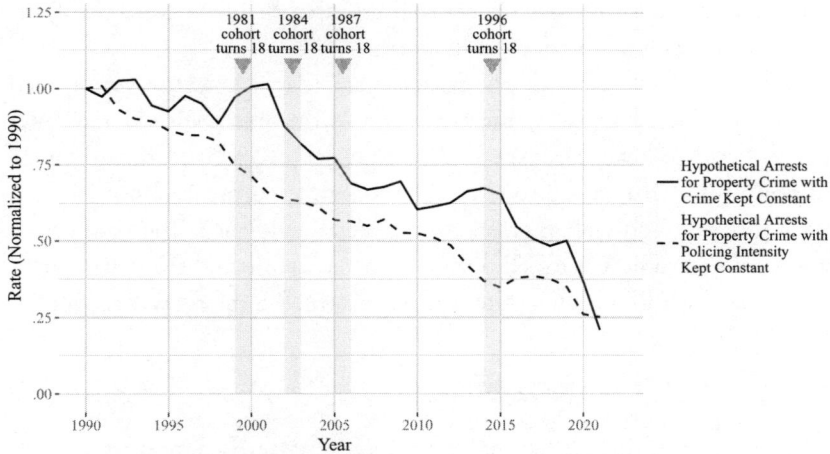

Figure 6.7. Property Arrest Patterns in Two Hypothetical Worlds. In these two hypothetical worlds, property arrest patterns largely align.

for violent and property offenses, respectively. One line represents the hypothetical arrests if police intensity had stayed the same and crime fell as it did, and the other line shows the hypothetical arrests if crime had stayed the same, but intensity varied as it did.

If one of these hypothetical scenarios produces a line that resembles the actual arrest line for that type of offense (property or violent), then we can identify that scenario as one that helps to explain the actual results. Figure 6.6 reveals that the decline in arrests for violence in the city of Chicago was driven primarily by changing violent behavior patterns rather than changes in policing intensity. We can see that even in a world of constant levels of police intensity, violent arrests would have plummeted by almost 75 percent, near to the actual value in Figure 6.4 of about 80 percent. But had crime remained at 1990 levels with varying policing intensity, the hypothetical arrest line looks nothing like the actual results (see again Figure 6.4), suggesting that changes in policing intensity had little impact on dropping arrest rates for violent crime.

Looking instead at property arrests, both hypothetical worlds predict less of a decline than occurred, and both are quite close to each other going back to the 1990s. Here, then, and considering again Figure 6.5's plot of observed trends, the results show that both changing crime and the intensity of police enforcement contributed about equally to the decline in property arrests, with changing crime being slightly more important. For violent crime, changes in reported criminal behavior were clearly the prominent driver of the decline in arrests.

The crucial takeaway of the patterns thus far is that the younger cohorts experienced a vastly different social world than their older counterparts. This world was almost equally composed of a sharply declining risk of arrest—for drug and property crimes—and sharply declining rates of both property and violent crime, but especially violence. The younger cohorts seemed to have escaped both a crime epidemic and the drug war, although as we will see, their fate was not destined to be forever favorable.

WHAT ELSE CHANGED?

Changes in criminal behavior and policing patterns may ultimately be driven by other, more distal social changes that distinguished the contexts through which the study's cohorts came of age. I thus focus here on factors outside the criminal justice system, though of course incarceration and policing itself are potential explanations of national crime trends.[21] Several of the topics discussed below were among the compositional and early-life factors I controlled for in Chapter 4, meaning that at least as measured, they cannot be substantive explanations for the cohort arrest gap. But they are topics of great interest in the criminological literature as well as pieces of the larger story about social change in the era that go beyond the Chicago cohorts. They are also relevant to later adolescence and early adulthood experiences, and I examine alternative measures of similar constructs at a more macrosocial level (such as economic factors) to see if something was missed in the earlier chapters. Put differently, I take a broader look at multiple factors of theoretical and policy interest, going beyond the family and neighborhood to include the wider Chicago and national context to help paint the larger picture of the changing world through which millennial cohorts grew up, came of age, and transitioned to adulthood.

Although there are many potential large social changes outside the criminal justice system in this era, one that typically comes to mind in public discourse about crime trends is poverty and the general state of the economy. Consider too that a major event during the period in question was the Great Recession that burst onto the scene in 2008. I have already considered exposure to poverty and socioeconomic disadvantage of the Chicago children within their families and neighborhoods when they were young, but what about larger societal economic changes as the cohorts later came of age?

The economy nearly collapsed after the Great Recession and the poverty rate went up, but not as much as we might think. The poverty rate in the United States increased from about 13 percent to 15 percent, a relatively minor change, kept so small in part by the American Recovery and Reinvestment Act of 2009.[22] Unemployment saw more of a jump because sudden job losses and foreclosures increased dramatically, but in the 1990s, poverty and unemployment had both fallen, and after 2010 would drop again.

To evaluate these changes more formally, Figure 6.8 shows normalized trends in unemployment and poverty, for both Illinois and the nation. There were fluctuations in these economic conditions from 1995 to 2021, but no clear trend or pattern. Gains in poverty reduction were offset by increases in unemployment. Of the economic fluctuations that did occur, the older cohorts in the PHDCN+ study were unluckier in their exposure to hardship, but not by much and unevenly so. The 1980 cohort members, for example, were ages fifteen to twenty in the late 1990s when poverty was dropping. The 1985 cohort passed through those same ages in the early 2000s when poverty was creeping back up, and the mid-1990s cohort turned fifteen near the height of the economic wreckage of the Great

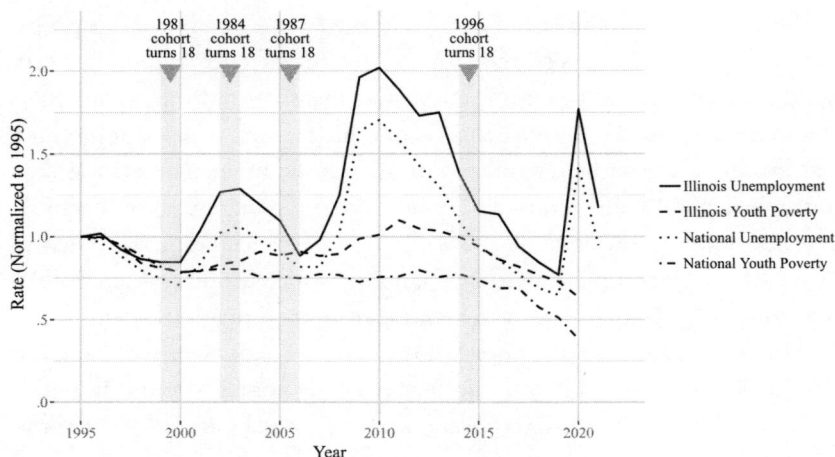

Figure 6.8. Unemployment and Child Poverty, Illinois and National. The trends in unemployment and child poverty in Illinois and at the national level do not follow a consistent pattern.

Recession in 2010, but then things turned for the better with poverty dropping again. These patterns do not make for a coherent explanation of cohort differentiation in arrest, especially considering that the economic conditions of every person at age nine, both neighborhood and family, were taken into account in the results of Chapter 4.

A different strategy is to examine the long-term data for the individuals in the respective birth cohorts and estimate changing exposure to poverty at the neighborhood level from ages eight to twenty-five, the ages at which we have comparable data on cohort members. The transition from adolescence to adulthood captures meaningful experiences of our study participants with respect to poverty exposure because arrest increases and reaches its peak in late adolescence and the early twenties, and we know that concentrated poverty is related to both crimes and arrests. I can study this life-course dynamic because we followed each person no matter where they moved in the United States, enabling us to match their neighborhood characteristics to the census and estimating the poverty rate for each year for each cohort. For simplicity, the cohorts born in the 1980s are combined into a single cohort ("older" cohort) to compare to the youngest cohort, born in the mid-1990s. I examine each race/ethnic group as well, since we also know that Black, white, and Hispanic individuals live in vastly different neighborhood contexts to begin with, so any averages would obscure racial differences.[23]

Figure 6.9 shows that there are some modest cohort differences in the experience of poverty during childhood and adolescence. Children coming of age more recently exhibit more advantaged neighborhood trajectories than those born earlier, up to about age fifteen, and there is a decline among the younger Black and Hispanic cohorts in living in neighborhood poverty after age twenty, whereas the youngest white cohort sees an increase. But the gaps are relatively small, especially up to about age twenty, and the overall trends are mostly flat for the majority of the ages observed.

What Figure 6.9 tells us, then, is that the main poverty story is one of *stable differences between racial groups* in childhood and adolescence, almost as if they are living in unchanging separate worlds.[24] Recall that neighborhood poverty in childhood was controlled for in all analyses in Chapter 4. The inescapable conclusion, then, is that differential exposure to concentrated poverty by cohort cannot form the story of why arrest trajectories diverge between cohorts so much in adolescence and early adulthood, for all racial groups.

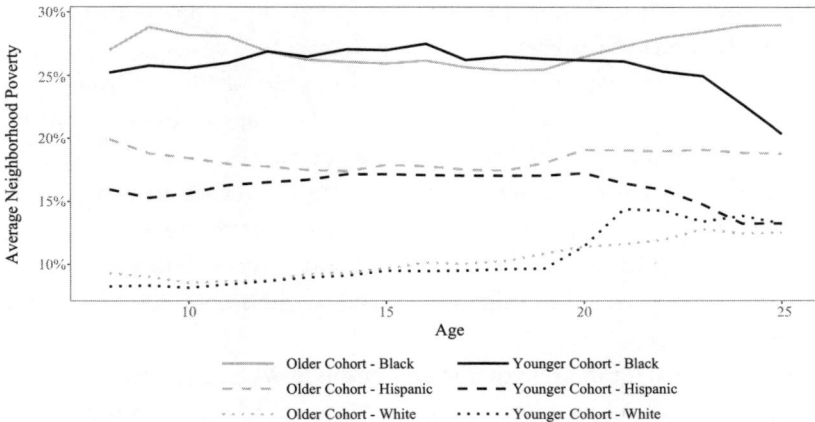

Figure 6.9. Varying Neighborhood Poverty Experiences. Neighborhood poverty experiences vary more by race than by cohort, both in childhood and in the transition to adulthood.

Urban Revitalization

Individual, neighborhood, and macro-level economic conditions such as poverty are not everything, however. Parts of Chicago and many other cities around the country underwent a broad form of urban revitalization arising from a mix of forces related to immigration, repopulation, and gentrification. What the economist Edward Glaeser more broadly calls "the triumph of the city" was a global phenomenon, as well.[25] Even neighborhoods largely bypassed by such revitalization processes have seen important changes. For example, supported by funding from the federal Hope VI program which began in the 1990s with the goal of developing mixed-income neighborhoods, many of the largest and most notorious public housing projects in Chicago, such as Cabrini-Green (the former home of Dantrell Davis) and the Robert Taylor Homes, were demolished. By some accounts, the transformation of public housing influenced the distribution of criminal behavior in Chicago.[26]

Yet, even though the economic and social improvement of cities must be part of the story, not all our cohort members remained in Chicago—and moreover, the chicken-or-egg question is whether improving conditions in cities were a cause or result of the large declines in violence. Surely, the crime improvements at least facilitated broadscale urban revitalization, again reinforcing the importance of more proximate trends in crime and crime control. It is also hard to see how changes in public housing would have had a direct bearing on the trends we have seen. For one thing, changes in public housing were concentrated in select areas of the city from which only a minority of the study's sample came (and again, many of the cohort members moved outside the city). The decline in arrests and reported crime is much too broad across Chicago and the nation to be driven by such small areas. The immigrant status of the cohort children's parents was also considered in Chapter 4, and there are few cohort differences in exposure to concentrated immigration at the neighborhood level over time, similar to poverty.[27]

Nonetheless, it might be that immigration flows, above and beyond the composition of study cohorts, indirectly influenced arrests through their effects on urban revitalization and general processes of urban renewal, which in turn depressed crime rates.[28] If immigration is one piece of the puzzle, and it probably is, it likely operated through a broad national and especially urban scale, with increases in first-generation Americans helping to bring down rates of crime in major cities over a long period starting in the 1990s, paving the way for safer cities and a safer society that the younger cohort inherited. This trend may not be as protective to younger cohorts going forward, however, as the context of immigration, and in particular, immigration-related arrests, is again changing. Immigration became a controversial topic in the 2016 election and into the second term of President Trump's administration, leading to a broad crackdown and a slowing of new migrants to the United States, along with the specific targeting of illegal immigrants for deportation. It is not clear at this writing what the future of immigration, and thus immigration's influence on future arrest rates, will look like.

The Lead Hypothesis

Lead exposure has been proposed by some as yet another cause of the crime decline in America during the 1990s and into the 2000s.[29] This is a plausible environmental hypothesis. Many studies show that lead exposure in children fosters low self-control and aggressive behavior, and national estimates indicate falling lead exposure prior to the crime decline, due in large part to the 1974 regulations imposed on leaded gasoline. A recent meta-analysis of over twenty studies estimates that the subsequent abatement of lead pollution may be responsible for between 7 and 28 percent of the drop in homicide in the United States in the latter part of the twentieth century.[30] It stands to reason then that more recent cohorts in America were lucky in being exposed to much lower levels of lead growing up than their older cohort peers, just by virtue of their birth year.

The data support this hypothesis for Chicago, as well: The percentage of children with elevated blood-lead levels in Chicago declined approximately 90 percent from 1995 to 2021. When we consider exposure to lead by when each cohort was in their early teens, the differences are substantial. For example, when the 1981 cohort was fourteen, the percentage of tested children in Chicago with dangerous levels of lead in their blood was approximately 50 percent, compared to less than 5 percent when the mid-1990s cohort was at the same age. Given this fact, along with national trends, we can assume that cohort differences even earlier in childhood were similarly stark. Recall also from Chapter 4's analysis of arrest trajectories that the older cohorts' exposure to high levels of lead in their home neighborhoods was more than double that of the younger cohort (Figure 4.3). Accordingly, in that chapter I adjusted for neighborhood lead exposure, along with other factors. Yet large cohort differences in arrest during adolescence and young adulthood still emerged.

The logical conclusion is that while variations in lead exposure are one part of the national puzzle of declining crime and they make a difference in the lives of individual children, neighborhood lead levels as measured in our study are not a major factor in explaining cohort differentiation in arrest in our data. Put differently, while there are differences in the level of local lead exposure in childhood by cohort, and while there is considerable evidence that lead increases developmental problems in children at the individual level, accounting for ecological differences in exposure still leads to different arrest rates between cohorts, as shown in Chapter 4; thus, while it could and does contribute some to the arrest gap, it does not fully explain it. Similarly, declining lead exposure does not appear to explain the majority of the aggregate crime decline in America, though as the meta-analysis revealed, it likely is a significant contributor. I revisit lead exposure more fully in Chapter 7 as a form of poisoned development that is both racially and economically stratified, in turn bearing on our understanding of character and social change.

Citizens and Communities Fight Back

Another often-overlooked hypothesis to consider is the power of community-based organizations and the leadership of citizens in fighting back on crime and improving the urban environment. In his book *Uneasy Peace,* Patrick Sharkey and colleagues show how community-based organizations emerged in the United States as a response to increases in neighborhood violence during the height of the crack cocaine epidemic and the surge of murders among youth in the late 1980s and early 1990s, proactively intervening to institute a variety of crime control initiatives, such as youth programs.[31] As Charles Lanfear has argued, a related but overlooked mechanism is collective efficacy, which can reduce crime indirectly through changing the built environment (for example, remediation of vacant homes, regulation of bars, and the greening of public spaces where children congregate).[32] Taken together, these accounts suggest that one plausible reason for the transformation of the public spaces inhabited by the younger cohorts in our study is the collective efficacy of residents and local organizations, including residents' participation in police-community problem solving and improving the built environment.[33]

It is hard to measure this kind of effect. In Chapter 4 I accounted for social organizational characteristics, including collective efficacy, of the neighborhoods where the PHDCN+ participants lived as children. But if active organizing on the part of residents in high-crime communities was responsible for driving down the crime rate and thereby exposing children of the mid-1990s birth cohort to a safer world as they hit the peak ages for crime in later adolescence and early adulthood, that would still be an important part of the story. The story would be one of indirect influences— growing up in a safer world, the children coming of age in the mid-2000s were less likely than their older-cohort counterparts to confront disputatious encounters, dangerous or unregulated environments, and criminality among peers, and in turn faced a lower risk of arrest, which as we have seen was declining despite expectations derived from drug-war and broken-windows policing. Citizen community engagement and community organizations thus likely worked through these channels in any impact on cohort differences in arrest.

Technology and the Supervision of Youth

A final set of explanations of declining crime rates that scholars have put forth turn on changing technology and routine activities, especially how they affect those at the high-risk ages for crime. Technology and supervision are not factors I controlled for in Chapter 4, since we do not yet have a strong grasp on them empirically in our measures for each cohort, but there are several pathways through which technological change might work. One has to do with the increasing efficiencies in policing, data collection, and surveillance, such as improvements in the recording and statistical analysis of crimes by the police (for example, in predicting "hot spots" of crime).[34] Another is the increasing prevalence of video cameras and users of cell phones that monitor public space, leading to crimes becoming more visible or reported. It is no accident that police brutality came to the fore of public attention in recent years because of exposure through citizen monitoring. The increased surveillance or monitoring of behavior of all kinds is a classic concern of social control and routine activity theories in criminology.

Systematic data are hard to come by on the effects of such technological changes on other behavior, but the number of persons arrested for a crime because of surveillance technology seems to be on the rise. If true, then the more recent birth cohorts faced a higher probability of getting caught and arrested for a given crime compared to the older cohorts who came of age before the constant presence of surveillance technology. Yet this expectation does not easily square with the vastly lower rate of arrests among the younger cohorts. An alternative view is that the rise of surveillance was a deterrent to crime, which in turn drove down the arrest rate because of its suppressing effect on individual criminal behavior.

Another technological pathway is that the rise of both household and automobile security measures have reduced opportunities for many crimes, such as the greater difficulty of stealing most cars nowadays without a key.[35] Consider too that with the rise in debit cards and apps like Venmo, less cash is circulating, meaning that there is simply less opportunity for easy robberies. The amount of time that children and adolescents spend on smartphones, video games, the internet, and social media may also reduce criminogenic situations, for example through teenagers spending more time at home on their devices watching videos rather than hanging out in the streets with peers, where conflicts frequently arise. The rise of social media may substitute digital conflict for physical confrontations as well.

As with other hypotheses, the data are incomplete and there is no scientific consensus on the influence of social media or technology on crime.[36] The one thing we can say for certain, however, is that there are large cohort differences in exposure to technology and a secular trend toward children spending more time in structured activities.[37] After all, the youngest birth cohort members were teenagers in the 2010s, when the prevalence of internet use and social media had already deeply penetrated American society—they are, in effect, the first iPhone generation, with all that entails.[38] By contrast, the 1980 cohort was already well into its thirties when social media became commonplace. How and why Instagram, Snapchat, Twitter, or videogaming has influenced crime in the United States is well beyond the scope of this book and there are no easy answers.

But if technological changes led to lower criminal behavior and a higher probability of detecting it, that would mean that the most proximate mechanisms influencing the chance of arrest in recent generations were offsetting, thus clouding explanations for how we got to a lower-crime and lower-arrest world. This is especially true given that national surveys show that recent cohorts of teenagers are more supervised or socially controlled by their parents than prior cohorts, perhaps precisely because of technological advances in the ability of parents to track their children. For example, national estimates of the percent of time that teens spent outside the control or knowledge of their parents ("unstructured time") declined dramatically from 1995 to about 2015.[39] One might say, based on this continuing trend, that today's youth are the most closely watched in generations. Helicopter parenting became a buzzword for good reason.

Changes in technology and supervision may yet prove to be meaningful factors in explaining changes in criminal behavior, which, as we have shown, constitute one of the foundations of the cohort arrest gap. Even with the countervailing effects and difficult quantification of the technology landscape, youth routines, and parental control, it is possible, or even likely, that these factors contributed in part to the lowered rates of certain types of crimes, and thus, the differences in arrest trajectories.

THE CHALLENGE OF SOCIETAL CHANGE

The reasons for the large crime drop in the United States starting in the 1990s remain a frustrating mystery to many scholars because there is no magic bullet to explain the sharp trend. The same goes for why crime increased dramatically in the 1960s and 1970s. Whether before or after the crime decline, multiple explanations are at work, rendering the idea of a one-cause explanation of change illusory.[40]

Moreover, while this book is concerned with why crime rates vary in the aggregate, its core focus is how social and environmental change affects children coming of age at different times, and with the impacts of certain turning points at critical ages that in turn shape other life outcomes, such as becoming marked with a criminal record and being exposed to violence. My ultimate unit of analysis is thus not society writ large but rather intra- and inter-cohort trajectories of youth as they meet up with a changing social world. That is why I worked logically through the most well-known hypotheses of aggregate change and assessed them in terms of observable implications that bear on my cohort focus. Despite the welter of possible causes, a clear yet at times counterintuitive story of the generative mechanisms of change comes into focus.

Two broad sets of factors—institutional changes in law enforcement practices (particularly the policing of drug- and disorder-based offenses), and behavioral changes in crime (especially in decreased property- and violence-based criminal behavior)—each account for about half of the cohort divergence in arrest trajectories, with more granular factors (including changing technology use, supervision, lead exposure, and immigration) likely shaping underlying rates of criminal activity.

Interestingly, however, one of the law enforcement mechanisms named most often for the rapid growth of mass incarceration—broken-windows policing—does not explain major difference in arrest patterns by cohort in the simple way many scholars and pundits alike have asserted. Additionally, while the war on drugs is often thought of as constantly escalating, the primary reason for its impact on cohort arrest differences is actually the downturn in enforcement. In 2005, drug enforcement became much less aggressive, effectively siloing the drug war arrests to the older cohorts and excluding the youngest cohort from its reach—though, as outlined earlier, drug arrests alone do not fully account for the differences in arrests. Drug enforcement is not the only way in which enforcement patterns eased up in ways that run counter to dominant accounts of the penal state. From 1990 to 2020, patterns of decline for non-drug and drug arrests were roughly the same, and the decline was greater for disorderly conduct arrests, which dropped over 90 percent despite the expectations of broken-windows policing and the common interpretation of policing in recent decades as uniformly aggressive. An added complexity is that stops and frisks of citizens by the police skyrocketed, but in a very restricted time frame—2013 to 2015—during which the arrest enforcement of drugs, disorder, and many other offenses continued collapsing.

Police force size was in a relatively constant state over the period, ruling it out as a major factor to explain these changes. Changes in police tactics over time, especially with respect to drugs and disorder, are instead organizational in nature and, as seen in Chicago, often divorced from crime itself and driven by the idiosyncratic decisions of successive police chiefs. Within the drug war era and, more broadly, the era of mass incarceration and broken-windows policing, locally and temporally specific enforcement patterns like these have real but often overlooked consequences. This is especially true in a city like Chicago, which has a reputation for ongoing high rates of crime but also experiences extremes of policing on a breathtaking scale, with large swings in frequently counterintuitive directions; the consequences of this organizational social change are unevenly experienced by birth cohorts.

The fact that property and violent arrest patterns track so closely with reported crimes is a different story. The data strongly indicate that changing arrests for these non-drug crimes are largely (though by no means entirely) driven by changes in criminal behavior. It follows that cohort differences in property and violent arrests reflect, in large part, differences between cohorts in the larger behavioral contexts of crime and violence experienced at the same age and not just institutional differences in criminal justice reactions.

* * *

The large reductions in arrest among the younger cohorts relative to the older cohorts mirror a more general pattern of reduced problem behaviors among American youth—at least until very recently, when both cohorts had passed through the critical years for arrest.[41] In addition to changes in law enforcement practices, the cumulation of collective efficacy by citizens, community-based organizations devoted to reducing violence and improving public spaces, increased youth supervision and informal social controls, technological advances in security, widespread urban revitalization, altered immigration flows, and reduced lead in the environment (to name just some of the more empirically plausible hypotheses) constituted a societal transformation across multiple domains. While the impact of many of these factors was controlled for in Chapters 4 and 5 at the family and neighborhood level when the PHDCN+ cohorts were children, they nevertheless likely had synergistic societal consequences beyond the children's own family and home neighborhood for reducing criminal behavior in the late twentieth and early twenty-first centuries. In addition, these influences operate not just during childhood but during the adolescent and early adult years of our study participants, when arrest risk is the highest. But no matter how we apportion the unique contribution of these explanatory mechanisms, the key message is that, taken as a whole, the birth lottery of history stands outside the early-life social conditions and childhood propensities that individual theories of crime and character typically emphasize.

Similar to narratives of societal decline, the idea of steady progress sits uneasily with the forces of social and environmental change; as we have seen, there are frequent ups and downs, and alas, violence declined until it didn't. Gun violence, the subject of Chapter 7, is a telling indicator of how things change when we least expect it—a sad example of how something that once seemed to be coming under control can take a terrible turn, quickly and dramatically.

Guns, Violence, and Poisoned Development

In 2015, Patrick Sharkey and I assessed the mounting evidence from multiple disciplines revealing how exposure to violence infiltrates the minds of children, disrupting cognitive functioning and academic performance, impulse control, and, more generally, long-term developmental trajectories.[1] Exposure to environmental hazards such as lead and air pollution can similarly disrupt children's developmental capacities in the long run, leading to reduced cognitive ability, reduced impulse control, and increased attention-deficit/hyperactivity disorder. Put simply, violence and environmental hazards shape *who* we are as individuals, seeping into our minds and bodies. Less appreciated is how much of the variance in exposure to violence and other toxic inequalities results from the birth lottery of history, or purely from *when* we are.

So far, this book has been primarily concerned with measuring and explaining the arrest gap between the older and younger cohorts, finding that social changes in underlying crime prevalence and police enforcement account for most of that gap. This chapter sets aside that focus on arrests to look instead at guns, death, and lead exposure, all of which display their own meaningful cohort gaps. The story of lead exposure maps onto the general trend line already seen, with worse outcomes for older cohorts and better outcomes for the younger. But in the case of gun violence, the cohort inequalities in life experience tell a more complex story. The trend is not a linear improvement, but an improvement followed by a reversal for the youngest cohort.

Social transformations do not invariably add up to a march of progress. A closer look at lead exposure and gun violence reveals that determined policy interventions have made the former story one of significant progress, while gun violence in the youngest cohort reveals the extent to which social change can run roughshod over our hopes.

GUN VIOLENCE OVER THE LIFE COURSE AND ERAS

Like arrest and incarceration, violence creates powerful collateral consequences. Sharkey demonstrated this by studying how local homicides affected children's cognitive performance in mid-1990s Chicago, when violence remained high.[2] He found that African American children living near recent homicides (within a week before their PHDCN interview) performed significantly worse on vocabulary and reading tests. Sharkey concluded that violence occupies the mind, crowding out learning. This relationship tragically manifested in one PHDCN participant, Devon Shantel, a young Black male from Uptown. When he was barely eleven years old, in 1998, his mother described to an interviewer how the shots he heard ringing out in the neighborhood affected him: "When he hears gunshots, he says he has dreams that he or the family has been killed. It happens [the dreams] about once a week." The recurring dreams would prove prescient: At age twenty-four, Devon was murdered in Chicago.

In another study conducted with the PHDCN children in Chicago, David Kirk found that exposure to neighborhood violence had both an acute and enduring effect on aggressive behavior.[3] And a separate Chicago study with a different dataset found that children exposed to a homicide in close proximity to their home exhibited lower levels of attention and impulse control within the classroom setting.[4] Going beyond Chicago, more evidence came from the 1990s federal experiment called Moving to Opportunity for Fair Housing, which tested how grants of housing vouchers that enabled families to move out of high-poverty public housing projects affected their later outcomes in housing, earnings, and education. Later analysis of the data showed that children's test scores improved most when residential changes led to major reductions in exposure to violent crime.[5]

This body of research supports the assertion that exposure to violent crime impairs children's behavioral self-regulation, attention span, and performance on high-stakes tests. Prolonged exposure to community violence is thus linked to cognitive development deficits, reduced reading achievement, lower grades, increased absenteeism, and decreased rates of high school graduation and college attendance.[6] Such effects of childhood violence exposure accumulate over time, reinforcing initial disadvantages and likely increasing subsequent delinquency, criminal behavior, personal victimization, and even premature death.

Seeing the process in this way reinforces the idea, noted in Chapter 2, that exposure to violence can constitute a negative turning point—an experience that knocks a child's social development off the course it would otherwise have maintained. But even within the larger category of violent acts, there are important distinctions, including the outcome—injury or death—and the instrument of violence, like fists, knives, or guns. I am particularly interested in children's first exposures to any form of gun violence, both in the life course and in the temporal stream of history. Large-scale swings in gun violence experienced by children are often set aside in developmental research. The focus instead is typically on how various individual, family, and neighborhood risk factors predict violence, or on the factors that shield children from harm, the so-called protective factors. These are undoubtedly important, but as with research on the criminal justice system, multi-cohort longitudinal studies of violence that separate traditional risk or resilience factors from social change are rare.

This chapter counters that imbalance by looking at cohort inequalities in multiple forms of gun violence—an American scourge whose mark on children's lives has dramatically changed over time. While previous chapters have noted the general phenomenon of violent crime trending downward across the past several decades—known as the "great American crime decline"—the trends are more complex for gun violence.

Based on collaborative research with Charles Lanfear and David Kirk, I start by portraying age and cohort differences in cumulative exposure to direct gun victimization over the life course. The left panel in Figure 7.1 depicts differences in the experience of being shot, as reported by the respondents themselves.[7] All cohorts show sharp increases in gun victimization

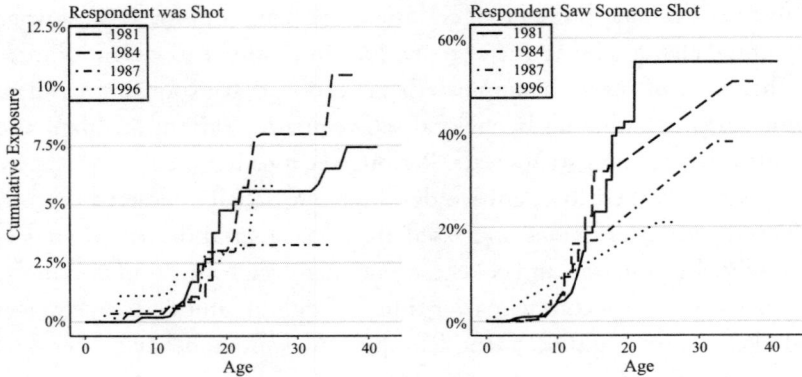

Figure 7.1. Cumulative Exposure to Gun Violence. Cumulative exposure to gun violence varies by age and cohort.

during their late teens, with one exception: The cohort born in the mid-1990s experienced an earlier, more gradual rise. Yet by the time its members reached their mid-twenties, this youngest cohort's cumulative gun victimization matched that of the oldest cohort (born around 1981, age fifteen at study start) and exceeded the lowest-exposure cohort (born 1987, age nine at study start).[8] The spike at age twenty-two for this youngest cohort is based on relatively few individuals getting shot at this age, however, and is not precisely estimated. The main takeaway is that cohort differences in the cumulative exposure to being shot are similar until participants' early to mid-twenties.

This pattern contrasts with arrest rates. While the mid-1990s cohort faced significantly lower arrest risks than those born in the 1980s, they gained no similar advantage in avoiding gun violence. Indeed, firearm violence shows markedly different life-course patterns than arrests, especially when comparing the two youngest cohorts, born just nine years apart.

Figure 7.1's right panel shows that the experience of witnessing a shooting—which happens earlier and more frequently than being shot—was highest among the two oldest cohorts. By age twenty, for example, over 40 percent of the 1981 cohort had witnessed a shooting, compared to about 20 percent of the 1987 cohort—a twofold difference between groups born just six years apart. Though the 1987 cohort experienced more gun exposure in early childhood, they reached adolescence and age twenty during the relatively peaceful early 2000s, while the 1981 cohort became teenagers in the more violent years of the 1990s.

By contrast, children from the infant cohort of the mid-1990s, born almost exactly when the great crime decline started, experienced a less violent world than the two oldest cohorts as young teenagers. By the end of the observation period, at approximately age twenty-six to twenty-seven, the cumulative exposure to witnessing shootings of the younger cohort matched what earlier cohorts experienced at just age fifteen. The patterns in Figure 7.1 persist even after controlling for race, poverty, family criminality, immigrant status, and childhood neighborhood disadvantage, ruling out conventional criminological risk factors as explanations. Cohort experiences with gun violence are driven largely by broader societal changes.

Death Foretold?

Not only did Devon Shantel hear gunshots, he also reported witnessing the shooting of someone else before he was eighteen—in fact, he first reported it at age nine. Unfortunately, this was not an uncommon experience among our study participants; the cumulative risk of witnessing a shooting, as shown in Figure 7.1, climbed to over 50 percent for the oldest cohort. The younger cohorts fared relatively better, but their corresponding prevalence of witnessing shootings was still over 20 percent. These high but distinct rates of exposure raise the question: How does this experience with violence in adolescence relate to a life's ultimate outcome, death?

Analysis of national CDC mortality records, described in Chapter 3, along with PHDCN interview notes, reveal that 112 of our 1996, 1987, 1984, and 1981 cohorts selected in the initial wave were deceased by the end of 2024—a rate of more than 3 percent. Focusing on the two oldest cohorts, for whom we can observe mortality risk up to at least age forty, as well as reliably measure direct and indirect gun victimization up to the age of eighteen, allows us to probe the associations between violence exposure while coming of age and later adult mortality.

The data reveal that individuals who were shot (and survived) before the age of eighteen were almost five times more likely to die by their early forties, with a death rate of 15.7 percent compared to 3.5 percent for those who had not been shot. But it isn't just being shot that is linked to increased mortality risk; witnessing a shooting by age eighteen, as Devon Shantel did, is also linked to higher mortality rates by age forty. Specifically, 5.4 percent of those who had witnessed a shooting as a minor died before reaching their fortieth birthday, compared to 2.4 percent of those who had not witnessed a shooting.[9] The 1981 cohort was particularly affected; for them, individuals who were either shot themselves or witnessed gun violence before eighteen faced a risk of adult death more than three times higher than those who were not exposed. By contrast, the mortality risk of violence-exposed individuals was lower for the 1984 cohort, just over two times higher than non-violence-exposed cohort members.[10]

Not all adult deaths reported were homicides. The majority were due to other causes, including accidents, drugs, alcohol, suicide, health issues, and more. A second question thus arises, directly pertinent to this chapter's focus: What happens when we zoom in on homicide? With just a three-year gap between the 1981 and 1984 cohorts, our data still show meaningful disparities in homicide. Though the 1981 cohort had a slightly lower overall death rate than the 1984 cohort, the homicide rate of those born in 1981 was more than five times higher, a significant difference even after adjusting for race and sex.[11] Across these two cohorts, there were ten homicide victims who had previously been asked about exposure to violence in PHDCN+ surveys. Of the ten, remarkably, nine had witnessed a shooting by the age of eighteen—meaning that only one eventual homicide victim had never seen someone else shot by age eighteen. While these homicide rates are too low to perform meaningful significance testing, it is clear that the majority of homicide victims in this study had already witnessed extreme violence before their own demise. In this sense, although death was not immediate, it was, just as for Devon, eerily foretold.

Figure 7.2 provides a hint as to why the 1981 cohort had a higher homicide rate as well as a strong association between exposure and later deaths. At the critical ages of adolescence and on the cusp of adulthood, the 1981 cohort lived in a world with a firearm homicide rate almost 50 percent higher than the cohort born just three years after them. When they were nineteen, for example, the rate was 17 per 100,000, compared to about 12 per 100,000 for the later cohort. To be sure, most of them were not killed at such a young age—still, a rising incidence of witnessing shootings marks a distinct trajectory of violence over time. This fact, combined with earlier findings, confirms that the oldest cohort faced a double disadvantage in

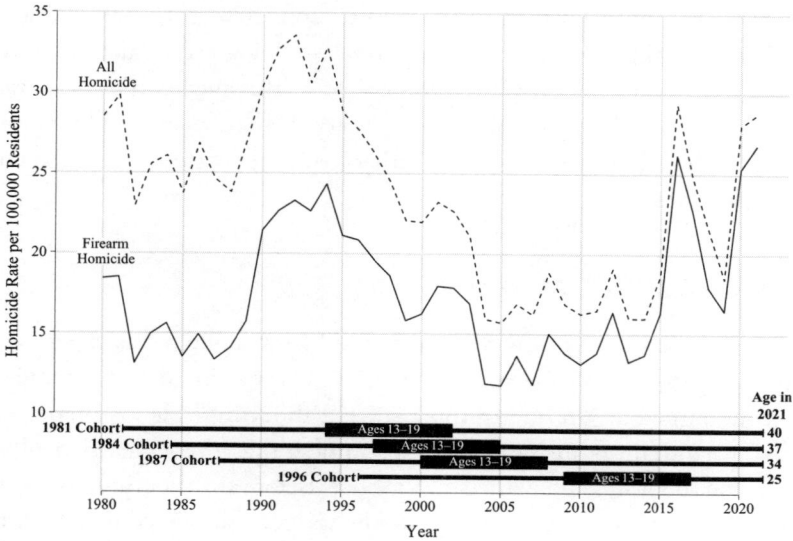

Figure 7.2. Firearm Homicide in Chicago. Variations in firearm homicide in Chicago distinguish the teenage years of the different birth cohorts. *Source:* Reformatted from Charles C. Lanfear, Rebecca Bucci, David S. Kirk, and Robert J. Sampson, "Inequalities in Exposure to Firearm Violence by Race, Sex, and Birth Cohort from Childhood to Age 40 Years, 1995–2021," *JAMA Network Open* 6, no. 5 (2023): e2312465, figure 1.

life, of both criminal legal involvement and violence exposure, largely due to growing up and coming of age during spikes of violence and mass criminalization.

As crime declined from its 1990s heights, later cohorts encountered a less violent world. Yet the crime decline did not continue perpetually, and the risk of being shot in the mid-1990s cohort reached similar if not higher rates than the 1987 cohort (Figure 7.1). The reversal in crime began around 2015 to 2016, when US violence, especially in Chicago, rose unexpectedly. While overall crime continued its decades-long decline, lethal gun violence in particular increased sharply. By 2021, Chicago's gun-related deaths peaked (seen in the second spike in Figure 7.2), with almost all homicides involving firearms—up from previous decades, including the high-violence era of the early 1990s. The mid-1990s cohort, though largely avoiding criminalization, as we saw in Chapter 4, thus faced the misfortune of experiencing their late teens and early twenties during the 2016–2021 surge in gun homicides. And while the mid-nineties cohort had higher survival rates

into their late twenties than older cohorts, consistent with national longevity trends, their murder risk conditional on dying was actually slightly
higher than either the 1987 or 1984 cohorts. This means that deceased
members of the youngest cohort were more likely to have died by homicide than those born just nine years earlier—another within-generation cohort difference.

GUN CARRYING AND USE

In one interview, seventeen-year-old Larry James spoke of his experience
witnessing violence as a teenager: "When I was walking down the street,
someone pulled a gun out and just started shooting." He also reported
carrying a gun for protection. It was a reminder that gun violence involves
more than shootings and witnessing violence. Before any shooting, someone
must possess and choose to use a gun—behaviors also shaped by exposure
to violence and changing historical experiences.

In another PHDCN+ study with Charles Lanfear and David Kirk, we
found that witnessing gun violence in adolescence directly predicted
carrying concealed weapons, independent of typical individual, family, and
neighborhood risk factors.[12] Those who carried weapons were also most
likely to brandish them or shoot someone. Concealed firearm carrying has
become remarkably common, with nearly one-third (32 percent) of our
Chicago study population having carried weapons by age forty—a concerning indication of guns' reach in American society. This pattern varies
significantly by demographics: About 48 percent of males versus 16 percent
of females had carried guns by age forty, and Black individuals carried at
rates more than double those of Hispanic or white individuals. Interestingly, while Hispanic rates started higher than whites in adolescence, they
converged by age forty. White respondents, though least exposed to gun
violence, were most likely to begin carrying after exposure.

My main interest here, though, is how the onset of gun carrying and
use differ by the birth-cohort lottery, for all races and sexes. The "truly disadvantaged" historically is again the oldest cohort, those born in the early
1980s and who became teenagers during the epidemic of violence in the
early 1990s. The left panel of Figure 7.3 shows that this cohort, which
included Larry James quoted earlier, reported the sharpest increase in
carrying during the teen years, followed by those born right after them,

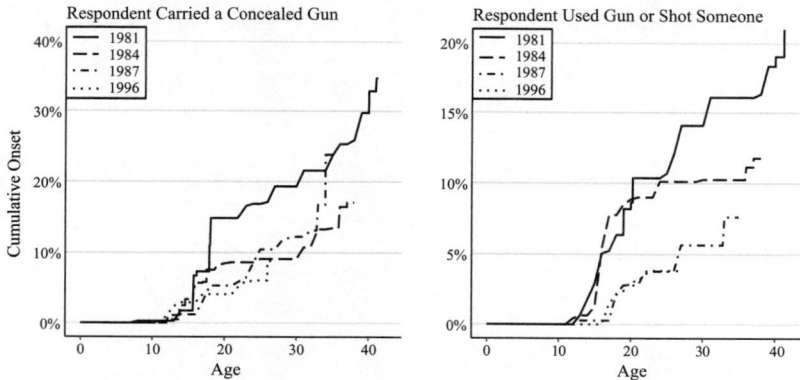

Figure 7.3. Percentage of Concealed Gun Carriers and Users, by Cohort. The oldest cohort had the highest proportion of concealed gun carriers and users at most ages after twenty years old. *Source:* Reformatted from Charles C. Lanfear, David S. Kirk, and Robert J. Sampson, "Dual Pathways of Concealed Gun Carrying and Use from Adolescence to Adulthood over a 25-Year Era of Change," *Science Advances* 10, no. 49 (2024), figures 2C and 3C.

in 1984. The younger 1987 and 1996 cohorts have low and similar rates of onset before adulthood.

Later-life patterns reveal a shift. The 1987 cohort's onset accelerates notably in their mid-thirties, during the COVID era, matching the 1981 cohort's rate—approximately 25 percent had carried concealed weapons. In a similar pattern, onset for the 1996 cohort reaches parity with the 1984 cohort at age twenty-six.

Gun use—whether for self-defense or crime—also distinguishes cohorts: As seen in the right panel of Figure 7.3, by their mid-twenties, about 10 percent of the two oldest cohorts had used guns compared to less than 5 percent of younger cohorts. The 1981 cohort stands out further—after age twenty-five, their gun use continued increasing while the 1984 cohort's rate plateaued. By age forty, one in five members of the 1981 cohort had brandished or used a gun. These patterns persist after adjusting for demographics and childhood conditions (race, sex, poverty, family criminality, and neighborhood composition).[13]

Figure 7.4 provides a broader historical perspective by illustrating how concealed gun carrying evolved across cohorts during the transformative quarter-century studied in this book, marking key historical events and each cohort's twenty-first birthday. Also demonstrated in this graph are the

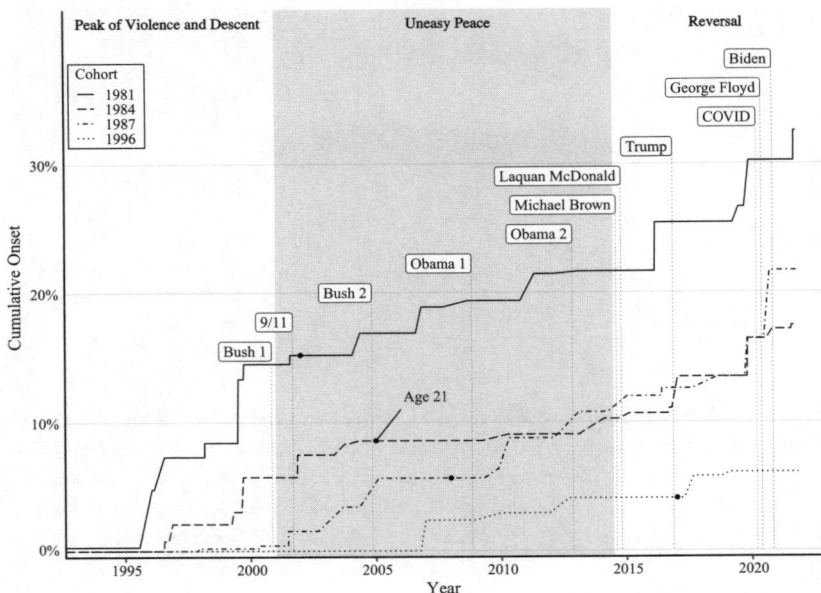

Figure 7.4. Concealed Gun Carrying by Cohort, 1995–2022. Timeline shows cumulative rates of concealed gun carrying by cohort, noting significant historical events, across twenty-seven years.

potential period- and age-specific effects of large changes in laws around gun carrying, since concealed carrying permits for those twenty-one or older became legal in Illinois starting in 2013. The 1996 cohort was thus the only cohort for which carrying was legal at twenty-one years old, and we see the largest increase in carrying right after their average twenty-first birthday.[14] Pre-2015 political and social events showed surprisingly little impact on gun carrying. Instead, two eras drove significant changes, particularly affecting minority males: the 1990s violence peak and decline, and the post-Ferguson policing crisis—triggered by the shooting of Michael Brown in Ferguson and culminating most visibly in George Floyd's murder—through the early pandemic years.

These social changes intersected with age differences in gun carrying. In 2021, approximately a quarter of gun carriers (about 3 percent of the total sample) were new to the practice—a notable shift among adults in their late twenties through early forties. This rise in "adult onset" carriers between 2016 and 2021 reveals a significant group overlooked by youth-focused research.[15] Our analysis also suggests distinct motivational patterns between age groups. For teenagers, carrying appears directly linked to immediate environmental threats, as illustrated by study participant Jose Rubio, who began carrying at sixteen "out of anger" and for "protection." Adult-onset carriers, however, seem driven by different concerns. Unlike the adolescent-onset group, their gun carrying shows less connection to personal experiences like witnessing gun violence. Instead, particularly during the pandemic, adult-onset carrying appears related to broader societal concerns: institutional distrust, fears of social unrest, and declining confidence in public safety.

These dual pathways of gun carrying by age emerged during a period of declining arrests and, for much of the time, declining violent offenses—highlighting social change's complexity. The 1996 cohort illustrates this paradox: Despite experiencing childhood during the early 2000s' relative calm—Sharkey's "uneasy peace"—and witnessing fewer shootings and lower arrest rates, they matched the 1981 cohort's shooting victimization rates when violence spiked around 2015. While these patterns await full explanation, evidence from other domains like lead exposure demonstrates how deliberate policy interventions can create positive cohort differences, even as significant challenges remain.

LEAD EXPOSURE AND ENVIRONMENTAL INEQUALITY

Environmental hazards like pollution and lead toxicity represent another crucial context for understanding children's development and the transmission of inequality over time. In a 2018 assessment in the *Annual Review of Sociology* with Christopher Muller and Alix Winter, we argued that lead exposure, though operating through biological mechanisms, demands social science attention because it is socially stratified and has broad social consequences—effects that extend beyond individual or family circumstances and depend partly on children's social environments.[16] While earlier chapters showed that neighborhood lead exposure alone doesn't explain the cohort arrest gap, this finding shouldn't minimize lead's significant social impact. Those previous analyses measured lead exposure only in children's home neighborhoods, not accounting for individual blood-lead levels or citywide patterns of change. A complete understanding requires examining both broader trends and individual-level exposure.

Lead is present in water, paint, and soil because of historically weak environmental regulations. Although they have strengthened over time, existing regulations have been insufficient to protect children from harm, as has been repeatedly revealed in cities around the country and during the pandemic.[17] Indeed, far from a relic of history books, prevalence estimates indicate that half of the US population as recently as 2015 has been exposed to adverse lead levels from gasoline in early childhood.[18] These are probably underestimates, moreover, because lead exposure, both historically and today, also comes from leaded paint in older homes, lead plumbing, brownfields, and hazardous industrial plants.

While I will continue to focus on cohort gaps in lead exposure as a means to discern the impacts of social change, I also want to open this portion of the analysis by pointing toward linked inequalities by race and socioeconomic status. As with gun violence, poor families of color are most at risk and they tend to live in neighborhoods of concentrated disadvantage and racial segregation, which often lack the resources and organizational access to eliminate environmental toxins from their homes and communities. For example, an investigation of Santa Ana, California, not typically thought of as an industrial city, found that lead levels in the soil were significantly elevated in a poor Latino neighborhood characterized by recycling plants and an industrial past, literally on the other side of the railroad tracks from advantaged neighborhoods.[19] Exposure to these kinds of toxic environments reinforce inequality and lead to further social stratification through its negative influences on child development and adult well-being.

Pilsen, a lower-income Latino community on the southwest side of Chicago that was home to over 150 of the PHDCN+ children, is a case in point of both historical and contemporary inequality. While leaded gasoline was banned in the early 1970s and airborne pollution declined thereafter, lead toxins in the soil remained in many neighborhoods like Pilsen, especially those near highly traveled roads or adjacent to old industrial plants. Even those smelter plants that had been long shuttered, often called "ghost factories," emitted lead toxins that remained in the soil.[20] In Pilsen, it was not until 2013 after many children became sick and developed behavioral problems that it was discovered that playing in abandoned lots, as children have always and will always do, was leading to high levels of children's lead exposure from the contaminated soil.[21]

Figure 7.5. Lead Exposure in Pilsen, Chicago. Lead exposure persists in Pilsen, Chicago, in 2013. Sign translates to: "Warning! Lead Contamination. Poison." *Source:* Courtesy of PERRO (Pilsen Environmental Rights and Reform Organization).

As captured in Figure 7.5, this area, close to apartment buildings with a high density of children who played in the area, was declared toxic and scheduled for cleanup, but only long after the damage was done from a smelting factory closed down decades earlier. Similar examples occurred in nearby East Chicago, Indiana, a poor community where an old smelter had spewed contaminants into the soil over many years.[22] And as widely reported in the media, Flint, Michigan became notorious for the shock of its lead-contaminated water. A study in 2024 demonstrated that the resulting increases in exposure to lead-in-water levels within classrooms in Flint increased disciplinary actions and led to a decline in the share of students testing proficient in both math and reading.[23] The ingestion of lead into the body is clearly not just a thing of the deep past, even though the ultimate sources of lead exposure have long-term historical roots.

Alix Winter and I approached childhood lead exposure from a contextual life-course perspective. As discussed in Chapter 3, we extended the PHDCN+ study by linking our survey, census, and other data to Chicago Department of Public Health blood tests. These infant blood tests were

matched to neighborhoods and individually to the youngest 1995 birth cohort members where records existed. We also measured each child's home
distance from abandoned smelter factories, identified through historical
records, regardless of neighborhood location.

We argued that while lead exposure's impact is age-graded, its origins
are structural and ecological. Infants and young children face higher exposure risks through normal behaviors—playing in outdoor areas (as shown
in Figure 7.5), or in houses, schools, and playgrounds—leading to ingestion of lead paint, contaminated dust, and dirt. We found that proximity
to ghost factory smelters predicted higher blood-lead levels in our sample,
after adjusting for poverty, race, housing conditions, and other risk factors.

Lead's biological impact is magnified by early exposure. Young children
absorb lead more efficiently than adults, and their developing brains show
greater vulnerability to its effects. Lead mimics calcium, disrupting brain
development and neurotransmitter systems, which impairs executive functioning and mood regulation. This leads to reduced impulse control and
diminished inhibition of aggressive behaviors. These neurological effects
are directly linked to decreased cognitive ability and increased rates of
attention-deficit / hyperactivity disorder—both established predictors of delinquent behavior.[24] This evidence reveals childhood lead poisoning as an
adverse transition in the early life course that becomes literally embodied
within a child's developing system. Like exposure to violence, lead poisoning functions as a turning point that can destructively alter long-term
development. Unlike traditional turning points that emerge in later life
(military service, marriage, employment) or even exposure to gun violence
in adolescence, lead exposure begins its damaging impact very early, typically between ages one and three.

Causality cannot be demonstrated in observational data, but this timing
of lead exposure offers an analytical advantage over traditional social science predictors. Unlike internal characteristics (attitudes, morality) or adult
transitions that may reflect individual choice (employment, marriage), very
young children do not control or select their lead exposure. Most contemporary exposure comes from lead-contaminated house dust and soil
particles, unknowingly tracked into homes and ingested through normal
toddler behavior. While parents can choose environments, they often remain unaware of environmental lead levels—and our analyses control for a
range of parental, family, and neighborhood characteristics. As an external

toxin, lead differs fundamentally from typical developmental factors. The term "ghost factories" aptly describes these invisible yet potent sources of contamination.

Analyzing blood-lead levels of Chicago children at ages one to three, Winter and I detected lasting consequences through adolescence: mental and physical health problems (anxiety / depression, obesity), low self-control, and antisocial behaviors including aggression.[25] While childhood blood-lead levels didn't directly predict adolescent arrests, they influenced known arrest predictors—low self-control and aggression—suggesting a potential indirect pathway to criminal justice involvement. The longer-term PHDCN+ data show modest connections between high blood-lead levels and violent arrests through age twenty-five, and the 2021 wave 5 interviews reveal significant links between childhood lead exposure and poor self-reported health at age twenty-five, controlling for multiple childhood disadvantage factors.

PHDCN+ data at the ecological level demonstrate that neighborhood lead exposure reduces test scores and educational achievement, intensifying concentrated poverty's effects.[26] Moreover, my work with Robert Manduca shows children from high-lead, high-violence, high-incarceration neighborhoods face reduced intergenerational mobility and increased adult incarceration—especially poor Black males—after accounting for poverty and racial composition.[27] These patterns extend to poor white children's mobility and teenage pregnancy rates across racial groups, while our additional research links neighborhood exposure to traffic-related air pollution and housing-derived lead to lower adult incomes and higher rates of teenage parenthood and incarceration, independent of socio-demographic and metropolitan-level factors.[28]

Evidence beyond the PHDCN+ study and around the world strengthens the poisoned development thesis. Studies show lead exposure negatively affects personality development in the United States and Europe, while New Zealand research documents cognitive and socioeconomic impacts into people's thirties.[29] Fascinating historical evidence also suggests that lead pollution contributed to homicide in the early part of the twentieth century in the United States, and possibly even to ancient Rome's decline—researchers estimate childhood lead exposure reduced intelligence quotients there by 2.5 to 3 points, potentially contributing to widespread cognitive decline.[30]

Inequality, Again

Lead exposure, like arrest and violence, varies significantly not only by co-hort but also by racial group. Figure 7.6 reveals more than just lead distri-bution—it shows how areas with the highest levels of lead exposure at the outset of the PHDCN+ study align with concentrations of poor and non-white residents, demonstrating an ecological pathway through which ra-cial inequality becomes physically embedded.

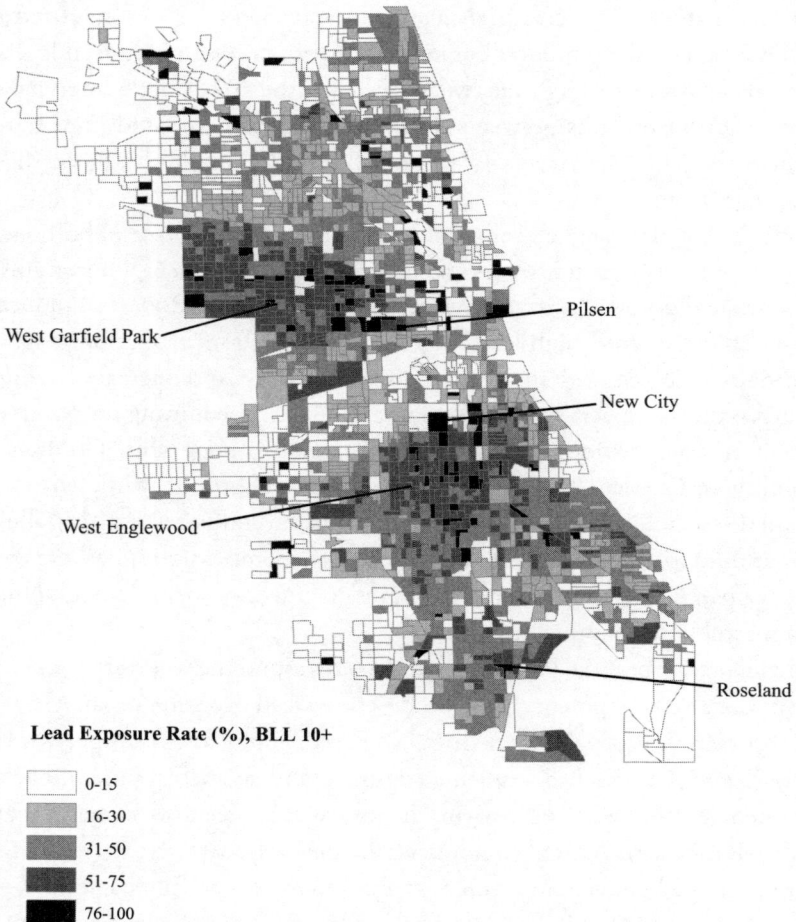

Figure 7.6. Children's Exposure to Lead in Chicago, 1995. Mapping children's ex-posure to dangerous levels of lead in Chicago in 1995 reveals a distinct ecology.

Using a blood-lead level (BLL) of 10 micrograms per deciliter (μg/dL) as a marker—far above traditional harmful levels of 5 μg/dL and current CDC guidance that no level is safe—we can see wide variations across Chicago's block groups (census-defined clusters of city blocks) in 1995 when the longitudinal study began. The west and south sides, including the Pilsen neighborhood of Figure 7.5 that contained many of our study's children, experienced the highest exposure to dangerous lead levels in 1995. Dozens of other block groups within poor, racially segregated communities in these sections of the city contained respondents to our study, like the South Side areas of West Englewood (home to Darnell and Andre) and New City (home to the infamous "Back of the Yards" neighborhood), West Garfield Park on the city's west side, and Roseland on the far South Side.

The geographic inequality seen in Figure 7.6 means that there is little overlap in exposure rates for Blacks and whites: Virtually all majority Black neighborhoods, and to a lesser extent Hispanic neighborhoods, in Chicago are more exposed to environmental hazards like lead than any majority white neighborhoods. The elevated exposure of Black, Hispanic, and poor areas to lead toxicity also remained after we accounted for the age of the housing stock, proximity to industry, density, and the presence of public housing.[31] These large, racialized differences in lead exposure plausibly account for a meaningful portion of racial disparities in intergenerational inequality according to one of our studies.[32]

At the same time, as discussed in Chapter 6, lead exposure dropped dramatically in the 1990s and 2000s across the country and in Chicago—a significant positive historical change. Children from poor Black and Hispanic neighborhoods gained the most. Figure 7.7 visualizes these improvements, showing extreme lead exposure by neighborhood poverty (greater than 30 percent poor residents) and racial composition (70 percent or more Black, white, or Hispanic) over time.[33] All neighborhood types show sharp downward trends, with poor Black neighborhoods experiencing the largest absolute declines—from over 50 percent of children with 10 micrograms per deciliter lead or more to under 5 percent. This pattern of improvements aligns with the reductions in arrest rates among Black disadvantaged respondents in our study (Chapter 5).

Despite these dramatic reductions, relative racial inequality in exposure persists at every level and across both poor and nonpoor areas, following a racial hierarchy of risk. In 1995, even Black nonpoor areas had lead toxicity

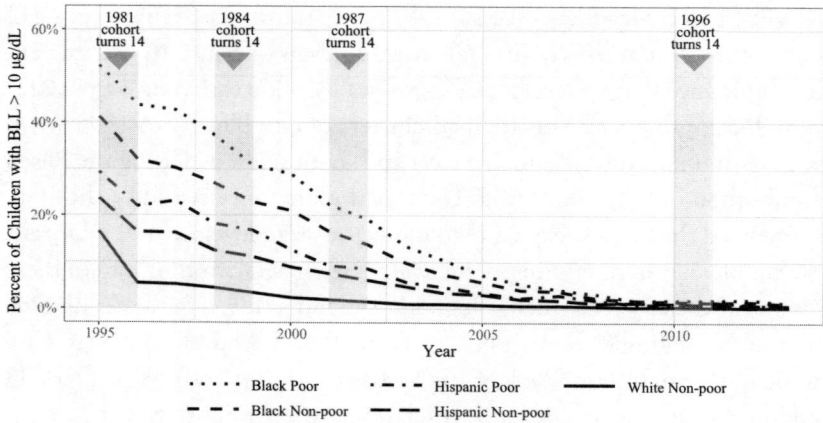

Figure 7.7. Lead Exposure by Neighborhood Race and Poverty Levels. Monitoring of lead exposure has documented large declines, by neighborhood race and poverty levels.

rates more than double those of white nonpoor areas (notably, no white neighborhoods had poverty rates above 30 percent). Combined with the ecology of lead contamination mapped in Figure 7.6, this pattern suggests that racial inequality and economic disadvantage, interacting with the birth lottery, largely determine individual experiences with toxic inequality across the life course.

Lead remediation's benefits varied by cohort too. The older PHDCN+ cohorts faced the greatest disadvantage, being infants in the early 1980s before enhanced Chicago regulations. As Figure 4.3 showed, 1980s cohort members were twice as likely to live in lead-poisoned neighborhoods as young children compared to the 1996 cohort, born when lead exposure began its massive decline. Given lead's documented detrimental effects on life-course development, we can conclude the younger cohort's lower exposure, especially among the poor, provided lifelong advantages unavailable to older cohorts.

This conclusion raises the question of why government interventions through soil remediation, code enforcement, and housing reinvestment efforts are not more widespread, especially given their proven effectiveness and poor families' lack of resources to eliminate environmental toxins. We know, for example, that the remediation of lead paint in rental properties can be powerfully influenced by city governments, should they choose to do so. Anna Aizer and colleagues demonstrated that Rhode Island's landlord mitigation requirements significantly reduced children's blood-lead levels and improved later academic performance.[34] Evidence also shows community organizing and local interventions can create positive change, suggesting policy reform's political dimension significantly affects children's outcomes.[35]

Through investment in disadvantaged neighborhoods, green space promotion, environmental poison remediation, safe housing access, and stronger regulations, we can reduce toxic exposure through deliberate policy interventions. Social change for the public good can be active and intentional, benefiting poor minorities most while improving entire cohorts' lives. Environmental policy thus serves as both crime-reduction and inequality-reduction policy. However, such efforts, along with other potential crime-reduction policy areas such as gun policy for children, remain sadly unprioritized, if not actively opposed.[36]

* * *

This chapter's examination of environmental toxins, violence, and death reveals how historically shaped exposures—what I have called poisoned development—interact with racial inequality and cohort timing to shape important life outcomes. Together with earlier findings about police enforcement and the cohort arrest gap, these patterns demonstrate how structural governance choices affect character development while acknowledging individual and family differences. The next chapter builds on this theoretical framework to reconceptualize our understanding of individual propensity and character in light of macrosocial change.

PART III

RECONCEIVING WHO WE ARE

CHAPTER 8

The Reign of Propensity and the Character Trap

We typically view character as an immutable core of personality traits guiding our actions and defining who we are, with a distinctly moral dimension that leads us to think about—or at least talk about—individuals as simply good or bad. The evidence presented in previous chapters challenges this logic, suggesting that character is neither as individual nor as static as commonly assumed.

Cohort inequalities in differential experiences of social change shape both personality traits—through lead exposure and violence—and societal responses, visible in the cohort arrest gap. A child born in the 1980s faced harsher police enforcement during adolescence than one born in the 1990s—clearly no reflection of individual character. Yet these cohort inequalities in lead exposure, violence, and policing shaped critical outcomes from academic achievement and incarceration to employment, income, and longevity.

Many PHDCN+ respondents were injured, arrested, poisoned, or punished not due to character flaws, but because of the birth lottery of history. Most tellingly, low self-control individuals from the youngest cohort had arrest chances similar to high self-control individuals from older cohorts. Even this hallmark of "good character"—high self-control—couldn't protect older cohorts from arrest. Understanding these patterns requires examining how concepts of character and propensity function in both criminology and law.

Consider how criminal behavior is commonly explained by invoking supposedly stable propensities in individuals' dispositions, characters, and, less frequently, social environments. When certain individuals or groups repeatedly commit or are arrested for crimes, they are typically deemed to possess a criminal propensity, or criminal nature, manifesting in terms like *chronic* or *predatory* offender, sometimes reaching fanciful extremes like *super-predator.*

Assumptions about criminal propensity have powerful implications not only for how we explain crime but also for how we go about controlling it. Scholars vary in their views on propensity's stability, its relation to age, and whether it stems primarily from internal or external sources. While most existing criminological theories (as opposed to legal ones) consider criminal propensity to be rooted in both internal characteristics and immediate social / cultural conditions, even these approaches typically build outward from internal characteristics.

The individualist bias is even starker in legal settings, where propensity is attributed almost exclusively at the level of the individual and their assumed internal tendencies. This bias drives the character trap—the self-reinforcing cycle that labels and punishes individuals using assumptions about their supposed innate qualities that can in turn lead them to conform to the same negative expectations. The character trap functions by focusing on individual acts and qualities while neglecting changing social environments.

Although propensity and character are intertwined in meaning, they have followed different intellectual paths in theory, research, and legal practice. Drawing on collaborative work with Ash Smith, this chapter first examines scholarly approaches and empirical evidence about criminal propensity before addressing character's broader implications and legal applications.[1]

THEORIES OF PROPENSITY

Though common in life-course theories of crime, criminal propensity is not universally defined. Some theorists define it primarily as an internal characteristic—focusing on constructs like antisocial personality traits or inability to exercise self-control. Gottfredson and Hirschi's influential self-control theory defines criminal propensity as "the tendency of individuals to pursue short-term gratification without consideration of the long-term costs."[2] Individuals with high criminal propensity have low self-control, which these authors describe as a skill that must be taught in childhood through effective parenting—thus presenting an argument for criminal propensity stemming from socialization. Without developing self-control, individuals become "impulsive, insensitive, physical (as opposed to mental), risk-taking, short-sighted, and non-verbal"—attributes that engender criminal propensity.[3]

Sociologist Callie Burt argues that low self-control is better conceptualized as impulsivity or "perhaps more narrowly as shortsightedness."[4] She emphasizes the external environment more than Gottfredson and Hirschi, arguing that low self-control is necessary but not sufficient for crime—it requires available opportunities for criminal activity. Burt's conceptualization offers a friendly amendment to self-control theory, viewing criminal propensity as arising from both low internal self-control (a character-adjacent concept) and one's external opportunity structure.

These accounts of criminal propensity are built around the idea of "latent traits"—stable, underlying internal characteristics (of which Gottfredson and Hirschi's self-control is an archetype) that vary throughout the population and generally lead individuals to engage in antisocial activity.[5] Those high in these traits possess high levels of criminal propensity or disposition. Such traits are believed relatively stable within individuals over time even though criminal acts may vary. Theories positing relatively stable latent traits typically place little, if any, theoretical weight on social change and, by implication, cohort differentiation.

Other life-course theorists focus more explicitly on the interplay between offender and environment in accounting for criminal propensities, moving away from purely individualistic explanations. In earlier work, I argued that criminal propensity is "forged in interactions with institutions of social control—family, school, peers, neighborhood, and the state."[6] Per-Olof Wikström's situational action theory similarly locates propensity both within and outside the individual: Criminal propensity is "the tendency to see and, if so, to choose acts of crime . . . as a viable action alternative in response to a motivation (temptation or provocation)."[7] Individuals with such propensities are deemed crime-prone (and those without, crime-averse), and criminality occurs when a crime-prone individual encounters a crimino-genic environment with reduced social control and cohesion. This frame-work specifies the environment more concretely than the general oppor-tunity structure argument of Burt or Gottfredson and Hirschi.

There are other approaches to the relationship between internal and ex-ternal factors, though all maintain some focus on individual internal qualities. Terrie Moffitt's developmental taxonomy explains criminal pro-pensity as inherent in certain individuals and expressed through environ-mental interactions. For her, the uniquely crime-prone are life-course-persistent offenders who—unlike adolescent-limited offenders—"show extreme, pervasive, persistent antisocial behaviour from early childhood to adulthood."[8] She attributes this to atypical psychological development stemming from the combination of a high-risk child's difficult behavior (internal) with a high-risk social environment (external). Internal factors include neuropsychological issues, difficult temperament, or cognitive def-icits; external forces include disrupted family attachments, inadequate parenting, maltreatment, and poverty. Adolescent-limited offenders are pri-marily driven by peer influences and other external factors. Her theory recognizes both internal and external influences on criminal propensity, though external influences remain largely proximate to the individual.

David Farrington's cognitive antisocial potential theory similarly posits that "the commission of offenses and other types of antisocial acts depends on the interaction between the individual (with an immediate level of [antisocial potential]) and the social environment (that provides criminal opportunities and victims)."[9] Like Moffitt and other interactionists, Farrington acknowledges social environmental influences on propensity, primarily through proximate factors like family poverty, unemployment, poor housing, family disruption, inadequate supervision, delinquent peers, high-crime neighborhoods, and negative life events such as school failure. Yet here too, antisocial potential functions as a stand-in for a stable, internal character that inclines one toward criminality.

"State dependence" theorists offer another variant, acknowledging so-cial influences on criminal propensity through feedback loops of cumula-tive adversity, particularly among those with prior criminal behavior. Here, propensity becomes a self-reinforcing state: Crime reduces inhibitors to delinquency—like "attachment to school, attachment to conventional others, perceived sanction risk, and moral beliefs that condemn criminal behavior."[10] Social control theories suggest that without these inhibitors, future antisocial behaviors recur, whereas strong social bonds can prevent individuals from acting on criminal inclinations. Consistent with classic social control theory, when stakes in conformity weaken in the absence of these inhibitors, individuals become "free to commit delinquent acts" more readily.[11] These theories give more attention to social context than others but still focus on individual behavior and proximate environment through the self-reinforcing quality of criminal acts.

Many life-course theories of crime thus present similar internal-external or interactionist theories of propensity. Internal factors include self-control, impulsiveness, future orientation, antisocial personality, morality, and honesty—often stemming from neuropsychological issues, cognitive deficits, or biological factors. External factors typically involve social institutions—parents, family, peers, neighborhoods, schools—and their conditions—poverty, poor housing, family disruption, delinquent peers, high-crime areas. When mutually reinforcing, these factors create cycles that strengthen crime-prone dispositions.

However, the broader social context—period effects, cohort influences, and especially macro-historical change at key developmental ages—rarely feature explicitly in classic criminological theories of propensity, despite environments being shaped by ongoing social changes. By focusing on individual proclivities toward criminality, mainstream life-course theories effectively reintroduce character through the back door. Though propensities may be more narrowly defined than character and employ statistical rather than moral language, both concepts share the same underlying assumption—that individual internal proclivities should be the primary unit of criminological analysis.

That said, academic criminology deserves credit for giving substantial (if insufficient) consideration to external factors. The individualist perspective and its assumption of stable, internal criminal proclivities is so central to the criminal justice system that adopting criminology's internal-external framework would represent a marked improvement in legal approaches.

CRIMINAL PROPENSITY IN POLICY AND PRACTICE

In contrast to its more precise, evidence-based conceptualization in social science, criminal propensity takes a different form in law and legal practice. Rather than linking propensity to empirically tested internal and external factors, legal definitions remain vague and malleable. This ambiguity

creates disparate applications of the law—those with greater legal resources can challenge harmful assumptions about their character, while
those with fewer resources are often overwhelmed by such assumptions.
Moreover, individuals with resources or perceived "upstanding" reputations
may avoid legal scrutiny altogether when their illegal behavior isn't interpreted as reflecting underlying criminal character. Legal practice would
better represent criminality by adopting less individualistic, less internally
focused conceptions of propensity and character, especially given how pervasive subjective character judgments are within the system.

While propensity in criminology typically refers to specific internal and
external characteristics involving an offender and their interaction with
their environment, in US criminal law, propensity refers broadly to either
an individual's internal character (ill-defined) or their prior bad acts (criminal history). The "propensity rule" in criminal law—Rule 404(b) of the
Federal Rules of Evidence—doesn't define propensity at all while deeming
propensity-related evidence generally inadmissible at trial (with exceptions).
Propensity evidence may include character evidence or information on prior
crimes, interpreted quite broadly.[12] Legal scholars have similarly defined
excludable propensity evidence vaguely as that which "is intended to establish an individual's general tendency to engage in certain conduct in
order to prove that he engaged in that conduct on a particular occasion."[13]

This vagueness might appear to favor defendants. After all, a fundamental principle of American criminal law holds that persons should be
punished for what they have done, not for what they are—which the propensity rule ostensibly supports.[14] If evidence suggesting proclivity, pattern,
or tendency constitutes propensity, one might expect all such evidence to
be excluded. But this conclusion would be wrong.

Such evidence is frequently admitted under various broad, ill-defined
exceptions. Defendants are not ultimately protected from assertions or implications that they possess stable, internal traits disposing them to criminal activity. Propensity-adjacent evidence may be admitted for an allegedly "proper" purpose under Federal Rule of Evidence 404(b)(2), including
establishing the defendant's "motive, opportunity, intent, preparation, plan,
knowledge, identity, absence of mistake, or lack of accident"—terms broad
enough to encompass almost any propensity-related evidence.[15] Federal
courts have affirmed trial courts' decisions to permit evidence of bad acts
in thousands of cases through these 404(b)(2) exceptions.[16] As Richard

Kuhns argues, any supposed difference between a mere propensity inference and a motive inference is illusory—they are essentially identical.[17] Other exceptions like knowledge and plan have similarly been criticized for functioning as disguised propensity inferences, as has credibility evidence, especially since "prior convictions and prior misconduct admitted as credibility evidence are notoriously misunderstood by jurors as criminal propensity."[18]

The result is a criminal process that effectively prosecutes defendants for who they are rather than what they've done—or at least treats propensity-like inferences as probative to guilt determinations, despite their prejudicial effect.[19] This undermines verdict accuracy, compromising the constitutional presumption of innocence, fundamental fairness, and due process. Beyond harming procedural justice, the variability in what constitutes admissible propensity evidence means individuals may lose their liberty based on inconsistently applied considerations. Inconsistent application of Rule 404(b)(2) exceptions leads to arbitrary and potentially discriminatory enforcement of the propensity rule—all stemming from vague, permissive legal definitions of criminal propensity.

In this justice system, defendants are effectively tried not even for who they are, but for who they are presumed to be. These presumptions persist because of our common understanding of criminal propensity as stable and internal—a view that doesn't align with the more nuanced, evidence-based definitions in life-course literature, even though these theories should, as I argue, give more attention to social and external factors.

We shouldn't underestimate the influence of ahistorical, internally-focused propensity constructs in explaining crime—both at the theoretical level (in academia) and at the practical level (in courts). But the courts would benefit from adopting scientifically grounded, clear definitions of propensity that recognize both its internal and external aspects, providing a means to limit conceptual abuse and reduce inequality and inconsistency in application.

CHARACTEROLOGICAL CRIMINOLOGY

Character is a pervasive concept in criminal law and theory as well, but it has some unique characteristics that give it more free and ultimately dangerous reign than propensity. Indeed, character also infuses the US criminal process, from the pretrial stage to the trial (if any), to sentencing and beyond. Further, character constructs—similar to those of propensity—are commonly misunderstood, variably defined and measured, and arguably unstable over time. These constructs may be, consequently, inaccurately and prejudicially levied against criminal defendants. In this way, even in our modern bureaucratic system of criminal justice, the moral concept of one's character suffuses myriad decision points—from the legislature's definitions of criminality, to whom to investigate and arrest under those statutes, to charging decisions, to pretrial bond determinations, to the fact-finding phases of a criminal trial, to sentencing, mitigation, and parole.

To buttress these claims, in this section I first define character in criminal justice spaces, echoing and extending the language around propensity I explored above. Second, I expose the pervasiveness of character judgments and assumptions in shaping decisions in the US criminal justice system by looking at the stages whereby an individual enters and exits the system, from arrest through parole. I conclude with implications for social-scientific theory and legal practice.

The Meaning and Prevalence of Criminal Character

Although precise definitions of character and character evidence vary across jurisdictions, character evidence typically addresses either an individual's propensity for certain behaviors, their credibility (trustworthiness), or both. In everyday language, character often refers to broad moral traits like honesty, violence, cruelty, and temperance.[20] Each trait represents "a self-contained packet of potential conduct" in which one is reasonably expected to engage—hence the connection to propensity.[21] John Rawls argued that a propensity to break the law is a "mark of bad character" even while he recognized external shaping factors such as family and social circumstances "for which we can claim no credit," or blame.[22]

Character in legal contexts generally indicates any behavioral propensity based on an individual's past behavior. The line between a behavioral tendency and morality or personality is easily blurred, as it often is in criminological theory, and legal definitions vary widely, giving the concept wide berth. Like propensity, the Federal Rules of Evidence do not define character at all, for example, and there is substantial variation in state-level definitions, too.[23] One legal scholar observes that the only attempted codification of character, in Model Code of Evidence Rule 304, defines it as "the aggregate of a person's traits, including those relating to care or skill and their opposites."[24] As this quite broad definition illustrates, legal constructs of character have been too general, confusing, and vague to be meaningfully applied with any consistency. Some legal scholars have even called the law's attempt to define character utter "nonsense."[25]

Despite definitional problems, character constructs appear at every stage of the criminal process—beginning with statutory definitions of crime and punishment. The late twentieth and early twenty-first century rise in mandatory minimums, three-strikes laws, and dangerous offender statutes reflect a renewed emphasis on criminal propensity constructs.[26] The US Sentencing Commission's 1991 Special Report to Congress stated: "Because a defendant's prior record is relevant to such important sentencing goals as general deterrence, just punishment, and the need to protect the public from *the defendant's propensity to commit crimes,* the guidelines evaluate criminal history" (emphasis added). They added that career offenders are always assigned the "highest criminal history category," a notion that was subsequently taken up by the states in enacting their own repeat offender laws.[27] Three-strikes laws operate either on propensity inference (offenders are likely to reoffend, justifying punishment) or character-based inference (repeat offenders morally deserve punishment).[28] Regardless of legislative intent, these statutes effectively regulate crime and punishment through inferences about the presumed recidivism of chronic offenders, treating character and propensity as stable, internal traits.

Each stage of criminal legal involvement, from initial police contact onward, utilizes propensity-adjacent character evidence. In encounters with juvenile suspects, police discretion is heavily influenced by perceived demeanor—a moral judgment linked to informal culpability prediction.[29] Law enforcement bases investigative decisions on criminal records and databases of former arrestees (convicted or not), assuming past actions predict future behavior due to stable, internal proclivities.[30] Prosecutors use character evidence in charging decisions, especially "where the *actus reus* [act of commission] is not in dispute and the only fact in issue is the *mens rea* [mental state] or identity" of the defendant, making them more likely to charge those with seemingly more culpable character traits.[31]

Judges similarly employ character concepts in bond determinations, with dozens of state laws expressly including defendant character evaluations (usually undefined) as considerations.[32] States that define character in bail statutes use either propensity language (such as having a "record of appearance . . . or [alternatively] of flight," as Ohio's Criminal Rule 46 phrases it) or credibility terminology, considering a defendant's "reputation for reliability."[33] Legislatures have acknowledged such terms' ambiguity and potential for bias, yet their use persists.[34]

Character may play its largest role in the fact-finding phase of the criminal trial—where a defendant's innocence or guilt is adjudicated—assuming there is a trial in the first place.[35] Evidence pertaining to the propensities and credibility of defendants, victims, and witnesses alike may be admitted.[36] Broadly, character evidence concerning "good qualities of the victim" is usable, and that of a witness can likewise be admitted under Federal Rules of Evidence, to determine their "general credibility . . . , rather than the believability of specific testimony"—a similarly broad rule.[37] For both victims and witnesses, past actions are assumed to stably inform present character.

Although character and propensity evidence is presumptively inadmissible at trial per Federal Rule of Evidence 404, character-like evidence regularly enters through Rule 404(b)(2) exceptions for motive, intent, knowledge, and similar purposes. It's also commonly admitted as evidence concerning the "habit[s] or routine practice[s]" of the defendant, which may, of course, go to character.[38] Character evidence can sometimes be admitted to inform recidivism predictions—the likelihood of committing the specific crime charged again, rather than a general propensity to criminality.[39] Jurors, however, likely perceive predictions of specific recidivism as indications of generally bad character.

Background evidence—including absence of prior arrests or convictions—is generally admissible, with trial courts having considerable discretion in distinguishing between background and character evidence.[40] Legal exceptions permitting evidence of a defendant's moral character are thus abundant.

Character also permeates sentencing and mitigation. Character judgments are common for both defendants (considering criminal histories to predict reoffending) and victims. The Supreme Court's notorious 1991 decision in *Payne v. Tennessee* (501 US 808) reversed the *Booth* precedent by allowing victim-impact evidence in capital sentencing hearings—despite potentially shifting focus from the defendant's guilt to "the relative worth of the victim's character—about which the defendant was unaware and that [was] irrelevant" to committing the crime.[41] Criticized for potentially resulting in arbitrary and capricious decisions in capital cases, *Payne* represents another shift toward moral character judgments in determining severe punishments—privileging victim character judgments over defendant guilt considerations.[42]

Implications in Law and Practice

Given its pervasiveness within the US criminal-legal system—albeit sometimes subtle and unintended—character's use has been widely critiqued for resulting in trial by character rather than by criminal acts.[43] Critics of character's expanding role in criminal justice argue that jurors misapply the character construct, leading to arbitrary and capricious punishment decisions, and that character is misunderstood as stable and internal, when in reality it can be unpredictable and situationally—or externally—driven.[44] Heavy reliance on character constructs may therefore undermine verdict accuracy and the right to a fair trial by increasing the likelihood of convicting innocent defendants.[45]

Social psychologists have found that character traits seemingly irrelevant to criminality—such as being perceived as lazy—lead people to judge individuals as more blameworthy for criminal activity, even when the trait has no relationship to the crime or motivation.[46] Both mock jury and real trial studies show increases in perceived guilt and guilty verdict likelihood when jurors learn of a defendant's previous similar conviction.[47] These studies demonstrate that jurors make propensity inferences even when explicitly instructed by judges not to use prior convictions as evidence of guilt for the current charge. Thus, character influences trial decisions even against explicit intentions (as in Federal Rule of Evidence 404).

Post-conviction, whether through plea or verdict, character constructs persist in the criminal-legal process, with guidelines loosening over time. The Federal Sentencing Guidelines represented a retributivist shift away from 1970s rehabilitative approaches toward "forced treatment of the criminally-diseased."[48] This pathological, character-based punishment model directs judges to consider—where relevant—a range of defendant characteristics including mental and emotional conditions, drug dependence, employment, family and community ties, criminal history, and dependence upon criminal activity for a livelihood, with options for additional penalties for multiple offenses even at different times. Those with two or more prior felony convictions receive "a substantial term of imprisonment."[49]

The influential Federal Sentencing Guidelines thus impose additional punishments on those with criminal records, presumably based on either (1) propensity reasoning that previous offenders are likelier to reoffend due to stable, internal criminal inclinations or (2) the retributivist notion that recidivists morally deserve greater punishment. Either way, the Federal Sentencing Guidelines embed character constructs in federal sentencing. States widely adopted similar sentencing grids, formalizing criminal history as a character judgment in sentencing policy. By allowing judicial discretion in considering factors like employment history, community ties, drug dependence, criminal history, and mental / emotional factors, existing guidelines effectively authorize character assessments during sentencing. Ironically, the Federal Sentencing Guidelines were created primarily to mechanize and streamline justice—producing more consistent outcomes for similarly situated defendants. Instead, they've likely introduced arbitrariness into sentencing through the ample discretion they give judges to determine punishments using character-related factors.[50]

Parole guidelines similarly incorporate character information—primarily through the weight assigned to criminal history, again presuming stable, internal propensities drive past offenders to future crimes.[51] In assessing offense severity, judges are encouraged to consider the entire criminal scheme—not just the charged act but all related conduct, which may reflect on character. Clinical risk evaluations factor into determinations of parole eligibility, and the Parole Commission can exercise discretion to grant or deny parole for various character-related reasons.[52] Thus, individuals may exit the criminal justice system as they entered it: through morally laden, scientifically questionable character judgments based on viewing character as stable and internal.

The widespread use of character constructs—throughout statutory construction, charging, trials, sentencing, and parole—raises serious concerns about accuracy and justice, particularly since people generally judge strangers' character poorly.[53] Our evaluations tend to be misguided and often incorrect. As life-course criminological theories indicate through their consideration of both internal and external factors, character constructs may be unstable across time and situations. Social psychologists specifically warn against confidently predicting single instances of behavior—yet this is precisely what legislators, jurors, judges, and parole officers do when using generalized character assessments (supposed stable, internal bundles of propensities, credibility, and personality) to determine guilt or innocence for specific charges.[54]

Psychological research further suggests that character is fragmentary and can change over time, even without changes in external circumstances. From the internal-external interactionist perspective discussed earlier, specific criminal actions may result from situational factors that don't translate easily to future behavioral predictions. Walter Mischel's landmark social-psychological experiments demonstrated that "even seemingly trivial situational differences may reduce correlations [of trait and behavior] to zero," casting serious doubt on connections between character traits and corresponding behaviors.[55] While a prior conviction might indicate future offending, it might instead reflect situational or temporal factors that no longer exist.[56] Useful, accurate conceptions of character and propensity must acknowledge behavioral motivations and the internal-external influences on criminal propensity that many life-course criminologists, myself included, consider essential to predicting criminal behavior.

* * *

The disconnect between social-scientific theory and legal practice is both wide and pernicious—prejudicing individual defendants while undermining the equal justice that American "law and order" claims to uphold. Nicola Lacey argues that character- and risk-based responsibility attribution has become "at once a symptom and a driver of expanded criminalization."[57] When criminality is understood as a property of bad-character individuals prone to future harm, it's unsurprising that risk-based criminalization mechanisms have both expanded and diversified over the last quarter-century. We see this in predictive policing, risk assessments for bail, recidivism evaluations in sentencing, and broader uses of propensity and character throughout the criminal justice system. These practices exemplify the character trap's self-reinforcing logic: Assumptions about stable, internal criminal propensities justify labeling and punishment, which preclude rehabilitation and further marginalize individuals.

Despite attempts at rationalization and increased bureaucratization, moral character continues to shape societal ideas, interests, and institutions.

Despite constitutional values of liberty and equal justice—and despite life-course theories emphasizing external forces—skewed perceptions of individual moral character permeate criminal law, policy, and practice. Fueled by criminal justice politicization and public preoccupation with insecurity, character- and propensity-based notions of criminality have become entrenched in our modern penal system. Even recent reductions in mass incarceration and increased reform efforts show little sign of displacing these notions. Now more than ever, we must place character and criminal propensity in broader context. Criminal justice must recognize both internal and external influences on criminal propensity, while life-course theorists must expand their vision beyond factors proximate to individuals to include social change and its dramatic temporal variations.

Chapter 9 examines prediction, and how these same faulty assumptions about propensity and character underlie quantitative models for predicting criminal activity and recidivism. Sophisticated statistical methods alone cannot solve the problem. For prediction, too, we must push definitions of character and propensity beyond their individual, internal focus toward better incorporating external factors—ultimately embracing social change itself.

CHAPTER 9

How a Changing Society Degrades Prediction

Politicians and criminal justice reformers across the political spectrum have embraced the idea that we can reliably separate high-risk from low-risk offenders. Prediction, a central goal in behavioral science, has a scientific aura that grants it increasing weight in these policy discussions. Even the US Congress endorsed the importance of prediction in the First Step Act, a 2018 law passed with bipartisan support mandating new, "objective" risk assessment and prediction tools.[1] The logic seems straightforward: We should be tough on career criminals (or "chronic" criminals) while reforming or ignoring the rest. But for policies like this to prevent crime, we need accurate prediction of future risk.

Chapter 8 explored theoretical and legal aspects of risk assessment, examining how concepts of criminal propensity and character endow multiple stages of the criminal justice system with an unrelenting predictive logic—one that assumes criminality to be a stable, internal characteristic. By now, most social science has moved beyond this assumption, with a recognition that both internal and external factors should be incorporated. Yet scholarship, law, policy, and criminal justice reform efforts must all go further to recognize the broader external forces of social change.

This chapter tackles the quantitative dimension of the predictive logic rooted in assumptions of stable criminal propensity, using several statistical analyses to test how accurately older cohort arrest data predicts arrest for younger cohorts. Measuring prediction accuracy is an important part of advancing this book's central argument—that social change has the power to alter life-course development. If social change powerfully distinguishes arrest patterns between cohorts, there is an even stronger reason to challenge assumptions about stable individual risk prediction.

Consider the ubiquity of empirical risk prediction in today's "actuarial age."[2] Risk assessment instruments (RAIs), whether they use simple methods—as is typically the case—or sophisticated machine-learning algorithms, now guide high-stakes decisions across healthcare, child welfare, and criminal justice. The influence of these instruments runs deep and wide; they determine life-altering medical treatments, judicial decisions, and social service interventions. In the realm of criminal behavior and legal system involvement, risk assessments typically combine data on individual characteristics, family background, and especially prior criminal history, reflecting the instrument designer's assumptions about how these factors affect propensities toward criminality.[3]

Here lies a fundamental flaw. The fact that individuals age and develop at the same time society is changing carries unsettling implications for prediction instruments if point-in-time relationships between risk factors and measures of criminality are not stable. As seen throughout this book, individuals' future behaviors depend not just on stable traits, early circumstances, prior behaviors, and age, but also on the continuous social changes happening around them, affecting entire birth cohorts. Consider how a criminal record itself—widely used to indicate propensity—has history embedded within it. While practitioners recognize that algorithmic performance can degrade over time, real-world implementations of RAIs typically ignore the implications of ongoing social change.

In a 2023 paper in the *Proceedings of the National Academy of Sciences* (PNAS), Erika Montana, Daniel Nagin, Roland Neil, and I examined how social change complicates predictive risk assessments of future criminal justice involvement.[4] We argued that social change poses distinct challenges because RAI accuracy assumes stable relationships between predictors and outcomes over time. A changing society undermines this stability in complex, unpredictable ways for people who grew up in different times, like the PHDCN+ children. Practically, this means an instrument built using one cohort's data may generate predictions that are dramatically off base for another cohort.

More specifically, as this chapter will show, risk assessments based on older PHDCN+ cohorts overpredict criminality among younger cohorts—creating "false positive" errors that unfairly point to individuals as likely perpetrators of crimes they will not actually be inclined to commit. This isn't a minor error: The overprediction is both substantial and universal, appearing across all racial groups and risk categories, whether defined by prior criminal record or classic risk factors like low self-control. What my colleagues and I identified as the "cohort bias" in risk assessment thus presents a major, underappreciated threat to even the most rigorous predictive models.

To see how cohort bias undermines prediction, we need to examine, using multiple PHDCN+ birth cohorts, two key types of RAI methods to predict future arrests: calibration and rank-ordering performance. Arrest represents both the first formal entry point into criminal legal processing and a widely used measure of future criminal risk. Most risk assessment tools rely primarily on relatively simple indicators of prior arrest when making predictions in criminal justice settings.[5] Predictions like these exemplify high-stakes applications where false negatives may allow harmful crimes to occur, while false positives can trigger miscarriages of justice. Using both simple and more complex methods, I show that cohort bias can work in either direction.

THREE QUESTIONS AND A STRATEGY

Guided by criminal propensity theories, much research on crime risk assessment has focused on identifying early-life, individual-level, psychosocial, and neighborhood predictors of criminal involvement in adolescence and beyond. Standard predictors include personal circumstances relating to family instability and poverty, psychological characteristics like low self-control, and contextual features such as growing up in poor neighborhoods.[6]

While the association between many of these features and later criminal involvement is well established, researchers have inadequately investigated whether their predictive strength remains constant across historical periods. This oversight is problematic, especially given that societal-level crime rates and broader social conditions vary considerably, as evidenced by the sustained crime drop beginning in the early 1990s across the United States and other countries. More specifically, as highlighted in Chapter 4, significant differences exist in age-specific arrests between Chicago birth cohorts separated by as little as ten years. Chapter 7 also showed how exposure to violence and gun-carrying varied among birth cohorts depending on when individuals came of age.

These findings motivate the central question of this chapter: Does a risk assessment instrument trained to predict arrest using known risk factors from an older cohort accurately predict arrest likelihood for a younger cohort that matured during a different era? Assuming we can adjust for compositional differences across cohorts, as in Chapter 4, we can credibly assess how social change influences prediction performance. While researchers commonly train prediction models on one group and evaluate performance on another (for example, comparing models for males versus females), my primary focus here is on temporal heterogeneity in prediction rather than demographic features like sex or race. In other words, I investigate whether when we are born—not who we are—contaminates prediction models. Because this focus highlights social change, I define cohort bias as the systematic difference between the younger cohort's actual arrest patterns and their predicted arrest patterns based on a risk assessment instrument trained on older cohort data.

Three specific questions guide my analysis. First, is there evidence of cohort bias—and if so, of what magnitude? Not only does cohort bias exist, it is substantial. Regardless of model type and feature specification, RAIs trained on the older cohort overpredict the younger cohort's arrest probability by as much as 89 percent—a substantial miss. Second, is this cohort bias related to racial bias, a more commonly studied form of bias in machine learning research?[7] I show that cohort bias exists within all three groups studied—white and others, Latinos, and Black individuals—establishing that cohort bias is distinct from racial biases. Third, can cohort bias be mitigated by targeting high-risk groups? I test two definitions of high risk: accounting for prior adolescent arrest, or limiting predictions to those with low self-control. The answer is *no*—cohort bias persists even when analyzing only high-risk participants.

This chapter again groups the PDHCN+ data into older and younger cohort groups. The infant (or age zero) cohort is the youngest cohort, containing individuals born in the mid-1990s. The cohorts who were nine, twelve, and fifteen years old at the outset of the study are combined into the older cohort, containing individuals born between 1979 and 1988, creating a six- to seventeen-year age difference between individuals in the younger cohort and any individual in the older cohort. As in Chapter 4's arrest analysis, the combined dataset includes rich features related to participants' personal, early-life family, and neighborhood characteristics, as well as arrest data for all participants, in all cohorts, at the same ages. The primary outcome is whether an individual was arrested as a young adult, typically between ages seventeen and twenty-four. For analysis including prior arrest history as an indicator, the age range shifts to arrests between nineteen and twenty-four years old.

Available predictors—or *features* in machine-learning terminology—include socio-demographic information (sex, race / ethnicity, caretaker's immigrant generation), psychosocial characteristics (anxiety / depression, aggression, low self-control), family characteristics (family size, household income, parental education level), and neighborhood characteristics (poverty rates, college education rates, violent crime rates). The dataset thus includes both standard and extended crime predictors from childhood, family, and neighborhood factors.[8] Except for time-stable features like race and sex, all features were measured at approximately the same ages across cohorts. The features span from childhood to just before age seventeen, which marks the initial age of the outcome variable: arrest between the high-risk ages of seventeen and twenty-four.

To identify the impact of different sets of covariates on observed cohort bias, we created two prediction sets. The "classic" risk-factor feature set includes characteristics that prior literature has consistently identified as strongly correlated with crime and legal system involvement, many of which are commonly used in RAIs.[9] These classic features measure characteristics of the individuals themselves and their immediate family—sex, race, adolescent self-control, family poverty (as indicated by receipt of public assistance), caregiver marital status, and caregiver immigrant generation.

The second feature set, the "full set," goes further by measuring over thirty features, including the classic risk-set factors set plus additional early-life indicators of future criminal involvement, individual psychosocial characteristics, and childhood community-level factors like concentrated poverty, racial segregation, and violent crime. Although not all these measures appear alongside criminal histories in real-world RAIs, we wanted to provide the strongest possible test, erring on the side of including the "kitchen sink" of risk factors. After all, we must assume that future AI systems will incorporate more and more information into RAIs, especially from administrative datasets. Testing comprehensive risk-factor bundles is also justified because we're concerned with overall predictive power rather than individual predictor effects (which cannot be interpreted causally). Our aim is to assess how well bundled features predict arrest across changing social contexts. Even if certain factors aren't used in current practice, we want to know how effectively we can, theoretically, predict future outcomes in a changing world.

PREDICTION PERFORMANCE RESULTS

I begin with the first of the three research questions, determining both the existence of cohort bias and its magnitude. Regardless of the method used or features included in the RAI, cohort bias consistently appears when predicting arrest from ages seventeen to twenty-four and for other age ranges as well. To simplify the presentation, Figure 9.1 shows basic prediction models using the classic and hence most common risk factors. In our original PNAS article, we evaluated RAI performance on both younger and older cohorts in several ways. Here, the focus is on "calibration plots," which evaluate shifts in predictive accuracy for models "trained" on one dataset (older cohort) and evaluated on another (younger cohort). Other sophisticated RAIs used by machine-learning researchers, such as random forest models, yield similar results.[10]

Figure 9.1 addresses the first research question with plots comparing the RAI's predicted probability of arrest from ages seventeen to twenty-four with the actual proportion arrested at those ages. These straightforward plots directly compare the predicted likelihood of arrest between ages seventeen to twenty-four (x-axis) to the observed likelihood of arrest (y-axis). With a perfectly calibrated RAI, predicted and observed likelihoods would be identical—a predicted value of .5 on the x-axis would correspond to an actual value of .5 on the y-axis, .1 with .1, .75 with .75, and so on. We represent this perfect calibration standard with a black line having a slope of 1. The key comparison is the difference between where the two dashed lines fall in the figure's two panels, noting cohort differences.

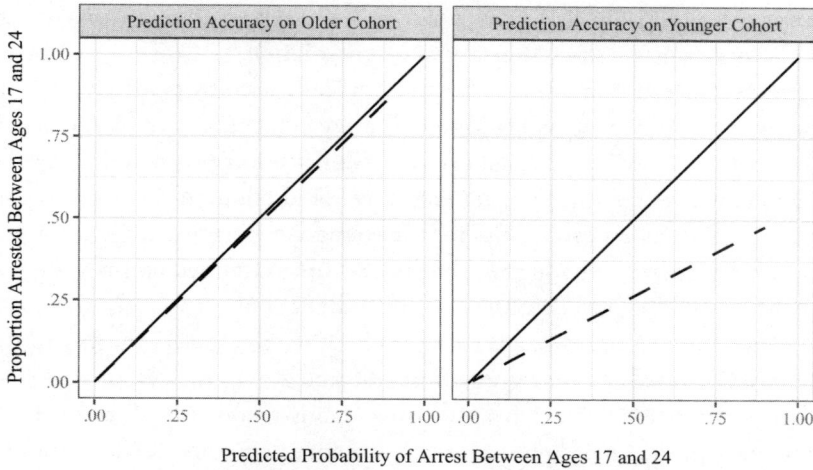

Figure 9.1. Varying Accuracy of Risk Prediction Models. Risk prediction models trained on older cohorts work well for older cohorts, but prediction accuracy lessens on younger cohorts. *Source:* Extracted and reformatted from Erika Montana, Daniel S. Nagin, Roland Neil, and Robert J. Sampson, "Cohort Bias in Predictive Risk Assessments of Future Criminal Justice System Involvement," *Proceedings of the National Academy of Sciences* 120, no. 23 (2023), figure 2.

This left-hand panel reveals that the RAI trained on the older cohort is well calibrated to that same cohort, producing a slope close to the baseline black line using the classic risk-factor set. Being well-calibrated means a model accurately correlates risk factors with arrest; for example, among individuals judged by the model to have a 50 percent arrest chance based on risk factors, approximately 50 percent were actually arrested. The older cohort result (left panel) confirms that our RAI effectively identifies who in our sample will and won't be arrested later in life, as indicated by the almost nonexistent gap between the solid and dashed lines.

When this same RAI is applied, however, to the younger cohort (right-hand panel), it systematically overpredicts arrest probability. This means that the RAI treats younger cohort members too harshly, predicting far more arrests than occurred. This result is visible in the regression line in the right panel falling well below the ideal 45-degree line (where the slope equals 1), indicating persistent overprediction of arrest likelihood for the younger cohort. More precisely, the slope estimate is 0.53, deviating from the well-calibrated slope of 1. This result implies that the older-cohort-trained RAI overpredicts arrest probability by nearly 90 percent for the classic model. Results using other techniques and with the extended list of predictors similarly show substantial overprediction.[11]

In short, RAIs that leverage features typically used by prediction tools, and even those that include additional, more comprehensive feature lists, show consistent evidence of cohort bias. While cohort bias could theoretically produce either underprediction or overprediction, in this application it overpredicts arrest probability for the younger cohort by a large amount. Conversely, these results suggest that an instrument trained on the younger cohort would underpredict arrest for the older cohort.

To test for further evidence of cohort bias, we conducted another form of statistical analysis that prediction research sometimes emphasizes— relative risk ranking—which allows direct comparison of RAIs trained on different cohorts. This approach works by first using one RAI to put all the members of one group in a list, ordering them from most to least likely to be arrested. Another RAI (in this case, one trained on another cohort) is then applied to that same group to produce a second ranked list, and the two lists are compared to assess agreement on order.

In conducting this analysis, we used the same main feature sets described above, classic risk-factor and full feature, to train RAIs on both the older cohort and younger cohort. We then tested how each RAI ordered the members of the younger cohort and compared the results. To cover varying ways to estimate risk, this analysis was conducted for four different estimation methods on both the classic risk-factor feature set and the full feature set. Across the resulting eight separate analyses, the average overlap of individuals' membership in the highest quartile of risk between the RAIs trained on the older cohorts and the RAIs trained on the younger cohort was only 53 percent, with a low of 44 percent to a high of 64 percent. While there is a clear positive association—meaning that the differently trained RAIs agree more than randomly—the variability around the 45-degree line is large. Across all quartiles in all eight analyses, the correlation in rank-order outcomes among differently trained RAIs ranged from 0.46 to 0.76.

Figure 9.2 shows results for just one of the eight analyses—the best-performing one based on the full feature set—representing the most agreement between RAIs and hence the most conservative test of their concordance. The figure compares two ranked lists, one from each RAI. The x-axis plots the younger cohort's risk rankings produced by an instrument trained on the older cohort. The y-axis plots risk rankings of the same

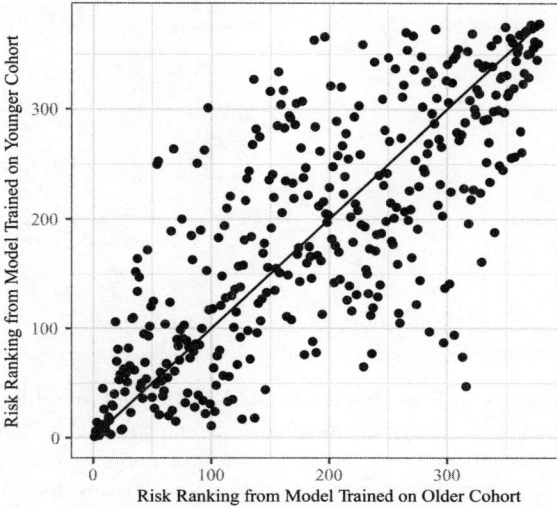

Figure 9.2 is a scatter plot with y-axis labeled "Risk Ranking from Model Trained on Younger Cohort" ranging from 0 to 300, and x-axis labeled "Risk Ranking from Model Trained on Older Cohort" ranging from 0 to 300.

Figure 9.2. Differences in Arrest Risk Rankings, by Prediction Model. Arrest risk rankings vary greatly based on whether risk prediction model was trained on younger or older cohort. *Source:* Reformatted from Montana, Nagan, Neil, and Sampson, "Cohort Bias in Predictive Risk Assessments of Future Criminal Justice System Involvement," figure 3.

younger cohort using an instrument trained on that same, younger cohort. Both the plot and the rank-order correlation value of 0.76 reveal that while the two rankings are correlated, there are substantial differences between the model produced by the older cohort and that produced by the younger cohort. The differences are stark—many cases clearly reside well above the regression line of prediction, and many below.[12]

Cohort Bias Is Distinct from Racial Bias

To test whether cohort bias is separate from racial bias, we applied the same analyses from Figure 9.1 to three non-overlapping racial / ethnic groups in the PHDCN+ data: whites and "others" (primarily Asians), Blacks, and Latinos. Again, we used an instrument trained on the older cohort, expecting the older cohort performance line to closely match the well-calibrated slope of 1. Figure 9.3 displays results for the classic risk factors that were also used in Figure 9.1. The ideal 45-degree prediction appears as a solid black line. The dotted line shows performance when the model

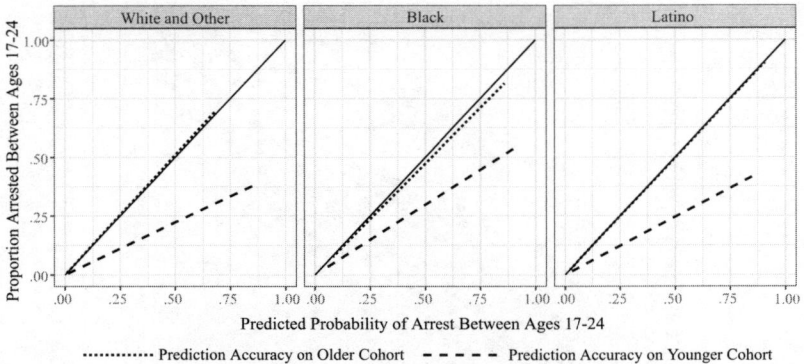

Figure 9.3. Accuracy of Risk Prediction Models Trained on Older Cohorts, by Race. Across races, when risk prediction models are trained on older cohorts, their accuracy weakens for younger cohorts. *Source:* Extracted and reformatted from Montana, Nagan, Neil, and Sampson, "Cohort Bias in Predictive Risk Assessments of Future Criminal Justice System Involvement," figure 4.

trained on the older cohort is applied to that same older cohort, while the dashed line shows performance when applied to the younger cohort.

Figure 9.3 demonstrates that the classic risk-factor RAI again substantially overpredicts arrest likelihood, but this time across all three racial groups. The same result holds for RAIs trained on the full feature set as well. While cohort bias magnitude varies somewhat by race, its persistence across groups thus indicates that observed cohort bias cannot be merely a manifestation of racial biases in data or algorithms. Instead, the data reveal cohort bias as a distinct form of algorithmic bias.

Assessing Cohort Bias within High-Risk Groups

One potential explanation for cohort bias is that it stems from differing cohort arrest patterns for low-risk groups. If arrest rates decreased for low-risk groups from older to younger cohorts without substantial decline among high-risk groups, then overprediction might happen only for low-risk individuals, creating the appearance of overall cohort bias. If true, cohort bias could be mitigated by training an instrument using high-risk group data or adding features identifying high-risk group membership. We therefore analyzed calibration shifts between cohorts using different high-risk group definitions.

In one test, we added a feature indicating prior arrest, allowing the model to adjust predictions for higher-risk participants using this common measure. In this specification, we examined multiple variations using different windows of arrest history (looking, for example, at arrests from ages seventeen to eighteen, arrests from seventeen to twenty-one, and arrests from ten to sixteen) and different windows of arrest prediction (predicting, for example, arrests at the ages of nineteen to twenty-four, arrests from twenty-two to twenty-four, and arrests from seventeen to twenty-four).[13] We also examined only individuals in the top quartile of arrest probability, based on a model trained on the older cohort. Cohort bias remained evident in these models, for individuals both with and without prior arrests.

Turning to another high-risk group of much interest, recall the central role assigned to self-control in criminological theory, developmental psychology, and commonsense definitions of grit. We incorporated this important construct by defining high-risk individuals as those scoring more than two standard deviations above the mean on tests of low self-control. Figure 9.4 shows prediction plots for high-risk groups defined in this way using the classic risk-factor model, with performance for older cohort

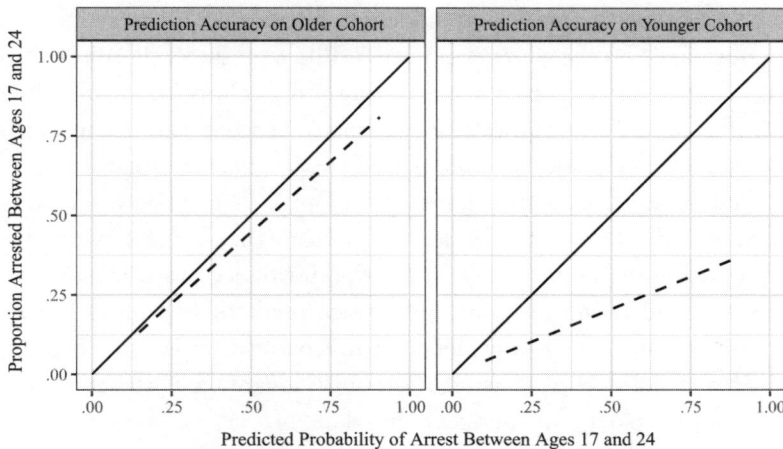

Figure 9.4. Accuracy of Risk Prediction Models among Low Self-Control Individuals. When risk prediction models are applied to individuals with low self-control, their accuracy worsens even more significantly for younger cohorts. *Source:* Extracted and reformatted from Montana, Nagan, Neil, and Sampson, "Cohort Bias in Predictive Risk Assessments of Future Criminal Justice System Involvement," figure 6.

individuals with low self-control on the left and younger cohort individuals with low self-control on the right.

Once again, cohort bias is clearly evident even in this extreme risk group, as shown by the wide gap between lines in the right-panel plots. Hence, regardless of how we define high-risk individuals—in this case by low self-control—models trained on the older cohort systematically and substantially overpredict future arrest likelihood for the younger cohort.

Assessing Predictive Stability of Risk Factors

Another potential explanation for cohort bias is that the prediction model's intercept changes over time, reflecting linear social change (such as a steady drop in crime), while parameters measuring the predictive impact of features remain stable. If true, cohort bias might be corrected by accounting for intercept movement reflecting changing arrest rates. Alternatively, feature parameters themselves might change across cohorts due to shifts in the underlying structure that links predictors with arrest, which would greatly complicate adapting an instrument trained on one cohort to perform accurately on another.

To identify the source of cohort bias, we examined classic risk features by again training the prediction model on the older cohort and evaluating its performance on the younger cohort. While we found a significant level shift reflected in the intercept, explaining some cohort bias as the direct result of an overall crime drop, we also found statistically significant changes in other coefficients. Notably, prediction coefficients for caregiver marital status, poverty, race, and immigrant generation all changed between models trained on different cohorts. These shifts indicate that features used in typical prediction methods change in their performance over time. In other words, the underlying relationship between predictors and arrest probability is not stable. We saw evidence of this pattern earlier, in Chapter 5, in the form of a declining association of disadvantage with arrest when comparing the older and younger cohorts.

A final possibility is that cohort bias is the result of shifting law enforcement practices, particularly in highly discretionary drug arrest patterns. While changes in drug enforcement practices (shown in Chapter 6) could contribute to cohort bias in RAIs, we repeated our analyses excluding drug arrests and found nearly identical results.[14] Cohort bias can thus be considered general and not specific to one type of criminal justice involvement.

WHAT ALL THIS MEANS

The running theme of this book is that societies, like the individuals who comprise them, change over time, and that social change should be taken into account by both social science and the criminal justice system. In this chapter, we have seen that social change poses an important and underappreciated challenge for predictive risk assessment instruments. The accuracy of their predictions depends on the assumption that relationships between outcomes and predictors remain stable over time.

Yet, when put to the test, our analyses showed that, in predicting arrest between the ages of seventeen and twenty-four (as well as other age ranges) for a representative population sample, this assumption is consistently violated for a variety of model types and feature sets. This result means that bias between cohorts separated by as little as ten years or fewer produces substantial overestimation of the probability of arrest for younger cohorts. We cannot simply trust an instrument trained on one cohort to work accurately on another.

Cohort bias also exists across all racial groups. This finding is important because it means cohort bias represents a potential source of inequality separate from racial or ethnic bias that requires its own considerations and remedies. When cohort bias generates crime risk overpredictions, individuals may be denied bail, sentenced more severely, or denied parole due to inflated risk assessments. Through these mechanisms, cohort bias can potentially trigger further criminalization, exacerbating existing racial inequalities.

While cohort bias might be attributable to unobserved individual- or neighborhood-level features, this explanation seems unlikely given both the magnitude of bias and the extensive set of predictors we used, including many well-established risk factors for arrest. Even if such unobserved characteristics were the root cause of the observed model degradation, knowing this would not solve the problem for real-world RAIs, which are constructed from much more limited feature sets that generally rely on observed administrative data.

The cohort differences in arrests in the PHDCN+ data reflect in part a widespread decline in Chicago arrests from the 1990s until recently, with major arrest types falling by at least two-thirds; similar declines occurred through the 1990s across most of America. Chicago is not unique, and nearly half our sample moved out of Chicago during the study. Many of these broad social trends have since flatlined or reversed, as shown in the gun violence analysis in Chapter 7. This shift in cohort fates underscores how the nature of cohort bias cannot be known in advance given social changes, which can be abrupt and contradictory. This result has implications for other policy fields such as addiction and teen pregnancy research, where similarly large cohort rate differences and fluctuations are well documented.[15] And it bears repeating that cohort bias can cut both ways, either overpredicting or underpredicting depending on the nature of social change and its interactions with the changing predictive power of risk factors over time.

In real criminal justice settings, RAIs typically predict relative risk tiers, showing where an individual's risk stands relative to peers; however, our results suggest that predictive error is substantial enough to cause outright misclassification at the relative risk tier level. But even a highly successful RAI could be dangerous in criminal justice settings. In the context of arrest, an algorithm that rank-ordered properly might successfully identify the highest risk individuals even if those people didn't actually pose a high risk. Put another way, even if a hypothetical cohort contained no one who would ever be arrested, variation in risk indicators within that cohort would still lead an instrument to label certain members as high-risk relative to others.

Errors in predicting absolute, rather than relative, risk levels can be equally hazardous and occur in other fields, such as health. For example, RAIs routinely used in high-stakes medical decisions, such as mortality scoring systems and organ failure assessments, predict mortality probability, not relative risk rankings.[16] This is because decisions like withdrawing life support are based on survival probability predictions, not on relative survival probability compared to other patients. While we found cohort bias in both relative and absolute rankings, these examples highlight why examining RAI performance in terms of absolute risk levels, not just relative ranking, is crucial.

Finally, the Chicago cohort findings have real-world implications for cost-benefit analyses of childhood interventions intended to prevent criminal offending and promote well-being. Cost-benefit experiments of childhood treatment interventions typically assign monetary values to outcome differences between treated and control groups observed years later. The Perry Pre-School Program, for example, concluded that efforts to improve cognitive functioning among children born in the 1960s yielded significantly lower rates of adult criminal involvement compared to nonparticipants, with crime reduction and other benefits exceeding program costs sevenfold.[17] The treatment and control groups aged, however, into sustained crime increases in the United States. Whether the estimated sevenfold benefit-to-cost ratio would hold for children born into later periods of declining crime rates, or different social worlds, remains uncertain.

To be clear, while these results are sobering, I'm not arguing that RAIs should be discarded wholesale as decision-making aids, or that early childhood interventions should be abandoned. After all, the alternative to RAIs is human decision-making (by judges, for example), which may also suffer from cohort bias. And since we can't predict the future, making investment decisions based on current conditions isn't unreasonable. As in the PNAS paper cited above, I argue for three complementary approaches to mitigate, if not remedy, cohort bias to ensure RAI tools are as effective and fair as possible.

The first is to construct measures of the changing social forces which influence the behavior of entire cohorts and include those measures as model features. This requires a new mindset that gets us outside the framework of individual risk. The identification and measurement of such macrolevel forces is not easy for the very reasons we have seen throughout the book, but we need investment in the science of studying societal and organizational changes, such as police effectiveness, both to improve RAI predictive performance and to advance knowledge about contextual influences on human behavior.

A second approach involves adapting the prediction instrument to account for changes in the structure of how predictors or potential features relate to outcomes. Although not straightforward or easy, such a method could, for example, involve reweighting or otherwise adjusting training data based on the age of each observation. The precise adaptation method would need to be tested and validated, but it's a path worth exploring.

Third, the most straightforward approach to mitigating cohort bias is to ensure that RAIs are updated frequently and reevaluated on a frequent basis. While further research is needed to determine the necessary update frequency, RAIs commonly go ten or even fifteen-plus years between updates. For example, the instrument used by the New York City Criminal Justice Agency to predict pretrial non-appearance risk was developed in 2003 and used without updating until 2020.[18] Sometimes the simplest solutions are the best and can seem obvious once acknowledged. Even here, however, the need to consistently update and reevaluate is no panacea. Frequent updating creates a trade-off with predictive accuracy as smaller training datasets result, and it threatens the stability and predictability necessary for legal fairness.

These practical changes are challenging but important because the stakes in prediction research are so high. Substantial social science research focuses on identifying predictive risk factors, and everyday policy relies heavily on prediction instruments. I've focused on criminal justice involvement, but crime correlates with many human outcomes, suggesting broad implications of cohort bias induced by social change. Our analysis also showed that relationships between identified risk factors and problem behaviors aren't stable over time. By implication, prediction models relying on these risk factors are unlikely to remain stable.

*   *   *

A case outside my research offers a telling parallel: Google Flu Trends severely overpredicted flu patterns when changes in Google's search algorithm altered the relationship between predictors and outcomes.[19] Crime is not the flu, but dynamic prediction faces similar challenges in both domains. As we've seen, risk assessment instruments for criminal justice involvement similarly fail when they ignore the dynamics of social change—which, unfortunately, happens all too often.

CHAPTER 10

Defining Character Up

To return to the observation by Heraclitus noted in the Introduction, no man steps in the same river twice—it's not the same river, and he's not the same man. Similarly, no birth cohort experiences the same society twice, nor do different cohorts face the same historical moment. Times change, and people change with them. While this entanglement of social change and individual lives seems obvious in retrospect, why has societal change been treated largely as background rather than a central force in how we think about criminal propensity and character?

As we have seen, commonsense notions of criminal propensity and character remain both misleading and deeply entrenched in society. While we readily acknowledge that the world changes, we paradoxically judge individuals as if they exist outside of time. Criminal justice policies, public discourse, and even many life-course theories continue to treat criminal propensity and character as internal and stable, or as an individual trait. Policymakers, scholars, and the public thus simultaneously recognize and ignore social change.

This contradiction is puzzling. Historians have long emphasized social change, and debates over mass incarceration have sparked rich analyses of criminalization's long-term dynamics. Political scientists and sociologists have also illuminated shifting patterns in punishment, examining how power, culture, institutions, and socioeconomic conditions shape crime and its control. These structural accounts locate criminality's causes in social environments rather than individual character. Meanwhile, studies of trends in incarceration and the "great American crime decline" have renewed public interest in societal change, while life-course research theoretically recognizes how larger forces shape individual experiences.

Nonetheless, the pull of individual propensity and character is strong in American culture, and as Heraclitus's aphorism reminds us, pulling apart individual change from social change is a hard problem. Perhaps this combination explains why the late twentieth and early twenty-first centuries have seen, in Nicola Lacey's words, "a resurgence of character- and (re)emergence of risk-based responsibility-attribution" in criminal justice organizations, and, I would argue, in many other institutional settings and in everyday thinking about the course of human lives.[1] I showed in Chapter 8, for example, that defendants still face serious consequences from assumptions about their supposedly innate, stable criminal character— even though some legal scholars dismiss the concept as "nonsense." Character assumptions are smuggled in at every stage of the criminal legal system—criminal statutes, citizen encounters with the police, pretrial practices, trials, sentencing, and parole—and they pervade many other walks of life as well, from making hiring decisions to buying insurance, getting financial credit, and even risk assessments of potential marriage partners.

Academic research shows similar limitations. Despite massive social changes over the past half-century, studies of crime and the life course remain heavily individualized. Single-cohort studies dominate, thwarting our ability to distinguish personal from societal change. Meanwhile, research on broader societal trends typically ignores variations within cohorts and life-course trajectories. While valuable, such macro-level analyses miss how individuals change along with society, and the complex dynamics of crime, punishment, and inequality challenge narratives of unidirectional change, such as the rise of the carceral state or a culture of control.

FROM WHO WE ARE TO WHEN WE ARE

The birth lottery of history motivates a distinctive way of asking about human development and the course of life. What if individuals who are born into the same socioeconomic and family conditions and experience similar childhood environments nonetheless face significantly different social worlds when coming of age or entering early adulthood? Andre and Darnell, introduced at the outset of the book, exemplify this situation. A common approach to understanding their different outcomes would be to intensify the search for the individual, family, and neighborhood features that set these boys apart—which is also the objective of resilience research. I accounted for such features but rejected this analytic approach, which is the reason these pages are not filled with uplifting narratives of how Darnell strove to escape a life of crime, or downbeat narratives of Andre's tribulations, or accounts that would be even more popular of how Andre confronted and worked to overcome the burden of his criminal record.

Instead, I drew on a venerable tradition in social science to study the lives of children from Chicago who grew up at different times over a three-decade period from the mid-1990s to the early 2020s. Across multiple chapters, we saw inequalities in the course of development that distinguished the life experiences of children born just ten years apart, and in some cases much less than that, overriding many of the individual, peer, family, and neighborhood risk factors highlighted in past research. This approach and its results provide new insights on how a birth cohort's unique location in the stream of history gives rise to a distinctive experience that shapes its members' life trajectories—which we can think of as shared life-histories. Cohort, in this view, is the key structural category and is distinct from generation, as demographer Norman Ryder emphasized a half-century ago in his influential essay on how social change both shapes and is shaped by cohort-specific experiences while growing up.[2]

Stated in its most general and strongest form, my thesis is that two groups of individuals whose only early-life difference is the year in which they are born will have immensely varied experiences over the courses of their lives, not because of who they are, but because of when they are. This thesis does not reject the idea that individual qualities matter or that individuals have agency, but being explicit about extracting the consequences of social change—a form of what Andew Abbott has called the "historicality of individuals," and of what we may think of as temporal individualism—is generative and has motivated this book's analytic perspective.[3]

The work of this final chapter is to synthesize the previous chapters' insights to reconceive who we are by charting a theory of when we are.

Building on this temporal understanding, I explore its implications for designing our future across research, policy, and conceptual development. Central to this discussion is a reimagining of a person's character as fundamentally social rather than individual. The text concludes with a coda arguing that any meaningful elevation of character must occur at the collective level. In essence, given these insights, this chapter confronts the crucial question: What do we do now?

Cohort Inequality

After accounting for a wide-ranging set of background measures in childhood, my results revealed the power of social change in shaping major turning points in life such as arrest, victimization by gun violence, and lead poisoning, which in turn shape long-term adolescent and adult development, and by implication, the future of society. The consequences of cohort inequalities in life experiences are extensive and enduring.

Take the mark of arrest. At the front end of the criminal legal system, arrest is the gateway to later experiences such as conviction and incarceration. As highlighted by the Chicago data, arrest triggers further involvement with the police in the form of future arrest, setting up a kind of vicious cycle of legal entanglement.[4] Much research, including from the PHDCN+ line of work, shows that arrest begets future trouble in many other life domains as well. For example, as we saw in Chapter 4, juvenile arrest curtails educational attainment, not just in high school but also the critical stage of graduating from college as an adult—for all racial and economic groups. Presumed individual characteristics such as self-control (or grit), IQ, sensation seeking, emotionality, and behavioral measures of violence, drinking, and drug use did not explain away this relationship. This result implicates institutionally-based disruptions in students' educational trajectories, rather than social-psychological factors or character. If higher education is the great demarcator of who gets ahead in life, arrest might be thought of as a stratifying factor along that pathway, a "great leveler" in sparing no group in exerting its educational penalty.

Another implication of this work is that individual-trait explanations of membership in arrest- or offender-groups are incomplete, if not substantially misleading. The famous "chronic offender" types from criminal career studies, and their successor, the "super-predators," turn out to have been contingent on their historical moments, if they ever truly existed, not ahistorical categories of people we should expect to find in all places and times. Whether they are called persistent or chronic offenders is less important than the power of their shared social environment coming of age, which shapes their group size and arrest patterns. Even if something like chronic offenders exist, and surely they do in the sense that some people are more criminally involved than others, predicting who belongs to this group by looking at past arrest records of individuals fails to explain a sizeable portion of their variation in later offending. And in fact, influential predictions from the 1980s and 1990s of a coming wave of super-predators were spectacularly wrong.

Strong as it is, the birth lottery of history goes well beyond the criminal legal system to influence a wide range of human development. In Chapters 6 and 7 we saw that poisoned development in the form of exposure to gun violence in childhood and adolescence, as well as exposure to environmental toxins, is similarly differentiated by birth cohort. In turn, early exposure to violence and toxic inequalities are linked to long-term consequences over the life course, including later gun use, problems with mental and physical health, delinquency, violent offending, incarceration, reduced economic mobility, and death.[5]

In many respects, then, *when* we are matters more than *who* we are for critical experiences and outcomes in life. The reason is that, as Stephen Raudenbush put it, "Shift Happens."[6] In the case of this book, large shifts occurred across three broad domains—punishment, community violence, and environmental inequality. As explored in Chapter 6, many sub-mechanisms within these three domains played a role, including the collapse of broken-windows policing and the drug war, changing norms of arrestable and punishable behavior, the rise of community-based organizations for youth, the improvement of public spaces, increased youth supervision and informal social controls, technological advances in security, widespread urban revitalization—including from immigration—and reduced lead in the environment. Although some mechanisms may have mattered more than others, historical change is not mono-causal. What matters most is how cumulatively, these social changes sharply differentiated the life chances of the lives of successive cohorts of children coming of age in the last quarter-century.

My argument doesn't reject the relevance of individual background characteristics or the idea that individuals are ultimately responsible for their actions in the eyes of the law. Instead, it emphasizes that social change and its mediating influences deserve independent theoretical consideration and require a different causal framework in public discourse, law, and social science. Life-course trajectories must be analyzed in conjunction with historical change, elevating our understanding of criminal propensity and character beyond purely individual factors.

Chapter 5 demonstrated how even self-control—typically viewed as highly individual—operates differently than commonly assumed. While self-control predicts arrest across all cohorts, confirming prior research, children with low self-control in one cohort faced the same arrest probability as high self-control children from an earlier cohort. This finding prompts a reconsideration of how individual characteristics function across changing historical contexts.

Changing Class and Racial Inequality

The interaction between social inequality and historical timing is another frontier for future research. Chapter 5 revealed how socioeconomic disadvantage—traditionally central to sociological and popular theories of crime and well-being—has lost predictive power for arrests over time. Among recent cohorts, poverty doesn't predict arrest rates as strongly as it did for older cohorts, while single parenthood has become more significant. Racial disparities in arrest have also shifted unexpectedly: Latino and Black individuals, particularly from disadvantaged backgrounds, show notably lower arrest rates in recent cohorts. Yet the underlying sources of racial disparities in arrest—early-life characteristics like parental education and neighborhood deprivation—remain influential across cohorts. These patterns show how cohort differentiation in socio-historical change is crucial for understanding both racial and class inequality dynamics.

The troubled history of race and criminal justice in America demonstrates the dangers of assumptions about stable criminal character. Historian Khalil Muhammad argues that racial calculations have long shaped views of criminal propensity and beliefs about who deserves official crime control. His study of early twentieth-century crime statistics and urban life shows how Blackness became "the singular mark of a criminal."[7] While other poor, discriminated-against white ethnic groups like Irish and Italians produced higher crime rates, assumptions about criminal character never stuck to them as they did to Black individuals—leading to lasting racial inequalities manifested in economic disadvantage and mass incarceration.

If there is good news to be had, it is that racial inequalities are not immutable over time. As we have seen, not only did arrests plummet, but Black male incarceration dropped markedly starting around 2010 and African Americans benefited the most from the 1990s crime decline, showing major life expectancy gains through about 2015. Combined, these results contradict causal misattributions of criminality to Blackness.[8]

Other social changes threaten these gains. As Chapter 7 showed, sharp increases in gun violence in 2016 and 2021 altered the youngest PHDCN+ cohort's trajectory, with Black youth facing the highest shooting risk. This disproportionate exposure to gun violence among African Americans has eroded life expectancy gains achieved during the crime decline's "uneasy peace."[9] Simultaneously, school and mass shootings increased, while COVID-19 disrupted an entire cohort's education, with lasting effects. Today's reading and math scores remain below pre-pandemic levels, with poor and racially segregated communities showing particular stress. This changing pattern of race and class-linked changes—part of what we might think of as the "stable disequilibrium" of society—is a defining feature of our times.

Intergenerational Transmission

Though not explicitly analyzed in this book, cohort variation among PHDCN+ children reveals important intergenerational implications. Parental involvement with the criminal justice system has been linked to children's delinquency, later arrest, and a wide range of behavioral troubles in my and others' data—what is known as intergenerational transmission.[10] This transmission likely extends beyond family criminal histories to include societal norms regarding law and criminality. Because parents aged through distinct social changes of their own compared to their children, the PHDCN+ children during the prison boom experienced what we might call the parental birth lottery of history.

Consider two children of the same age and risk characteristics whose parents (and extended family) differ in age. Our data, for example, include parents spanning up to thirty years in age difference within each birth cohort. These parental cohorts faced very different life experiences—like

mass incarceration's onset and the crack epidemic—affecting family structure, legal attitudes, trauma exposure, and the risk of intergenerational
criminal labeling. Coming of age in the 1950s also carried vastly different
implications for criminal records than it did in the 1970s, even before mass
incarceration. The parental birth lottery and its intergenerational transmission mechanisms represent an overlooked pathway for propagating social
change.[11]

This framework challenges conventional wisdom about inequality dynamics in other ways as well. While intergenerational research on crime
and socioeconomic mobility typically emphasizes cumulative disadvantages
and rising inherited inequality, this book's evidence suggests a more complex and perhaps hopeful view. The short-term but fundamental changes
documented here appear to counteract increasing disadvantage, at least
regarding crime and punishment. The younger cohorts' lower arrest risk,
despite having parents who came of age at a later stage of mass incarceration than those of the older cohorts, illustrates this pattern. Additionally,
research shows declining wage inequality from 2015 to 2022 among young
workers—drawn from these same birth cohorts in other data—with significant gains at the earnings distribution's bottom.[12]

Indeed, although the youngest Chicago cohort faced increased gun violence in the late 2010s and pandemic era, their reduced criminal justice
contact along with evidence of improved wage equity and economic
mobility for younger cohorts, especially Black Americans, deserve recognition.[13] These findings suggest that public policy and improved social
environments can overcome parental disadvantage, requiring revisions to
current theories of intergenerational transmission and challenging a dominant thread of pessimism or determinism in discussions of contemporary
social change, particularly regarding mass incarceration.

Social Movements and Changing Legal Cynicism

Social change not only creates cohort differences, but these differences
themselves drive future social change. This book implies that such change
occurs not just through shifting age distributions or period effects at all
ages, but also because historical contexts powerfully shape adolescence and
young adulthood. In the language of this book, when it comes to social
movements and significant cultural events, we might think of the "age
eighteen to twenty-five lottery of history." These are critical ages when so-

cietal events leave lasting imprints on memories and perceptions of life, with implications for how cohorts later transform society.[14]

This insight and the social changes analyzed in this book may help explain broad shifts in political and cultural landscapes, such as the Black Lives Matter movement and cynicism toward the law. The founders of Black Lives Matter, born in the early 1980s just like the PHDCN+'s older cohorts, grew up during endemic policing and surging violence that disproportionately harmed Black communities—experiences that may have shaped their later collective activation in response to events like Ferguson. These observations, viewed through this book's life-course historical framework, suggest promising avenues for future research: how different cohorts promote democratic ideals, how cohort replacement influences civic participation and views on criminal justice reform, and how cohorts differently organize against crime.[15]

This theoretical framework also illuminates how disorienting social changes have opened political and normative divisions about law in previously unimagined ways. Who predicted, even a decade ago, the January 6th Capitol riots, widespread beliefs about imminent civil war, mass pardons for those who attacked police and legislators, or a president declaring "He who saves his Country does not violate any Law"?[16] A deep cynicism about the rule of law and governmental institutions has grown. Could it also be, paradoxically, that the cohort least likely to be arrested and witness violence is now the most alienated from law and mainstream institutions?

Our data support this possibility through patterns of changing trust in police and neighbors. The youngest mid-1990s birth cohort experienced the Ferguson protests and George Floyd's murder, the related policing crisis, revelations about Chicago police torture, and pandemic disruptions during the critical ages of eighteen to twenty-five.[17] Figure 10.1 reveals a trust divide between this younger cohort and the older (1987) birth cohort at the same life stage, obtained by matching cohorts in their mid-twenties using the wave 4 and wave 5 PHDCN+ surveys. Adjusting for individual, family, and neighborhood factors, including parental criminal history and personal arrest history before age twenty-five, the differences are striking.[18] In 2021, only 42 percent of the mid-1990s cohort reported trust in police and 40 percent in neighbors at age twenty-five—down substantially from 2012, when 72 percent of the 1987 cohort at almost the exact same age expressed trust in police and 71 percent in neighbors. This pattern extends beyond Robert Putnam's thesis in *Bowling Alone* about declining generalized

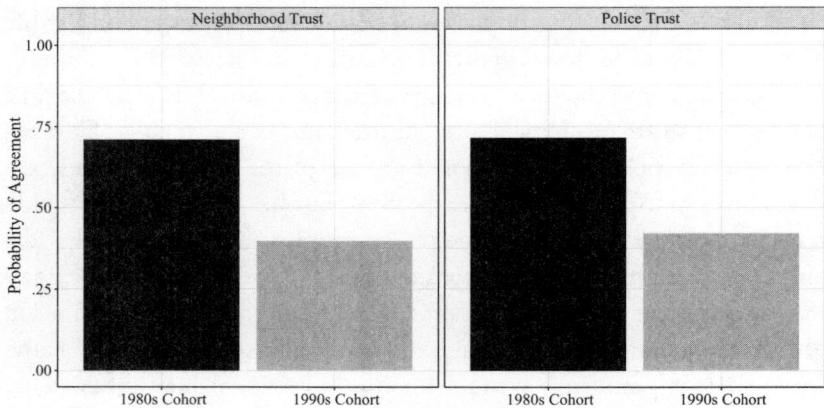

Figure 10.1. Trust in Police and Neighbors at Age Twenty-Five. Despite having much higher arrest rates, the cohort born in 1987 has greater levels of trust in police and neighbors at age twenty-five than counterparts in the cohort born just nine years later, adjusting for multiple background factors and early-life conditions.

trust—it suggests an age-period interaction specific to local contexts and police.[19]

This stark shift over a short period reveals a surprising fact: Despite experiencing much lower arrest rates, less toxic childhood environments, and even maintaining more personal ties as adults than older cohorts, the younger cohort shows significantly greater distrust in neighbors and the police. Their exposure to the social upheavals of the policing crisis and the COVID-19 pandemic during critical developmental years (recall also Figures 1.3 and 7.4) appears to have counteracted their lower likelihood of arrest by the police to produce heightened cynicism. As harbingers of future change, these cohort differences point toward continued social turbulence.

DESIGNING RESEARCH FOR CHANGING TIMES

The theoretical perspective and empirical approach of this book suggests a new criminological imagination which—to borrow from C. Wright Mills—enables us to better grasp the relationship between history and biography within society.[20] Rather than examining only what was wrong (or virtuous) with individuals in a particular cohort, we must consider what was wrong (or virtuous) with the larger social environment during the historical period when they came of age. This pivot requires a shift in theoretical vision, one that offers a number of ideas for designing future studies, policy, and ultimately how we conceptualize character.

At a minimum, the study of crime and its control needs an infusion of new research on cohort differences in life-course trajectories. Pragmatically, existing datasets offer untapped potential for testing competing explanations for cohort inequalities not only in delinquency, violence, exposure to toxins, and criminal justice contact, but also in domains like social support, adult well-being, and mortality. Many studies focused on developmental patterns within cohorts inadvertently conflate aging and historical change—not from data limitations, but because investigators' theoretical preferences for individual explanations lead them to overlook it.[21] Multi-cohort studies of crime in Philadelphia, Pittsburgh, Racine (Wisconsin), and Denver could be reanalyzed to test for the cohort differences and competing hypotheses proposed here.[22] Combined with multi-cohort designs like the Project on Human Development in Chicago Neighborhoods and recent European studies, we may have the footings of a new social scientific movement dedicated to foregrounding social change in the life-course perspective.[23]

The rich measurement of individual, family, and neighborhood characteristics in longitudinal studies conducted at different times suggests further potential for advancing research on social change and human development, even where multi-cohort designs are rare. Consider the opportunities for pseudo cohort-sequential designs—aligning indicators across different studies that followed same-age individuals through different historical periods and international settings. The Cambridge Study in Delinquent Development, for example, though typically viewed as a single-cohort study of London boys, shares many measures with other single-cohort studies worldwide from different eras: delinquency, education, health, employment, and intergenerational transmission. An imaginative analytic approach to harmonizing measurements across same-age groups could open new lines of inquiry in the social and perhaps even biological sciences, enhancing our understanding of human development in changing times.[24] While there remains a great deal of work to do, I have already begun pursuing this strategy with an international team of investigators whose common interests in life-course trajectories of crime and justice are set within the context of social change.[25]

This book's findings are also actionable in research that has direct policy import. We've seen real limits to predicting individual crime trajectories or rehabilitation prospects under conditions of largescale social change. This result challenges a growing movement in criminal justice that seeks to distinguish high-risk from low-risk offenders based on prior criminal histories, even as we've abandoned overtly problematic language like "super-predators." Indeed, as Chapters 8 and 9 revealed, today's influential policies and practices still rest on traditional assumptions about individual character and criminal propensity measured through legal involvement. The main difference lies in using larger datasets, predictive risk assessment instruments, and sophisticated tools like machine learning. The popular Public Safety Assessment, for example, relies primarily on arrest data, prior convictions, pending charges, failures to appear, and prior imprisonment. Yet algorithms trained on past data can make inaccurate predictions, particularly when failing to account for historical change. I showed that even the most advanced algorithm trained on 1980s cohorts overestimates risks for the 1995 cohort by at least 50 percent—an error of kind, not degree, that minor algorithmic refinements cannot fix. Social change fundamentally undermines prediction itself.

Cohort bias of this kind differs from typical risk assessment biases. While research on algorithmic bias in criminal justice has focused on racial, class, and gender discrimination—illustrated by controversies over racial bias—over- or underprediction extends to entire cohorts across all demographic groups. Beyond traditional bias categories, we must therefore prioritize identifying the type and magnitude of cohort-based inequalities in prediction. Given that birth cohorts are heterogeneous, there are likely substantial but unrecognized biases in how race and other social characteristics interact with cohort inequalities.

Changing crime prevalence across birth cohorts further means that cost-benefit calculations based on earlier cohorts may not apply to future ones in ways we assume. For example, the well-known Perry Pre-School Program was deemed a cost-effective initiative for improving cognitive functioning and significantly lowering criminal involvement in adulthood, but the participants were born around 1960 as American crime rates began sustained increases. The benefits of such programs for children born during declining crime rates or other rapidly shifting social conditions are unclear. More broadly, the promise of early childhood interventions may be overestimated given today's social and physical environments, so vastly altered since the 1960s and 1970s. Even randomized experiments prove vulnerable to the effects of social change.[26]

Perhaps more challenging are cognitive biases in how we conceptualize social change and prediction. How do people recognize and understand cohort bias? How do criminal justice professionals develop and update their mental models of how the world works? Likely not very effectively, though no worse than the general population. Cohort bias in our thinking transcends political ideology, manifesting on left and right, just in different ways. Humans struggle to update their beliefs to account for social change—it seems to confound human cognition.

These cognitive consequences extend beyond individual predictions or experiences to shape macro-level penal policies and theories of penalty. On the right, memories of past crime increases (with "chronic offenders" looming large) often drive policy, no matter what the present conditions may be. Crime policies initiated by the White House in 2025 might even be read as re-unleashing the super-predator logic and prison-filling mandate of prior decades, despite falling crime and incarceration.[27] And on the left, some influential theories of punishment don't seem to have incorporated actual declines in incarceration and racial disparities. Many still write of increases in the carceral state despite clear evidence of incarceration's substantial ongoing decline, especially among African Americans.

The findings and framework presented in these pages therefore highlight the need to broaden our theories of human development, punishment, and predictive crime control policies to account for social change's inexorable flow and its interaction with individual change. Pragmatically for future research, this means frequent updates to information systems, which remain outdated in many jurisdictions. Even sophisticated agencies like New York City's used pretrial risk assessment instruments unchanged for nearly two decades. Yet updating alone cannot solve the problem when major risk factors like poverty and family structure show changing relationships to future behavior across successive birth cohorts.

For these reasons, cohort bias presents a challenge requiring more than algorithmic adjustments or tweaks to current research practices—it demands radical rethinking. While this mandate may seem broad and general, it remains crucial given persistent cognitive biases in our mental models of a changing world and the prevalence of approaches that effectively ignore social change's power. Beyond pragmatic revisions to predictive tools, what might a different approach look like? I believe the essential step involves redefining (or rediscovering) our understanding of character and propensity in ways that allow us to move beyond individual prediction models in criminal justice altogether.[28] It is to this final and more abstract theoretical challenge that I now turn.

CULTIVATING SOCIAL CHARACTER

Common usage of character follows dictionary definitions of the mental and moral qualities or attributes that distinguish an individual, as does much criminal justice policy.[29] While social science theories have more carefully defined criminal propensity, definitions vary widely, and measures invariably use crime or criminal justice contact to reflect individual propensity, especially among the disadvantaged. Yet when operational measures like arrest result from substantial social changes in criminal justice practices and societal norms that differentiate cohorts—independent of individual or family differences—inferring stable individual-level propensity risks error.

If we are to maintain the concept of propensity and escape the character trap that has plagued much of our thinking, we must integrate conceptions of social change and what we might think of as the social foundations of character. My evidence shows how the violence epidemic, compounded legal entanglements, and toxic exposures profoundly disrupted the lives of children born in the 1980s as they came of age. Children growing up not much later, in the early twenty-first century, experienced much lower societal violence, fewer arrests, and improved environmental conditions for self-control and character development. Yet they still aged into a different regime of criminal justice controls (such as stop and frisk), along with increasing income inequality, the 2020 pandemic, and an associated period of increased violence that, in some cases like firearm deaths, reached historic levels. Cohort fates shifted dramatically, often suddenly and without warning.

Although traditional understandings pin character and criminal propensity to individuals, along with blame, this book's evidence challenges "defining character down" to this level.[30] Character can instead be seen as deeply rooted in changing social conditions. While criminological and sociological theories acknowledge individual-environment interactions to varying degrees, most empirical measures, policy treatments, and criminal

justice practices remain targeted on individuals or their immediate sur-
roundings. Social change operates on a much larger scale. The propensity
to criminality and criminal character should therefore be "defined up,"
reconceptualized to account for social change's power in shaping life
courses, societal reactions to character, and what I have elsewhere called
the "characterological imperative" of society.[31]

The evidence base is small, but it is revealing that levels of self-control
among American adolescents are significantly lower than those in Northern
European societies like Sweden, Norway, and Denmark.[32] Some might
point to the aggregated character deficits of individuals or lack of early
childhood self-control training in the United States as the explanation.
While these might contribute, this book points instead to factors like exposure to violence, concentrated disadvantage, toxic environments, aggressive policing, and other contextual features that arise and fluctuate largely
through public policies. In other words, the United States itself might be
said to have low self-control, not just its millions of individuals. By this
logic, we should be trying to reset the short-sightedness and impulsivity—
dare I say, character—of American policies.

Foremost, we should focus on eradicating the toxicities of poisoned development, reforming criminal justice policies on policing and incarceration, and enhancing socially supportive conditions across the life course.
Environmental policy offers a crucial starting point. Vigorous governmental
remediation of degraded physical environments—including industrial
waste sites, buildings containing lead paint, and abandoned lots lacking
green space—constitutes an underappreciated and cost-effective mechanism for improving population well-being, with far-reaching implications.[33]
Emerging evidence further suggests that citizen-based collective efficacy
and community organization can catalyze interventions to reduce toxic
exposures, especially in poor minority neighborhoods, potentially reducing
both criminal justice contact and its racial disparities.[34] Once we recognize environmental policy as effective crime control policy, or that eliminating environmental controls is essentially pro-crime policy, new avenues of
progress become possible without necessarily requiring wholesale changes
in society's economic or racial structure or changes in crime's purported
individual- or family-level root causes.[35]

Criminal justice legal reforms and community-based crime prevention
also show promise. Reductions in mandatory sentence lengths and
geographically-focused selective policing—generating fewer arrests than

blanket "broken windows" policing—can maintain community safety while reducing incarceration.[36] While we lack rigorous scientific evidence of their effectiveness, innovative citizen-based alternatives to violence prevention merit further investment. As Monica Bell notes, community alternatives to traditional policing have received far less funding and evaluation than criminal justice interventions.[37] And while cost-benefit estimates shift with social change, the science of supporting investment in childhood and adolescent development, especially among the disadvantaged, remains strong.[38] Combined, such approaches are forward-looking, feasible, and focus on aspects of reform external to individual-level prediction.

My primary aim, however, is not so much to advocate specific existing policies, though promising ones exist, but to encourage a shift in thinking—one that contrasts directly with the dominant approach, consistent over decades, of looking backwards to classify individuals who, by the birth lottery, unevenly experienced the enduring marks of violence, criminalization, environmental degradation, and other challenges to growing up in the last American quarter-century. Children have been differentially exposed to toxic environments that are socially produced rather than inevitable, with enduring consequences for their life-course development. It follows that nurturing human capacity depends heavily on the interaction between circumstances and historical timing—growing up in favorable conditions during favorable times—motivating a more expansive conception of character's sources.[39]

Importantly, this position doesn't mean we must deny individual agency or hold people blameless for crimes. In his recent work *Determined,* renowned scientist Robert Sapolsky argues that free will is an illusion, with every behavior resulting from an intricate web of biological, environmental, and social factors.[40] His metaphor of "turtles all the way down" illustrates how no decisions or actions are truly independent, but rather part of an endless chain of causation. While I share much of his structuralist perspective as a social scientist, and cohort is certainly a structural category, there is no world I can imagine that would or should let the fact of birth year alone erase culpability. Still, social change's consequences, like many life factors, can play a mitigating role in reforming criminal justice and determining fair, proportionate punishment.

This perspective on individual agency and social causation has pragmatic and potentially far-reaching implications for structural legal reform. One area involves creating more safety valves and "off-ramps," including resentencing reviews. Following this book's logic, judicial review policies could allow judges to revisit sentences of those who have served long periods due simply to their sentencing's timing. Consider the change in crack cocaine laws that arose from recognizing—belatedly—that significantly harsher penalties for crack versus powder cocaine offenses had disproportionately harmed African American communities. The 2010 Fair Sentencing Act reduced this disparity going forward, and the 2018 First Step Act made this change retroactive, allowing individuals sentenced under old crack cocaine laws to seek reduced sentences.

Should those sentenced under harsher laws during the war on drugs and violence epidemic, or those who grew up during intense exposure to environmental toxins, get their sentences reduced or vacated, without application? Not because of who they are, but because of when they were? This is a difficult and no doubt controversial question, but this book's logic demands we ask it. While the Supreme Court has generally resisted revisiting sentences under now-overturned laws, a more permissive view of retroactivity—allowing individuals to benefit from new rules unavailable when sentenced—could help reform sentencing to better reflect the macro social changes and conditions that affected entire birth cohorts.[41]

A mechanism bypassing courts is the pardon, which can be reconceived to account for cohort disadvantage. President Biden's end-of-term commutation of thousands of drug offenders and certain pandemic-era crimes, though not framed as such, could be seen as cohort reparations. These actions align with mitigating adversity for those who paid exaggerated dues merely through an unlucky draw in history's birth lottery. More generally, while a national conversation about racial reparations has addressed deep inequalities from slavery and its legacy, this book points to a different but compatible reparation mechanism deserving consideration.[42]

CODA: CONFRONTING STABLE DISEQUILIBRIUM

Early in the movie *Saturday Night Fever,* John Travolta's character Tony Manero is angling for a pay advance to dance on the weekend. His boss demurs, saying: "Save a little, build a future." Exasperated, Tony, who exuded low self-control, responds: "Fuck the future!" To which his boss responds: "No, Tony, you can't fuck the future. The future fucks you."

This book might not provide a magic-bullet policy implication, but it offers something perhaps more practical—a fundamental shift in perspective.

We can't control the Tonys of the world or predict the future, and as we've seen, the birth lottery of history weighs heavily on life chances in ways that weaken or sometimes negate individual characteristics while challenging theories focused on proximate contexts like family poverty or community disadvantage.

If we truly want to elevate character, we should do so first at the social level, prioritizing justice in the here and now while preparing for whatever the future brings. Judgments about individual character or deservedness should be secondary to achieving societal character—pursuing socially integrative policies that mitigate past damage, maximize present justice, and prepare for a more equitable future.

The radical implication suggests eliminating all prediction, all thinking about individual risk factors, and all attempts to cater to individual character. Motivations for crime and bad behavior will always exist, and as shown, attempts to predict them are rife with social change-induced error. Instead of focusing on the offender supply side, we should keep our eyes on the real prize—societal character that cultivates our shared fate.

Although the great theologian Reinhold Niebuhr would presumably be pessimistic about such an idea, perhaps he had the title backward in his classic book from nearly a century ago, *Moral Man and Immoral Society*.[43] He emphasized individuals' capacity for morality and self-control, compared to the power dynamics that hold society hostage to group interests. But societies vary tremendously in basic ethics and the ways in which they support their citizens through difficult times. While we can't control individual futures, we can set collective priorities.

In this sense, John Rawls's thought experiment of viewing justice from behind the veil of ignorance was on the right track all along. He invited us to imagine making choices about justice without knowing our personal circumstances—our race, gender, or social status.[44] I suggest we extend this thought experiment: Since none of us can know our future circumstances, even current advantages provide no guaranteed protection, making the design of a just society our shared imperative. We are all marked by time.

Building for the future is, ultimately, a moral choice. Constantly striving for a just society—struggles and all—offers our best protection against future uncertainty—even for Niebuhr. This is both our challenge and our promise. Tony and his boss might even agree.

NOTES

ACKNOWLEDGMENTS

INDEX

Notes

INTRODUCTION

1. Andre Lewis and Darnell Jackson are pseudonyms used here to preserve the anonymity of individual study subjects.

2. Only fragments remain of the writings of Heraclitus, so quotations like the river analogy, while widely accepted by scholars, are imperfect paraphrases. Classics scholar Daniel Graham notes that although Heraclitus was obscure in his statements, he was according to Plato, Aristotle, and many of his modern interpreters foremost a philosopher of change, seeing all things in flux. Hence the idea of the constancy of change, and the attributed statement that it is not possible to step twice into the same river. Daniel W. Graham and P. Curd, "Heraclitus: Flux, Order, and Knowledge," in *The Oxford Handbook of Presocratic Philosophy* (Oxford, UK: Oxford University Press, 2008), 170, 173.

3. Ralph Waldo Emerson, *Essays: Second Series* (Boston: James Munroe, 1844), 106. He also asserted that character "repudiates intellect," 114.

4. In psychology, for example, see Angela Duckworth, *Grit: The Power of Passion and Perseverance* (New York: Scribner, 2016); Angela Duckworth, "The Significance of Self-Control," *Proceedings of the National Academy of Sciences* 108 (2011): 2639–2640. For an influential review on self-control, see Roy Baumeister, Todd F. Heatherton, and Dianne M. Tice, *Losing Control: How and Why People Fail at Self-Regulation* (New York: Academic Press, 1994). In economics, the Nobel Laureate James Heckman has championed the cause of character building in childhood, focusing on preschool and family interventions that build "soft" or "noncognitive"

skills like self-control and the ability to inhibit criminal behavior, which he argues constitutes an important quality of character that shapes the development of human capital. James J. Heckman, John Eric Humphries, and Tim Kautz, eds., *The Myth of Achievement Tests: The GED and the Role of Character in American Life* (Chicago: University of Chicago Press, 2014). See also James J. Heckman, "Skill Formation and the Economics of Investing in Disadvantaged Children," *Science* 312 (2006): 1900–1902. There is evidence that the importance of soft skills is increasing over time. David J. Deming, "The Growing Importance of Social Skills in the Labor Market," *Quarterly Journal of Economics* 132 (2017): 1593–1640.

5. See Roger Crisp, ed., *Aristotle: Nicomachean Ethics* (Cambridge, UK: Cambridge University Press, 2014).

6. John Rawls, *A Theory of Justice: Revised Edition* (Cambridge, MA: Harvard University Press, 1999), 277.

7. A major work in this vein is Devah Pager, *Marked: Race, Crime, and Finding Work in an Era of Mass Incarceration* (Chicago: University of Chicago Press, 2009). For a systematic and definitive review of the literature on mass incarceration, see Jeremy Travis, Bruce Western, and Steve Redburn, eds., *The Growth of Incarceration in the United States: Exploring Causes and Consequences* (Washington, DC: National Academies Press, 2014).

8. Marvin E. Wolfgang, Robert M. Figlio, and Thorsten Sellin, *Delinquency in a Birth Cohort* (Chicago: University of Chicago Press, 1972).

9. James Q. Wilson, *Thinking about Crime* (New York: Basic Books, 1975), 209. For additional discussion of his thoughts on crime and character, see James Q. Wilson, *On Character* (Washington, DC: AEI Press, 1995), 5.

10. The super-predator concept is widely attributed to William J. Bennett, John J. Dilulio Jr., and John P. Walters, *Body Count: Moral Poverty—and How to Win America's War against Crime and Drugs* (New York: Simon and Schuster, 1996). For a discussion of the link between Wilson's notion of wicked people and the emergence of the super-predator concept, see Jens Ludwig, *Unforgiving Places: The Unexpected Origins of American Gun Violence* (Chicago: University of Chicago Press, 2025), chapter 3. For a discussion of super-predator policies that disproportionately harmed the African American community through incarceration, see Elizabeth Hinton, *From the War on Poverty to the War on Crime: The Making of Mass Incarceration in America* (Cambridge, MA: Harvard University Press, 2016). For the first apparent use of the term "ravenous wolves" and a review of subsequent literature on it, see William Spelman and John E. Eck, "Sitting Ducks, Ravenous Wolves, and Helping Hands: New Approaches to Urban Policing," *Public Affairs Comment* 35, no. 2 (1989); Natalie N. Martinez, YongJei Lee, John E. Eck, and SooHyun O, "Ravenous Wolves Revisited: A Systematic Review of Offending Concentration," *Crime Science* 6, no. 1 (2017).

11. Avshalom Caspi, Renate M. Houts, Daniel W. Belsky, Honalee Harrington, Sean Hogan, Sandhya Ramrakha, Richie Poulton, and Terrie E. Moffitt, "Child-

hood Forecasting of a Small Segment of the Population with Large Economic Burden," *Nature Human Behaviour* 1, no. 1 (2016); Terrie E. Moffitt, Louise Arseneault, Daniel Belsky, Nigel Dickson, Robert J. Hancox, HonaLee Harrington, Renate Houts, Richie Poulton, Brent W. Roberts, Stephen Ross, Malcolm R. Sears, W. Murray Thomson, and Avshalom Caspi, "A Gradient of Childhood Self-Control Predicts Health, Wealth, and Public Safety," *Proceedings of the National Academy of Sciences* 108 (2011): 2693–2698. On self-control and character in studies of crime, see Michael R. Gottfredson and Travis Hirschi, *A General Theory of Crime* (Stanford, CA: Stanford University Press, 1990); Per-Olof Wikström, Kyle Treiber, and Gabriela Roman, *Character, Circumstances, and Criminal Careers: Towards a Dynamic Developmental and Life-Course Criminology* (Oxford, UK: Oxford University Press, 2024).

12. Cesare Lombroso, ed., *Crime: Its Causes and Remedies,* trans. Henry P. Horton (Boston: Little, Brown, 1911). See also Mary Gibson and Nicole Hahn Rafter, eds., *Criminal Man: Cesare Lombroso* (Durham, NC: Duke University Press, 2006).

13. Adrian Raine, *The Anatomy of Violence: The Biological Roots of Crime* (New York: Random House, 2013).

14. David Eagleman, "The Brain on Trial," *The Atlantic,* July / August 2011; Lizzie Buchen, "Science in Court: Arrested Development," *Nature* 484 (2012): 304–306; Alexandra O. Cohen and B. J. Casey, "Rewiring Juvenile Justice: The Intersection of Developmental Neuroscience and Legal Policy," *Trends in Cognitive Sciences* 18, no. 2 (2014): 63–65.

15. Caspi et al., "Childhood Forecasting." Low intelligence, the preeminent cognitive skill, was identified by the authors as another of the predictors of being in this chronic group, similar to Wolfgang et al.'s Philadelphia study of chronic criminals. A recent study also finds that brain structure predicts the long-term course of criminal offending. Christina O. Carlisi, Terrie E. Moffitt, Annchen R. Knodt, Honalee Harrington, David Ireland, Tracy R. Melzer, Richie Poulton, Sandhya Ramrakha, Avshalom Caspi, Ahmad R. Hariri, and Essi Viding, "Associations between Life-Course-Persistent Antisocial Behaviour and Brain Structure in a Population-Representative Longitudinal Birth Cohort," *Lancet Psychiatry* 7, no. 3 (2020): 245–253.

16. Robert Plomin, *Blueprint: How DNA Makes Us Who We Are* (Cambridge, MA: MIT Press, 2018). Polygenic scoring of DNA has been linked to educational attainment, which Plomin argues is because genetic differences tap into traits needed to succeed, such as grit.

17. Cade Metz and Adam Satariano, "An Algorithm That Grants Freedom, or Takes It Away," *New York Times,* February 9, 2020.

18. Farah Stockman, "How 'End Mass Incarceration' Became a Slogan for D.A. Candidates," *New York Times,* October 25, 2018.

19. The federal reform bill defined a risk and needs assessment tool as an "objective and statistically validated method" to assess, among other things, "the risk that

a prisoner will recidivate upon release from prison." First Step Act of 2018, Public Law no. 115-391, 132 Stat. 5194, 38.

20. The corresponding figures for white male dropouts are only 11 and 4 percent. These data come from Becky Pettit and Bruce Western, "Mass Imprisonment and the Life Course: Race and Class Inequality in U.S. Incarceration," *American Sociological Review* 69 (2004): 151–169.

21. Patrick T. Sharkey, *Uneasy Peace: The Great Crime Decline, the Renewal of City Life, and the Next War on Violence* (New York: W. W. Norton, 2018); Patrick T. Sharkey and Michael Friedson, "The Impact of the Homicide Decline on Life Expectancy of African American Males," *Demography* 56 (2019): 645–663.

22. Jeffrey J. Arnett, "Getting Better All the Time: Trends in Risk Behavior among American Adolescents since 1990," *Archives of Scientific Psychology* 6 (2018): 87–95. Drawing on large, nationally representative surveys, researchers have also found that adolescents in birth cohorts since 2000 are less likely to engage in adult-like activities than older cohorts of adolescents who grew up in previous decades. Jean Twenge and Heejung Park, "The Decline in Adult Activities among U.S. Adolescents, 1976–2016," *Child Development* 90 (2019): 638–654.

23. Jason DeParle, "Expanded Safety Net Drives Sharp Drop in Child Poverty," *New York Times*, September 12, 2022, 1.

24. John Gramlich, "America's Incarceration Rate Falls to Lowest Level since 1995," Pew Research Center, August 16, 2021, https://www.pewresearch.org/short -reads/2021/08/16/americas-incarceration-rate-lowest-since-1995/; James Forman Jr., "The Juvenile Justice Revolution," *New York Times*, February 2, 2025, 20–25, 46–47.

25. Neil MacFarquhar, "Murders Spiked in 2020 in Cities across the United States," *New York Times*, September 27, 2021. For data from the US Centers for Disease Control and Prevention, see Scott R. Kegler, Thomas R. Simon, Marissa L. Zwald, May S. Chen, James A. Mercy, Christopher M. Jones, Melissa C. Mercado-Crespo, Janet M. Blair, Deborah M. Stone, Phyllis G. Ottley, and Jennifer Dills, "Vital Signs: Changes in Firearm Homicide and Suicide Rates—United States, 2019–2020," *Morbidity and Mortality Weekly Report* 71, no. 19 (2022): 656–663.

26. Federal Bureau of Investigation, "Active Shooter Incidents in the United States, 2021," US Department of Justice report prepared in collaboration with the Advanced Law Enforcement Rapid Response Training Center at Texas State University (Washington, DC: US Department of Justiec, 2022); Olga Khazan, "Why People Are Acting So Weird," *Atlantic Monthly*, March 30, 2022.

27. William Brangham and Sam Lane, "Chicago Sees Historic Drop in Violent Crime during First Half of 2025," *PBS News Hour*, July 3, 2025; Roseanna Ander, Thomas Ballard, Katie Hill, Javier Lopez, Kim Smith, and Greg Stoddard, "2024 End-of-Year Analysis: Chicago Crime Trends," University of Chicago Crime Lab,

December 2024, https://crimelab.uchicago.edu/resources/2024-end-of-year-analysis-chicago-crime-trends/.

28. Thomas Piketty, *Capital in the Twenty-First Century* (Cambridge, MA: Harvard University Press, 2014).

29. Raj Chetty, David Grusky, Maximilian Hell, Nathaniel Hendren, Robert Manduca, and Jimmy Narang, "The Fading American Dream: Trends in Absolute Income Mobility since 1940," *Science* 356, no. 6336 (2017): 398–406.

30. Raj Chetty, Nathaniel Hendren, Patrick Kline, and Emmanuel Saez, "Where Is the Land of Opportunity? The Geography of Intergenerational Mobility in the United States," *Quarterly Journal of Economics* 129, no. 4 (2014): 1553–1623.

31. Geoffrey T. Wodtke, Kerry Ard, Clair Bullock, Kailey White, and Betsy Priem, "Concentrated Poverty, Ambient Air Pollution, and Child Cognitive Development," *Science Advances* 8, no. 48 (2022): eadd0285.

32. Angelina R. Sutin, Yannick Stephan, Martina Luchetti, Damaris Aschwanden, Ji Hyun Lee, Amanda A. Sesker, and Antonio Terracciano, "Differential Personality Change Earlier and Later in the Coronavirus Pandemic in a Longitudinal Sample of Adults in the United States," *PLoS ONE* 17, no. 9 (2022): e0274542. More generally on the disruption of the pandemic, see Eric Klinenberg, *2020: One City, Seven People, and the Year Everything Changed* (New York: Knopf, 2024).

1. CHANGING LIVES, CHANGING TIMES

1. Karl Mannheim, "The Problem of Generations," in *Essays on the Sociology of Knowledge: Collected Works,* vol. 5, ed. Paul Kecskemeti (New York: Routledge, [1928] 1952), 276–322.

2. Norman Ryder, "The Cohort as a Concept in the Study of Social Change," *American Sociological Review* 30, no. 6 (1965): 843–861. See also Matilda White Riley, "On the Significance of Age in Sociology," *American Sociological Review* 52, no. 1 (1987): 1–14.

3. C. Wright Mills, *The Sociological Imagination* (New York: Oxford University Press, 1959).

4. Glen H. Elder Jr., *Children of the Great Depression: Social Change in Life Experience* (Chicago: University of Chicago Press, 1974).

5. Glen H. Elder Jr., "The Life Course as Developmental Theory," *Child Development* 69, no. 1 (1998): 1–12. There is a long history of work on generations, but typically in the sense of familial and kinship-based networks or, more frequently, on the supposed cultural identity of different generations, such as Baby Boomers or Gen X. These approaches do not take up the questions asked in this book. For the classic work on generations, see Mannheim, "The Problem of Generations." For a popular account and critique of overwrought conceptions of generational differences in health, attitudes, economic conditions, marriage, and other non-crime outcomes,

see Bobby Duffy, *The Generation Myth: Why When You're Born Matters Less than You Think* (New York: Basic Books, 2021).

6. Richard A. Easterlin, *Birth and Fortune: The Impact of Numbers on Personal Welfare* (New York: Basic Books, 1980).

7. Riley, "On the Significance of Age in Sociology," 4.

8. Ryder, "The Cohort as a Concept," 852.

9. For more on how cities and crime changed in this era, see Robert J. Sampson, "Neighborhood Effects and Beyond: Explaining the Paradoxes of Inequality in the Changing American Metropolis," *Urban Studies* 56, no. 1 (2019): 3–32. There are some fluctuations in the nature of trends in crime depending on the data source, type of crime, and year, especially prior to the 1990s, but the general pattern of increasing violence from the 1960s to the 1990s followed by a large decline is uncontested.

10. David Garland originally coined the term *mass imprisonment* in his essay "Introduction: The Meaning of Mass Imprisonment," *Punishment and Society* 3, no. 1 (2001): 5–7. For a discussion of the stability of incarceration prior to 1975, going back to the early part of the twentieth century, see Alfred Blumstein and Jacqueline Cohen, "Theory of the Stability of Punishment," *Journal of Criminal Law and Criminology* 64, no. 2 (1973): 198–207.

11. James Q. Wilson and George L. Kelling, "Broken Windows," *The Atlantic Monthly,* March 1982, 29–38.

12. Ben Austen, *High Risers: Cabrini-Green and the Fate of American Public Housing* (New York: Harper / HarperCollins, 2018), 218.

13. William Julius Wilson, *The Truly Disadvantaged: The Inner City, the Underclass, and Public Policy* (Chicago: University of Chicago Press, [1987] 2012).

14. Terrence McCoy, "Freddie Gray's Life a Study on the Effects of Lead Paint on Poor Blacks," *Washington Post,* April 30, 2015.

15. Franklin E. Zimring, *The Great American Crime Decline* (New York: Oxford University Press, 2006). See also Alfred Blumstein and Joel Wallman, *The Crime Drop in America* (New York: Cambridge University Press, 2009).

16. Robert J. Chaskin and Mark L. Joseph, *Integrating the Inner City: The Promise and Perils of Mixed-Income Public Housing Transformations* (Chicago: University of Chicago Press, 2015). Just three years after Dantrell Davis's murder, the demolition of Cabrini-Green began. For a documentary history, see Ronit Bezalel, dir., *70 Acres in Chicago: Cabrini-Green* (Ronitfilms, 2016).

17. Englewood and West Englewood, where Darnell and Andre were raised, are "low-rise" poor communities on Chicago's South Side that continue to struggle, too, but there has been tangible improvement. Annie Sweeney, "As Shootings and Homicides Drop in Englewood, a New Optimism Grows," *Chicago Tribune,* December 8, 2017. For Sandtown-Winchester in Baltimore, transformation is also a work in progress, but homeownership has grown and hope remains. Michael S. Rosenwald and

Michael A. Fletcher, "Why Couldn't $130 Million Transform One of Baltimore's Poorest Places?," *Washington Post,* May 2, 2015; Peter Rosenblatt and Stefanie DeLuca, "What Happened in Sandtown-Winchester? Understanding the Impacts of a Comprehensive Community Initiative," *Urban Affairs Review* 53, no. 3 (2017): 463–494.

18. Patrick T. Sharkey, *Uneasy Peace: The Great Crime Decline, the Renewal of City Life, and the Next War on Violence* (New York: W. W. Norton, 2018).

19. Charles C. Lanfear, Rebecca Bucci, David S. Kirk, and Robert J. Sampson, "Inequalities in Exposure to Firearm Violence by Race, Sex, and Birth Cohort from Childhood to Age 40, 1995–2021," *JAMA Network Open* 6 (2023): e2312465; Chris A. Rees, Michael C. Monuteaux, Isabella Steidley, Rebekah Mannix, Lois K. Lee, Jefferson T. Barrett, and Eric W. Fleegler, "Trends and Disparities in Firearm Fatalities in the United States, 1990–2021," *JAMA Network Open* 5 (2022): e2244221. The most recent data available on causes of childhood mortality in the United States is from 2022: Jason E. Goldstick, Rebecca Cunningham, and Patrick Carter, "Current Causes of Death in Children and Adolescents in the United States," *New England Journal of Medicine* 386, no. 20 (2022): 1955–1956. See also Robert Geboloff, Danielle Ivory, Bill Marsh, Allison McCann and Albert Sun, "Childhood's Greatest Danger," *New York Times Magazine,* December 14, 2022, 14, 22, 32, 40.

20. Aleksandr I. Solzhenitsyn, *The Gulag Archipelago* (New York: Harper and Row, 1985), 3.

21. The strategy used to produce this figure is explained further in Chapter 4.

22. On the Supreme Court's reliance on psychological research, see Alexandra O. Cohen and B. J. Casey, "Rewiring Juvenile Justice: The Intersection of Developmental Neuroscience and Legal Policy," *Trends in Cognitive Sciences* 18, no. 2 (2014): 63–65.

2. BECOMING CRIMINAL

1. Matthew G. Yeager, "Frank Tannenbaum: The Making of a Convict Criminologist," *Prison Journal* 91, no. 2 (2011): 177–197.

2. "The process of making the criminal, therefore, is a process of tagging, defining, identifying, segregating, describing, emphasizing, making conscious and self-conscious; it becomes a way of stimulating, suggesting, emphasizing, and evoking the very traits that are complained of." Frank Tannenbaum, *Crime and the Community* (New York: Columbia University Press, 1938), 19–20.

3. Tannenbaum, *Crime and the Community,* 20.

4. Later theorists pushed these ideas further. Edwin Lemert, for example, made the distinction between primary deviance—criminal behavior that occurs for any number of reasons—and secondary deviance, which occurs in response to official reactions (such as arrest or incarceration) to the primary deviance. Edwin M. Lemert,

Social Pathology: A Systematic Approach to the Theory of Sociopathic Behavior (New York: McGraw-Hill, 1951). Using early waves of the Chicago study, others have found evidence of the "secondary deviance" effect of first arrest on the chances of a future arrest and for the subsequent commission of a crime: Akiva M. Liberman, David S. Kirk, and Kideuk Kim, "Labeling Effects of First Juvenile Arrests: Secondary Deviance and Secondary Sanctioning," *Criminology* 52, no. 3 (2014): 345–370. Increased surveillance of one's behavior because of a prior offense can, in this view, be a direct cause of further labeling.

5. Howard Becker, *Outsiders: Studies in the Sociology of Deviance* (New York: Free Press, 1963). For a general audience description, see Adam Gopnik, "The Outside Game: How the Sociologist Howard Becker Studies the Conventions of the Unconventional," *New Yorker,* January 12, 2015.

6. Becker famously wrote: "Deviance is not a quality of the act the person commits, but rather a consequence of the application by others of rules and sanctions to an 'offender.' The deviant is one to whom that label has been successfully applied; deviant behavior is behavior that people so label." Becker, *Outsiders,* 9.

7. Becker, *Outsiders,* 129. See also Nachman Ben-Yehuda, Richard A. Brymer, Steven C. Dubin, Douglas Harper, Rosanna Hertz, and William Shaffir, "Howard S. Becker: A Portrait of an Intellectual's Sociological Imagination," *Sociological Inquiry* 59, no. 4 (1989): 467–489.

8. John Hagan, "Extra-Legal Attributes and Criminal Sentencing: An Assessment of a Sociological Viewpoint, " *Law and Society Review* 8, no. 3 (1974): 357–384.

9. Jeremy Travis, Bruce Western, and Steve Redburn, eds., *The Growth of Incarceration in the United States: Exploring Causes and Consequences* (Washington, DC: National Academies Press, 2014); Bruce Western, *Punishment and Inequality in America* (New York: Russell Sage Foundation, 2006).

10. Michelle Alexander, *The New Jim Crow: Mass Incarceration in the Age of Colorblindness* (New York: New Press, 2012); Elizabeth Hinton, *From the War on Poverty to the War on Crime: The Making of Mass Incarceration in America* (Cambridge, MA: Harvard University Press, 2016), 35–36.

11. For a review of labeling research in the 1960s and 1970s, see Walter Gove, ed., *The Labelling of Deviance: Evaluating a Perspective* (Beverly Hills, CA: Sage, 1980). For a later take, see David P. Farrington and Joseph Murray, eds., *Labeling Theory: Empirical Tests* (New Brunswick, NJ: Transaction Books, 2014).

12. Travis Hirschi and Michael R. Gottfredson, "Age and the Explanation of Crime," *American Journal of Sociology* 89, no. 3 (1983): 552–584.

13. The life-course tradition spans multiple disciplines and empirical approaches too extensive to review comprehensively in one book. I focus on basic concepts relevant to crime and criminalization, providing reference sources and additional details in the notes. For those seeking broader assessment, one excellent resource is Michael Shanahan, Jeylan Mortimer, and Monica Kirkpatrick Johnson, eds., *Handbook of*

the Life Course, vol. 2 (New York: Springer, 2016). For a concise intellectual history of the life course, see Glen H. Elder Jr., "Time, Human Agency, and Social Change: Perspectives on the Life Course," *Social Psychology Quarterly* 57, no. 1 (1994): 4–15. For a distinctly sociological view, see Dale Dannefer, "Adult Development and Social Theory: A Paradigmatic Reappraisal," *American Sociological Review* 49, no. 1 (1984): 100–116.

14. For the initial statements of our life-course approach to crime, see Robert J. Sampson and John H. Laub, "Crime and Deviance over the Life Course: The Salience of Adult Social Bonds," *American Sociological Review* 55, no. 5 (1990): 609–627; Robert J. Sampson and John H. Laub, "Crime and Deviance in the Life Course," *Annual Review of Sociology* 18, no. 1 (1992): 63–84.

15. The original sample consisted of one thousand boys followed from age fourteen. We also conducted a thirty-five-year follow-up with a sample of fifty-two of the men, up to age seventy. Robert J. Sampson and John H. Laub, *Crime in the Making: Pathways and Turning Points through Life* (Cambridge, MA: Harvard University Press, 1993); John H. Laub and Robert J. Sampson, *Shared Beginnings, Divergent Lives: Delinquent Boys to Age 70* (Cambridge, MA: Harvard University Press, 2003).

16. This idea drew its inspiration from the social control theory of Travis Hirschi, *Causes of Delinquency* (Berkeley: University of California Press, 1969). His ideas were in turn rooted in Émile Durkheim's theory that suicide resulted from the loosening of an individual's attachment to society. Whereas suicide is typically thought to be an individualistic or personal act, Durkheim saw it as a quintessentially social act. Émile Durkheim, *Suicide* (New York: Free Press, 1897 [1951]). These theories share an emphasis on relationships among individuals, as opposed to characteristics *of* individuals, whether unchanging (like temperament) or changing (like income).

17. Laub and Sampson, *Shared Beginnings, Divergent Lives,* 135.

18. For a contemporary assessment of research, see Chester L. Britt, "Age and Crime," in *The Oxford Handbook of Developmental and Life-Course Criminology,* ed. David P. Farrington, Lila Kazemian, and Alex R. Piquero (New York: Oxford University Press, 2019). On criminal careers, see Alex R. Piquero, David P. Farrington, and Alfred Blumstein, "The Criminal Career Paradigm: Background and Recent Developments," *Crime and Justice* 30, no. 1 (2003): 359–506.

19. The Cambridge Study in Delinquent Development, which West launched in 1961, is a is a longitudinal survey of hundreds of males in London, first studied that year at age eight, as well as their parents and their children. Donald West and David P. Farrington, *The Delinquent Way of Life* (London: Heinemann, 1977); Alex R. Piquero, David Farrington, and Alfred Blumstein, *Key Issues in Criminal Career Research: New Analyses of the Cambridge Study in Delinquent Development* (Cambridge, UK: Cambridge University Press, 2007).

20. The social environment affects "life-course-persistent" offenders differently, mainly through interactions with neuropsychological deficits, as when harsh

punishment of impulsive children with low cognitive skills increases the risk of persistent criminality. Terrie E. Moffitt, "Adolescence-Limited and Life-Course-Persistent Antisocial Behavior: A Developmental Taxonomy," *Psychological Review* 100, no. 4 (1993): 674–701. For a more recent assessment, see Terrie E. Moffitt, "Male Antisocial Behaviour in Adolescence and Beyond," *Nature Human Behaviour* 2, no. 3 (2018): 177–186.

21. For a review of longitudinal studies on group-based crime trajectories, see Alex R. Piquero, "Taking Stock of Developmental Trajectories of Criminal Activity over the Life Course," in *The Long View of Crime: A Synthesis of Longitudinal Research,* ed. Akiva M. Liberman (New York: Springer, 2008). For assessments of research on turning points and desistance from crime, see John H. Laub, Zachary R. Rowan, and Robert J. Sampson, "The Age-Graded Theory of Informal Social Control," in *The Oxford Handbook of Developmental and Life-Course Criminology,* ed. David P. Farrington, Lila Kazemian, and Alex R. Piquero (New York: Oxford University Press, 2019). Bianca E. Bersani and Elaine Eggleston Doherty, "Desistance from Offending in the Twenty-First Century," *Annual Review of Criminology* 1, no. 1 (2018): 311–334. Holly Nguyen and Thomas Loughran, "On the Measurement and Identification of Turning Points in Criminology," *Annual Review of Criminology* 1, no. 1 (2018): 335–358. For a critical review of turning point theory with respect to marriage, see Torbjørn Skardhamar, Jukka Savolainen, Kjersti N. Aase, and Torkild H. Lyngstad, "Does Marriage Reduce Crime?," *Crime and Justice: An Annual Review of Research* 44, no. 1 (2015): 385–446.

22. This section builds on ideas discussed in John H. Laub and Robert J. Sampson, "Life Course and Developmental Criminology: Looking Back, Moving Forward," *Journal of Developmental and Life-Course Criminology* 6, no. 2 (2020): 158–171.

23. Laurence Steinberg, *Age of Opportunity: Lessons from the New Science of Adolescence* (New York: Houghton Mifflin Harcourt, 2015).

24. William Julius Wilson, *The Truly Disadvantaged: The Inner City, the Underclass, and Public Policy* (Chicago: University of Chicago Press, 1987); William Julius Wilson, *When Work Disappears: The World of the New Urban Poor* (New York: Knopf, 1996).

25. Robert D. Crutchfield, *Get a Job: Labor Markets, Economic Opportunity, and Crime* (New York: New York University Press, 2014).

26. Becky Pettit and Bruce Western, "Mass Imprisonment and the Life Course: Race and Class Inequality in U.S. Incarceration," *American Sociological Review* 69, no. 2 (2004): 151–169.

27. Disclaimer: I served as one of over a dozen members on the National Academy of Sciences committee. The Academy's report primarily reviewed studies on crime, employment, and earnings, though individual outcomes linked to incarceration also included diminished mental health and elevated stress. Travis, Western, and Redburn, *The Growth of Incarceration,* 130–156, 233–259.

28. Robert J. Sampson, *Great American City: Chicago and the Enduring Neighborhood Effect,* 2nd ed. (Chicago: University of Chicago Press [2012] 2024), 114.

29. A list of notable works, far from exhaustive, would include Alexander, *The New Jim Crow;* James Forman Jr., *Locking Up Our Own: Crime and Punishment in Black America* (New York: Farrar, Straus and Giroux, 2017); Marie Gottschalk, *Caught: The Prison State and the Lockdown of American Politics* (Princeton, NJ: Princeton University Press, 2016); Katherine Beckett and Steve Herbert, *Banished: The New Social Control in Urban America* (New York: Oxford University Press, 2010); Hinton, *From the War on Poverty to the War on Crime;* David Garland, *Law and Order Leviathan: America's Extraordinary Regime of Policing and Punishment* (Princeton, NJ: Princeton University Press, 2025); Loïc Wacquant, *Punishing the Poor: The Neoliberal Government of Social Insecurity* (Durham, NC: Duke University Press, 2009); Jonathan Simon, *Governing through Crime: How the War on Crime Transformed American Democracy and Created a Culture of Fear* (New York: Oxford University Press, 2009).

30. John Pfaff, *Locked In: The True Causes of Mass Incarceration and How to Achieve Real Reform* (New York: Basic Books, 2017), 5.

31. We should also consider earlier points in history. Racial differences in incarceration date back to the early twentieth century—well before the drug wars of the 1980s. Christopher Muller, "Northward Migration and the Rise of Racial Disparity in American Incarceration, 1880–1950," *American Journal of Sociology* 118, no. 2 (2012): 281–326. Note, too, that even if all drug offenders were removed from prison, strong racial disparities would still be evident. See Travis, Western, and Redburn, *The Growth of Incarceration.*

32. US President's Commission on Law Enforcement and the Enforcement of Justice, *The Challenge of Crime in a Free Society* (Washington, DC: US Government Printing Office, 1967), 8–9.

33. The main exception for conviction is pretrial detention in jail. One can also be thrown in jail before being formally charged, although in almost all cases jail comes after an arrest.

34. As an earlier report concluded, "The police are the principal gatekeepers of the justice system and play a central role in the processing of youths in both the criminal and juvenile justice systems. They have a great deal of contact with youthful offenders and at-risk youth, perhaps more than any other officials do in the justice system. Most of these contacts are undocumented and of low visibility." Joan McCord, Cathy Spatz Widom, and Nancy A. Crowell, eds., *Juvenile Crime, Juvenile Justice* (Washington, DC: National Academy Press, 2001), 162.

35. Juvenile arrest cuts short educational attainment, for example, one of the primary pathways to adult success. David S. Kirk and Robert J. Sampson, "Juvenile Arrest and Collateral Educational Damage in the Transition to Adulthood," *Sociology of Education* 86, no. 1 (2013): 36–62. Another study finds that arrest and conviction account for at least half of the observed association of incarceration with

poor mental health outcomes. Naomi F. Sugie and Kristin Turney, "Beyond Incarceration: Criminal Justice Contact and Mental Health," *American Sociological Review* 82, no. 4 (2017): 719–743. More generally, some political scientists assert that the reach of the criminal justice system goes far beyond the currently or formerly incarcerated, creating what they term the "custodial citizen." See Amy E. Lerman and Vesla M. Weaver, *Arresting Citizenship: The Democratic Consequences of American Crime Control* (Chicago: University of Chicago Press, 2014). On the social organization of the policing of minorities and the poor, see Victor Rios, *Punished: Policing the Lives of Black and Latino Boys* (New York: New York University Press, 2011); Forrest Stuart, *Down, Out, and Under Arrest: Policing and Everyday Life in Skid Row* (Chicago: University of Chicago Press, 2016). The evidence on the potential positive and harmful effects of policing is reviewed in the National Academies of Sciences, Engineering, and Medicine, *Proactive Policing: Effects on Crime and Communities* (Washington, DC: National Academies Press, 2018). Crime rates, according to the report, were lowered by hot-spot policing. For a more pessimistic assessment of policing, see National Academy of Sciences, Engineering, and Medicine, *Reducing Racial Inequality in Crime and Justice: Science, Practice, and Policy* (Washington, DC: National Academies Press, 2023).

36. Christopher Uggen, Mike Vuolo, Sarah Lageson, Ebony Ruhland, and Hilary K. Whitham, "The Edge of Stigma: An Experimental Audit of the Effects of Low-Level Criminal Records on Employment," *Criminology* 52, no. 4 (2014): 627–654. See also Issa Kohler-Hausmann, *Misdemeanorland: Criminal Courts and Social Control in an Age of Broken Windows Policing* (Princeton, NJ: Princeton University Press, 2018).

37. James B. Jacobs, *The Eternal Criminal Record* (Cambridge, MA: Harvard University Press, 2015).

38. Andrea M. Burch, *Arrest-Related Deaths, 2003–2009* (Washington, DC: US Bureau of Justice Statistics Special Report, 2011).

39. Andrew Papachristos, Christopher Wildeman, Elizabeth Roberto, "Tragic, but Not Random: The Social Contagion of Nonfatal Gunshot Injuries," *Social Science and Medicine* 125 (2015): 139–150.

40. On the science of predicting the next shooting death, see Michael Friedrich, "How to Uproot a 'Tree of Death,'" Bloomberg CityLab, February 19, 2017, https://www.citylab.com/equity/2017/02/uprooting-a-tree-of-death/516402/.

41. Linda Teplin, Gary M. McClelland, Karen M. Abram, and Darinka Mileusnic, "Early Violent Death among Delinquent Youth: A Prospective Longitudinal Study," *Pediatrics* 115, no. 6 (2005): 1586–1593. Some studies, however, show that Black men's mortality risk is lower in prison, whereas for white men it is higher. See Evelyn J. Patterson, "Incarcerating Death: Mortality in U.S. State Correctional Facilities, 1985–1998," *Demography* 47, no. 3 (August 2010): 587–607.

42. See, for example, Charles R. Tittle, "Labelling and Crime: An Empirical Evaluation," in *The Labelling of Deviance: Evaluating a Perspective,* ed. Walter Gove

(Beverly Hills, CA: Sage, 1980). Michael J. Hindelang, Travis Hirschi, and Joseph G. Weis, "Correlates of Delinquency: The Illusion of Discrepancy between Self-Report and Official Measures," *American Sociological Review* 44, no. 6 (1979): 995–1014. It should be noted that Howard Becker was himself critical of labeling theory and resisted being categorized as a labeling theorist, preferring the term *interactionist theory*. He never claimed deviant behavior was unimportant; rather, he focused on how deviant acts are socially constructed and how others react to them through social interactions. On these points, see Ben-Yehuda et al., "Howard S. Becker," 476–477.

43. Alexander, *The New Jim Crow*, 215.

44. For certain population subgroups, such as Black men without high school education, recent cohorts face quite high cumulative lifetime incarceration risk by young adulthood (Western, *Punishment and Inequality in America*). At any earlier point in the life course, however, prevalence remains much lower with substantial individual variation. The early onset of criminalization in the current era is evidenced by the fact that average age at first arrest occurs before high school completion.

45. Forman, *Locking Up Our Own*. See also David Garland, "Penal Controls and Social Controls: Toward a Theory of American Penal Exceptionalism," *Punishment and Society* 22, no. 3 (2020): 321–352; John Laub, "Understanding Inequality and the Justice System Response: Charting a New Way Forward" (New York: William T. Grant Foundation, 2014).

46. Bruce Western, *Homeward: Life in the Year after Prison* (New York: Russell Sage Foundation, 2018).

47. Notable exceptions include the sustained focus of David Garland and Nicola Lacey. See, for example, Garland, "Penal Controls and Social Controls"; Nicola L. Lacey, David Soskice, and David Hope, "Understanding the Determinants of Penal Policy: Crime, Culture, and Comparative Political Economy," *Annual Review of Criminology* 1, no. 1 (2018): 195–217.

48. For a recent overview of research on criminal justice contact that is consistent with this conclusion, see Kristin Turney and Sara Wakefield, "Criminal Justice Contact and Inequality," *Russell Sage Foundation Journal of the Social Sciences* 5, no. 1 (2019): 1–23.

49. David P. Farrington, Geoffrey Barnes, and Sandra Lambert, "The Concentration of Offending in Families," *Legal and Criminological Psychology* 1, no. 1 (1996): 47–64.

50. Fox Butterfield, *In My Father's House: A New View of How Crime Runs in the Family* (New York: Knopf, 2018).

51. Elder, "Time, Human Agency, and Social Change."

52. John Hagan and Alberto Palloni, "The Social Reproduction of a Criminal Class in Working-Class London, Circa 1950–1980," *American Journal of Sociology* 96, no. 2 (1990): 265–299. For an extensive review on this point, see Christopher

Wildeman, "The Intergenerational Transmission of Criminal Justice Contact," *Annual Review of Criminology* 3, no. 1 (2020): 217–244.

53. Sara Wakefield and Christopher Wildeman, *Children of the Prison Boom: Mass Incarceration and the Future of American Inequality* (Oxford, UK: Oxford University Press, 2013).

54. Classic examples include the longitudinal studies of Boston boys born in the Great Depression: Sheldon Glueck and Eleanor Glueck, *Delinquents and Nondelinquents in Perspective* (Cambridge, MA: Harvard University Press, 1968). See also the 1945 Philadelphia birth cohort study of Marvin E. Wolfgang, Robert W. Figlio, and Thorsten Sellin, *Delinquency in a Birth Cohort* (Chicago: University of Chicago Press, 1972). In Europe, see West and Farrington, *The Delinquent Way of Life,* a seminal study of boys in Cambridge, England born in the 1950s. There are almost no contemporary birth cohort studies in the United States that are representative of the population. A partial exception is a set of three longitudinal studies funded by the Office of Juvenile Justice and Delinquency in Pittsburgh, Denver, and Rochester, but that research began with teenagers in the 1980s, and to date the authors have not focused on the life-course theory of criminalization highlighted in this book. See David Huizinga, Terence P. Thornberry, Kelly E. Knight, Peter Lovegrove, Rolf Loeber, Karl Hill, and David P. Farrington, *Disproportionate Minority Contact in the Juvenile Justice System: A Study of Differential Minority Arrest/Referral to Court in Three Cities* (Washington, DC: US Department of Justice, Office of Juvenile Justice and Delinquency Prevention, National Criminal Justice Reference Service, 2007). National-level studies, like the National Longitudinal Study of Adolescent to Adult Health and the National Longitudinal Survey of Youth, have produced important data sources, as well, but they are not primarily focused on crime or criminal records, nor do they focus on birth cohort as a major analytic category. For a review on longitudinal studies in crime, see Akiva M. Liberman, ed., *The Long View of Crime: A Synthesis of Longitudinal Research* (New York: Springer, 2008).

55. For reviews of these issues, see Joseph Murray and David P. Farrington, "The Effects of Parental Imprisonment on Children," *Crime and Justice* 37, no. 1 (2008): 133–206; Christopher Wildeman, "Parental Incarceration and Child Wellbeing" (Boston: Sills Family Foundation, 2014); Wildeman, "The Intergenerational Transmission of Criminal Justice Contact."

56. This concern was raised by the National Academy panel, which concluded that the correlation of incarceration with an array of other measures of social and economic marginality is dense, with all factors so interrelated that it is difficult to draw causal linkages among them. Travis, Western, and Redburn, *The Growth of Incarceration,* 429–430.

57. The idea behind legal cynicism is that laws and general norms against lawbreaking are perceived as irrelevant or not binding in the present everyday lives of citizens, as measured, for example, by asking respondents to affirm or disagree with

statements such as "It is OK to do anything you want" and "Laws are meant to be broken." See Robert J. Sampson and Dawn Jeglum Bartusch, "Legal Cynicism and (Subcultural?) Tolerance of Deviance: The Neighborhood Context of Racial Differences," *Law and Society Review* 32, no. 4 (1998): 777–804. For other work on legal cynicism using data from the Project on Human Development in Chicago neighborhoods, including attitudes about law enforcement, see David S. Kirk and Andrew V. Papachristos, "Cultural Mechanisms and the Persistence of Neighborhood Violence," *American Journal of Sociology* 116, no. 4 (2011): 1190–1233; David S. Kirk and Mauri Matsuda, "Legal Cynicism, Collective Efficacy, and the Ecology of Arrest," *Criminology* 49, no. 2 (2011): 443–472.

3. MEASURING WHAT MATTERS AND WHEN

1. My description of the research procedures and logistics of carrying out the longitudinal design and its other components, such as criminal history and lead exposure, draws from the following sources: Robert J. Sampson, David S. Kirk, and Rebecca Bucci, "Cohort Profile: Project on Human Development in Chicago Neighborhoods and Its Additions (PHDCN+)," *Journal of Developmental and Life-Course Criminology* 8 (2022): 516–532; Roland Neil and Robert J. Sampson, "The Birth Lottery of History: Arrest over the Life Course of Multiple Cohorts Coming of Age, 1995–2018," *American Journal of Sociology* 126, no. 5 (2021): 1127–1178; Robert J. Sampson and Alix Winter, "Poisoned Development: Assessing Lead Exposure as a Cause of Crime in a Birth Cohort Followed Through Adolescence," *Criminology* 56, no. 2 (2018): 269–301; Robert J. Sampson and Alix Winter, "The Racial Ecology of Lead Poisoning: Toxic Inequality in Chicago Neighborhoods, 1995–2013," *Du Bois Review: Social Science Research on Race* 13, no. 2 (2016): 261–283. These papers provide more details on the main points summarized here.

2. Patricia Cohen, "Long Road to Adulthood Is Growing Even Longer," *New York Times,* June 12, 2010. On extended adolescence and the changing schedules of adulthood, see Frank F. Furstenberg Jr., "On a New Schedule: Transitions to Adulthood and Family Change," *The Future of Children* 20, no. 1 (2010): 67–87.

3. For more description of the design, content, and logistical details of carrying out the community surveys, observational data, and community leader interviews, see Robert J. Sampson, *Great American City: Chicago and the Enduring Neighborhood Effect,* 2nd ed. (Chicago: University of Chicago Press, [2012] 2024), chapter 4.

4. To date, there have been over eight hundred publications based on the early stages of PHDCN data, the first three waves of which are publicly available at the University of Michigan's Inter-university Consortium for Political and Social Research. For further information on data access and publications, see https://www.icpsr.umich.edu/web/NACJD/series/206/publications.

5. For a description of the Los Angeles study, see Narayan Sastry, Bonnie Ghosh-Dastidar, John Adams, and Anne R. Pebley, "The Design of a Multilevel Survey of Children, Families, and Communities: The Los Angeles Family and Neighborhood Survey," *Social Science Research* 35, no. 4 (2006): 1000–1024.

6. Research Support Services was the firm selected to carry out the data collection after a national process of selecting bids. Alisú Schoua-Glusberg, formerly a survey director at the University of Chicago's National Opinion Research Center, is the principal there and was the designer of the follow-up strategy.

7. This measurement protocol was designed to be virtually identical in the Los Angeles portion of the study, allowing comparative analyses across sites for certain questions. For example, see Robert J. Sampson, "Individual and Community Economic Mobility in the Great Recession Era: The Spatial Foundations of Persistent Inequality," in *Economic Mobility: Research and Ideas on Strengthening Families, Communities and the Economy* (St. Louis: Federal Reserve Bank, 2016); Robert J. Sampson, Jared N. Schachner, and Robert D. Mare, "Urban Income Inequality and the Great Recession in Sunbelt Form: Disentangling Individual and Neighborhood-Level Change in Los Angeles," *RSF: The Russell Sage Foundation Journal of the Social Sciences* 3 (2017): 102–128. Although the measurement was comprehensive, about 10 percent of the Chicago interviews are missing information, a lapse attributable to one interviewer. This missingness was not disparate by cohort or for all these items, however, and we used multiple imputation methods to recover information for key analyses and to assess the robustness of results.

8. Funding constraints, logistical difficulties, and institutional review board hurdles dissuaded us from pursuing direct interviews with children. This was a limitation, but because the data on antisocial behavior collected from the children's parental caretakers directly parallelled data collected in prior waves, we were provided with consistent measures over time. These were, moreover, based on the "gold standard" of measurement—the Child Behavior Checklist—widely used in prior research.

9. David S. Kirk, "A Natural Experiment on Residential Change and Recidivism: Lessons from Hurricane Katrina," *American Sociological Review* 74, no. 3 (2009): 484–505; David S. Kirk, *Home Free: Prisoner Reentry and Residential Change after Hurricane Katrina* (Oxford, UK: Oxford University Press, 2020).

10. Christopher Wildeman at Duke University was also among that promising next generation; his intergenerational research will be discussed in Chapter 10.

11. The vast majority of respondents completed the survey on the web (71 percent), followed by phone (24 percent) and a small percentage in-person (5 percent). Both the phone and in-person contacts often led to a survey's being completed online, suggesting the advantages of a multi-mode design.

12. Given the difficulties in contacting currently incarcerated or otherwise incapacitated persons (for example, those hospitalized or with serious injuries), such individuals were considered out of scope at waves 4 and 5. Seventeen individuals were

incarcerated during the wave 4 interview period, and sixteen respondents from wave 4 were ineligible for wave 5 because they were deceased.

13. Sampling weights at baseline adjust for the original stratification of the PHDCN by neighborhood socioeconomic status and racial composition, along with age-cohort selection and post-stratification to match Chicago's demographic distribution of children in 1995. To account for participant attrition in follow-up studies, we also calculated attrition weights by first estimating the probability of non-response by wave. This model included indicators of the primary caregiver's gender, citizenship status, age, socioeconomic status, home ownership, household size, marital status, and social ties; the subject's gender, race / ethnicity, immigrant generation, and age; and neighborhood characteristics (including racial and socio-economic composition and collective efficacy). Some analyses also included whether participants were arrested prior to follow-up. (Surprisingly, juvenile arrest was not significantly related to wave 4 attrition.) Attrition weights were then calculated as the reciprocal of each subject's probability of response. Depending on the research question, some analyses in this book are unweighted—for example, in those cases where our main interest is not the broader Chicago population but rather the descriptive characteristics of our sample. In many longitudinal analyses, person-level weights also either are not possible or unduly reduce estimate precision, and to align with typical risk assessment practices, our main prediction models use unweighted data. Nonetheless, results using sampling design and attrition weights in analyses where weighting is appropriate and where we are more interested in population estimates yield similar conclusions, unless otherwise noted. For more on this issue, see Sampson, Kirk, and Bucci, "Cohort Profile."

14. These data were based on arrests in the late 1990s. David S. Kirk, "Examining the Divergence across Self-Report and Official Data Sources on Inferences about the Adolescent Life-Course of Crime," *Journal of Quantitative Criminology* 22 (2006): 107–129.

15. Because the computerized CHRI database extends back to the mid-1990s, our search captured the period before first arrest for the birth and nine-year-old cohorts, allowing us to construct complete prospective histories of criminal sanctioning for these cohorts. For the older cohorts, we captured criminal histories from approximately age twelve and fifteen, respectively. The Illinois Criminal Justice Information Authority researchers developed probabilistic matching algorithms using the Merge Toolbox software, based on University of Chicago expert recommendations. (See Christine Devitt Westley and Erika Hughes, "Assessing the Quality of Illinois Criminal History Record Information [CHRI] System Data on Juveniles" [Chicago: Illinois Criminal Justice Information Authority, 2016].) Over 80 percent of matches yielded a 100 percent probability of accuracy, and over 90 percent were 99 percent or higher. We individually verified remaining cases using demographic characteristics, family names, and locations.

16. Another potential concern is record expungement. Some individuals may have applied as adults to expunge eligible juvenile records. However, due to burdensome laws, lengthy waiting periods, expensive fees, complicated forms, and lack of knowledge about options, this occurrence is negligible—less than 0.005 percent of juvenile records were expunged between 2004 and 2014.

17. According to ICJIA analysis: "Overall, findings led to the conclusion that juvenile CHRI arrest records are representative of overall juvenile arrest activity in Cook and surrounding counties," where most PHDCN children lived (Devitt Westley and Hughes, "Assessing the Quality of Illinois Criminal History Record Information [CHRI] System Data on Juveniles," 7). Juvenile disposition data, however, were unevenly filed in the 1990s by the State Attorney's Office, which motivated our additional searches in 2017, 2019, and 2021. A related technical issue is that arrests before 1995 were not reliably entered into the system, primarily affecting the oldest (age fifteen) cohort. Prevalence estimates of juvenile arrests may also be slightly lower during the first few years of measurement (mid-to-late 1990s) before live scan fingerprinting technology was adopted. My analyses adjust for these differences.

18. The blood lead levels were tested following the CDPH's recommended schedule of four tests by thirty-six months of age, with additional testing until six years of age if test results were high or if children moved to a new address. The majority of lead tests were conducted using venous blood samples, and the remainder using capillary blood samples.

19. We performed matching on first name, last name, and date of birth for children whose caregivers had consented to health record checks (over 92 percent) at baseline. Consistent with the Chicago Department of Public Health's (CDPH) focus on higher-risk children, those with matching test results were more likely to be Black or Hispanic and from lower socioeconomic backgrounds compared to the overall wave 4 birth cohort. We calculated coverage rates for 1995, 1996, and 1997 by mapping all tested Chicago children (N = 54,703, 82,222, and 79,874, respectively) to their home census block group and dividing by the estimated total number of children ages one to three years residing in each block group each year, based on Decennial Census data. Most blood lead tests are conducted within this age range, though our results remained robust when using children ages one to four or one to five as the denominator. We estimate CDPH's average block group-level testing coverage was between 30 and 50 percent. When calculating these rates, we first removed children in wave 4 with blood lead tests in 1995 to 1997 from their neighborhoods' counts to prevent confounding between the lead testing coverage rates and individual-level exposure measures.

20. To minimize potential measurement error, we used children's average blood lead level (measured in µg/dL) across all test results as our main exposure measure. Because lead is most harmful when ingested during early development, we excluded

tests conducted at age six or older before calculating each child's average. As CDPH's testing recommendations aren't always strictly followed, children in our sample averaged 2.6 blood lead tests before age six. The average ages at first and last blood tests were 2.08 and 3.92 years, respectively, aligning with the ideal window for capturing lead exposure. Bruce P. Lanphear, Richard Hornung, Mona Ho, Cynthia R. Howard, Shirley Eberly, and Karen Knauf, "Environmental Lead Exposure during Early Childhood," *Journal of Pediatrics* 140 (2002): 40–47. The average blood lead level in our sample is 6.20µg/dL, higher than the CDC's monitoring threshold.

21. Scott Frickel and James R. Elliott, *Sites Unseen: Uncovering Hidden Hazards in American Cities* (New York: Russell Sage Foundation, 2018).

22. The data on social outcomes, which indicate levels of child mobility over time, come from the Opportunity Atlas, a tool constructed by Raj Chetty at Harvard based on linked data from the IRS, the Decennial Census, and the American Community Survey. This dataset covers approximately 96 percent of the 1978–1983 birth cohorts in the United States, meaning that the data overlap with the oldest Chicago cohorts born in the early 1980s. Children were matched to parents based on who claimed them as dependents on tax returns for each census tract in the country. In total, our analyses included data for nearly 75,000 census tracts, or neighborhoods. For air pollution, we estimated particulate matter (for both PM_{10} and $PM_{2.5}$ sized particles) as well as levels of nitrogen dioxide and carbon monoxide.

23. These maps display the most recent location of each participant who completed at least wave 4. While most of these addresses come from wave 5 or post-wave 5 updates (2021 to 2024), locations of individuals who only completed wave 4 come from 2012 addresses. Two additional wave 5 respondents live outside of the US mainland and are not represented in Figure 3.2.

4. THE ARRESTED YEARS

1. Travis Hirschi and Michael R. Gottfredson, "Age and the Explanation of Crime," *American Journal of Sociology* 89 (1983): 552–584.

2. Michael R. Gottfredson and Travis Hirschi, *A General Theory of Crime* (Stanford, CA: Stanford University Press, 1990). Their book has been cited over 18,000 times in the scholarly literature, a remarkable achievement widely recognized as a classic. In a follow-up nearly thirty years later, they assess the expansive literature on age, self-control, and crime, holding to their main age-invariance thesis. See Michael R. Gottfredson and Travis Hirschi, *Modern Control Theory and the Limits of Criminal Justice* (New York: Oxford University Press, 2019).

3. Alex R. Piquero, "Taking Stock of Developmental Trajectories of Criminal Activity over the Life Course," in *The Long View of Crime: A Synthesis of Longitudinal Research,* ed. Akiva M. Liberman (New York: Springer, 2008); Julien Morizot, "Trajectories of Criminal Behavior across the Life Course," In *The Oxford Handbook of*

Developmental and Life-Course Criminology, ed. David P. Farrington, Lila Kazemian, and Alex R. Piquero (New York: Oxford University Press, 2019). For a critique of the age-invariance argument for neglecting historical period and cohort effects, see David F. Greenberg, "Age, Crime, and Social Explanation," *American Journal of Sociology* 91 (1985): 1–21; David P. Farrington, "Age and Crime," *Crime and Justice* 7 (1986): 189–250; Darrell J. Steffensmeier, Emilie Andersen Allan, Miles D. Harer, and Cathy Streifel, "Age and the Distribution of Crime," *American Journal of Sociology* 94, no. 4 (1989): 803–831. For later empirical tests of cohort effects at the aggregate level, see Robert M. O'Brien, Jean Stockard, and Lynne Isaacson, "The Enduring Effects of Cohort Characteristics on Age-Specific Homicide Rates, 1960–1995," *American Journal of Sociology* 104 (1999): 1061–1095; Matt Vogel, Kristina J. Thompson, and Steven F. Messner, "The Enduring Influence of Cohort Characteristics on Race-Specific Homicide Rates," *Social Forces* 99 (2019): 1–30. These studies are nonetheless distinct from studying cohort differentiation in life-course patterns of crime and criminal legal contact.

4. Gary Sweeten, Alex R. Piquero, and Laurence Steinberg, "Age and the Explanation of Crime, Revisited," *Journal of Youth and Adolescence* 42 (2013): 921–938.

5. Stephen W. Raudenbush, "How Do We Study 'What Happens Next'?," *Annals of the American Academy of Political and Social Science* 602 (2005): 131–144.

6. John H. Laub and Robert J. Sampson, "Crime and Context in the Lives of 1,000 Boston Men, Circa 1925–1955," in *Current Perspectives on Aging and the Life Cycle,* vol. 4, *Delinquency and Disrepute in the Life Course,* ed. Zena Smith Blau and John Hagan (Greenwich, CT: JAI Press, 1995), 119–140; Robert J. Sampson and John H. Laub, "Socioeconomic Achievement in the Life Course of Disadvantaged Men: Military Service as a Turning Point, Circa 1940–1965," *American Sociological Review* 61, no. 3 (1995): 347–367; John H. Laub and Robert J. Sampson, *Shared Beginnings, Divergent Lives: Delinquent Boys to Age 70* (Cambridge, MA: Harvard University Press, 2003).

7. Repeated cross-sectional studies are a valid strategy for studying social change, but they lack the repeated measures on the same individuals over time that is necessary to map individual trajectories in relation to changing social circumstances. For a methodological assessment of scholarship on age, period, and cohort effects, see Ethan Fosse and Christopher Winship, "Analyzing Age-Period-Cohort Data: A Review and Critique," *Annual Review of Sociology* 45, no. 1 (2019): 467–492.

8. In this chapter and portions of Chapters 5 and 6, I extend the data and analysis strategies in Roland Neil and Robert J. Sampson, "The Birth Lottery of History: Arrest over the Life Course of Multiple Cohorts Coming of Age, 1995–2018," *American Journal of Sociology* 126 (2021): 1127–1178.

9. Karl Mannheim, "The Problem of Generations," in *Essays on the Sociology of Knowledge: Collected Works,* vol. 5, ed. Paul Kecskemeti (New York: Routledge, [1928] 1952), 276–322; Howard Schuman and Jacqueline Scott, "Generations and

Collective Memories," *American Sociological Review* 54, no. 3 (1989): 359–381; Amy Corning and Howard Schuman, *Generations and Collective Memory* (Chicago: University of Chicago Press, 2015), 77.

10. Paul E. Tracy, Marvin E. Wolfgang, and Robert M. Figlio, *Delinquency Careers in Two Birth Cohorts* (New York: Plenum Press, 1990). An earlier study in England for the Home Office also focused on cohort differences, studying delinquency in relation to the age at which children experienced the disruptions of World War II. See Leslie T. Wilkins, *Delinquent Generations, 1960, Home Office Research Unit Report* (London: Her Majesty's Stationery Office, 1960).

11. Anthony Fabio, Rolf Loeber, G. K. Balasubramani, Jeffrey Roth, Wenjiang Fu, and David P. Farrington, "Why Some Generations Are More Violent Than Others: Assessment of Age, Period, and Cohort Effects," *American Journal of Epidemiology* 164, no. 2 (2006): 151–160. For a review and discussion of a small set of studies in Australia, Britain, and Sweden focusing on multiple birth cohorts and crime over the life course, see Robert J. Sampson and L. Ash Smith, "Rethinking Criminal Propensity and Character: Cohort Inequalities and the Power of Social Change," *Crime and Justice* 50 (2021): 13–74. One study in Britain, for example, examined how political change influenced criminal careers: Stephen Farrall and Emily Gray, *The Politics of Crime, Punishment and Justice: Exploring the Lived Reality and Enduring Legacies of the 1980's Radical Right* (London: Routledge, 2024). Another study focused on criminal careers in two birth cohorts in Australia: Jason Payne and Alexis R. Piquero, *Developmental Criminology and the Crime Decline: A Comparative Analysis of the Criminal Careers of Two New South Wales Birth Cohorts* (Cambridge, UK: Cambridge University Press, 2020). Chapter 10 will return to the value of international comparative research on social change and the life course.

12. Alex R. Piquero, David P. Farrington, and Alfred Blumstein, "The Criminal Career Paradigm: Background and Recent Developments," *Crime and Justice* 30 (2003): 359–506, 410.

13. For a review, see Philip J. Cook and John H. Laub, "After the Epidemic: Recent Trends in Youth Violence in the United States," *Crime and Justice* 29 (2002): 1–37.

14. Bruce Western, *Punishment and Inequality in America* (New York: Russell Sage Foundation, 2006); Becky Pettit and Bruce Western, "Mass Imprisonment and the Life Course: Race and Class Inequality in U.S. Incarceration," *American Sociological Review* 69 (2004): 151–169. In more recent cohort-based studies, Porter and colleagues showed that changes in the age distribution of the prison population are primarily driven by birth cohorts who entered young adulthood—the prime ages of both crime and incarceration—when substance use was at its peak. A related study found that the birth cohorts that became young adults during the 1990s crime wave have elevated rates of incarceration throughout their observed life course. See Lauren C. Porter, Shawn D. Bushway, Hui-Shien Tsao, and Herbert L. Smith, "How

the U.S. Prison Boom Has Changed the Age Distribution of the Prison Population," *Criminology* 54, no. 1 (2016): 30–55; Yinzhi Shen, Shawn D. Bushway, Lucy C. Sorensen, and Herbert L. Smith, "Locking Up My Generation: Cohort Differences in Prison Spells over the Life Course," *Criminology* 58, no. 4 (2020): 645–677.

15. Jeremy Travis, Bruce Western, and Steve Redburn, eds., *The Growth of Incarceration in the United States: Exploring Causes and Consequences* (Washington, DC: National Academies Press, 2014).

16. It is simultaneously true that conditional on arrest, substantial increases in incarceration can and did occur because of changes in the probability of being sentenced to prison for any given offense and changes in the severity of sentences. See Travis, Western, and Redburn, *The Growth of Incarceration;* Shawn Bushway, Andrew Jordan, and Steven Raphael, "Understanding Race Disparities in Criminal Court Dispositions," *RSF: The Russell Sage Foundation Journal of the Social Sciences* 11, no. 3 (2025).

17. Although the focus here is on the PHDCN+ sample itself, the result in Figure 4.1 also holds if data are weighted to account for the survey design and attrition.

18. Akiva Liberman, David S. Kirk, and KiDeuk Kim, "Labeling Effects of First Juvenile Arrests: Secondary Deviance and Secondary Sanctioning," *Criminology* 52 (2014): 345–370; David S. Kirk and Robert J. Sampson, "Juvenile Arrest and Collateral Educational Damage in the Transition to Adulthood," *Sociology of Education* 86 (2013): 36–62.

19. Garrett Baker, David S. Kirk, Robert J. Sampson, "The Great Leveler? Juvenile Arrest, College Attainment, and the Future of American Inequality," *Sociology of Education* 98 (2025).

20. This analysis is robust to survey- and attrition-weighted data that provide a more population-based estimate of the percentage reduction in college graduation associated with juvenile arrest. If anything, arrest's negative consequences are even larger with weighted data, so we can consider Figure 4.2's estimates as conservative. And while there are some nonsignificant variations by group in Figure 4.2, that could be in part due to the relatively small sample sizes; the only result that would undermine the "great leveler" argument would be a precisely estimated null or a *positive* association for any one group, which is not the case. Only for whites, the smallest subgroup, does the range of confidence in the estimate include zero, and only marginally so, making it highly improbable that the true association is a precise zero.

21. Howard Becker, *Outsiders: Studies in the Sociology of Deviance* (New York: Free Press, 1963), 33–34.

22. Devah Pager, *Marked: Race, Crime, and Finding Work in an Era of Mass Incarceration* (Chicago: University of Chicago Press, 2009); Christopher Uggen, Mike Vuolo, Sarah Lageson, Ebony Ruhland, and Hilary K. Whitman, "The Edge of Stigma: An Experimental Audit of the Effects of Low-Level Criminal Records on

Employment," *Criminology* 52, no. 4 (2014): 627–654. Many existing studies rely on self-reports of arrest instead of defining criminalization based on official criminal histories. For example, one study used data on cohorts from the 1979 and 1997 versions of the National Longitudinal Survey of Youth to examine how the relationship between self-reported crime and self-reported arrest varied with the rise of mass incarceration. The authors found a decoupling between offending and arrest among the more recent cohorts, possibly due to policing practices, which constitutes a potential reason that arrest patterns may vary across cohorts. Vesla M. Weaver, Andrew Papachristos, and Michael Zanger-Tishler, "The Great Decoupling: The Disconnection between Criminal Offending and Experience of Arrest across Two Cohorts," *RSF: The Russell Sage Foundation Journal of the Social Sciences* 5, no. 1 (2019): 89–123. However, the most recent cohort in this study was born in 1984, and no data past 2002 were analyzed. Socio-historical or cohort compositional changes since then may differentiate the arrest patterns of more recent birth cohorts. As noted in Chapter 3, researchers have also raised concerns about the validity of self-reports of arrest and criminal behavior by age. See, for example, Janet L. Lauritsen, "The Age-Crime Debate: Assessing the Limits of Longitudinal Self-Report Data," *Social Forces* 77 (1998): 127–154; David S. Kirk, "Examining the Divergence across Self-Report and Official Data Sources on Inferences about the Adolescent Life-Course of Crime," *Journal of Quantitative Criminology* 22, no. 2 (2006): 107–129.

23. Graham C. Ousey and Charis E. Kubrin, "Immigration and Crime: Assessing a Contentious Issue," *Annual Review of Criminology* 1 (2018): 63–84; Robert J. Sampson, "Immigration and America's Urban Revival," *The American Prospect* 26, no. 3 (2015): 20–24.

24. Thomas M. Achenbach, *Manual of the Young Adult Self-Report and Young Adult Behavior Checklist* (Burlington: University of Vermont, Department of Psychiatry, 1997). I discuss further details on measurements on self-control at various ages in Chapter 5. For the older cohorts, a longer list of items was available and thus utilized. Although less studied than self-control or antisocial aggression, anxiety and depression assessments have been linked to adolescent crime. See Delbert S. Elliott, David Huizinga, and Scott Menard, *Multiple Problem Youth: Delinquency, Substance Use, and Mental Health Problems* (New York: Springer-Verlag, 1989).

25. See Lauritsen, "The Age-Crime Debate"; Jaeok Kim and Shawn Bushway, "Using Longitudinal Self-Report Data to Study the Age-Crime Relationship," *Journal of Quantitative Criminology* 34, no. 2 (2018): 367–396.

26. Measures for cohorts 0 and 9 pertain to exposure around ages five to six, whereas those for cohorts 12 and 15 pertain to the ages of about nine and eleven. Census tract measures prior to the 1990s are unavailable for Chicago. Incarceration and crime data are also not available for children born in the 1990s who moved out of Chicago before the early 2000s (about 23 percent of the 1995 birth cohort),

forcing me to restrict analyses that use these measures to the individuals of all co-horts who spent their childhood in Chicago.

27. Robert J. Sampson and Stephen W. Raudenbush, "Systematic Social Obser-vation of Public Spaces: A New Look at Disorder in Urban Neighborhoods," *Amer-ican Journal of Sociology* 105, no. 3 (1999): 603–651; Robert J. Sampson, Stephen W. Raudenbush, and Felton Earls, "Neighborhoods and Violent Crime: A Multilevel Study of Collective Efficacy," *Science* 277, no. 5328 (1997): 918–924.

28. For details on the statistical methodology using earlier data, see Neil and Sampson, "The Birth Lottery of History," 1141–1143. This paper also shows that unweighted and weighted analyses of arrest trajectories yield similar conclusions.

29. Recall from Chapter 3 that the data collection unfolded over several years in the mid-1990s and that the sample was clustered on the target ages of "zero," nine, twelve, and fifteen. So for example, the youngest infant cohort contained individuals born in both 1995 and 1996, while the age-nine cohort was born primarily in 1987 but also contained adjacent years. In other cases in this book, I refer to results using the modal birth year, depending on the analysis question. In Figure 4.4, the pattern of results is insensitive to which birth year within age cohorts is highlighted.

30. These differences are significant in statistical terms. To simplify the visual presentation, I do not show estimates with confidence intervals that pinpoint signifi-cance bands. Confidence intervals are a marker of estimated accuracy, but the figure with confidence intervals reveals the same conclusion on cohort differences. For more details of measurement procedures and statistical methodology, along with an analogous figure showing confidence intervals for data up to 2018, see Neil and Sampson, "The Birth Lottery of History," 1141–1152.

31. All differences in the probability of arrest from ages eighteen to twenty-three between the 1995 birth cohort and the 1980 and 1985 birth cohorts are statistically significant at the $p < .05$ level, meaning there is less than a 5 percent chance this finding would be obtained assuming a null relationship.

32. Patrick Sharkey and Robert J. Sampson, "Destination Effects: Residential Mobility and Trajectories of Adolescent Violence in a Stratified Metropolis," *Crimi-nology* 48 (2010): 639–681.

33. As noted earlier, crime-related factors, policing, and exposure to toxic lead in the environment of children are available only for children who stayed in Chicago.

34. These data are less precise because of a smaller sample size and because out of state arrests will likely lead to an undercount. Nonetheless, the older cohorts outside Chicago still have rates of arrest at peak ages roughly two times higher than the youngest cohort.

35. Marvin E. Wolfgang, Robert M. Figlio, and Thorsten Sellin, *Delinquency in a Birth Cohort* (Chicago: University of Chicago Press, 1972).

36. This analysis uses the latent-class or group-based trajectory method described in Roland Neil, Robert J. Sampson, and Daniel S. Nagin, "Social Change and Co-

hort Differences in Group-Based Arrest Trajectories over the Last Quarter-Century," *Proceedings of the National Academy of Sciences* 118, no. 31 (2021): e2107020118.

37. Terrie E. Moffitt, "Adolescence-Limited and Life-Course-Persistent Antisocial Behavior: A Developmental Taxonomy," *Psychological Review* 100, no. 4 (1993): 674–701.

5. RACE, CLASS, AND GRIT MEET THE MARK OF TIME

1. Feinian Chen, Yang Yang, and Guangya Liu, "Social Change and Socioeconomic Disparities in Health over the Life Course in China: A Cohort Analysis," *American Sociological Review* 75, no. 1 (2010): 26–150. Scholars have also examined how trajectories of political attitudes and work interact with large-scale economic transitions and cultural change. See, for example, Duane F. Alwin, Ronald L. Cohen, and Theodore M. Newcomb, *Political Attitudes over the Life Span: The Bennington Women after Fifty Years* (Madison: University of Wisconsin Press, 1991); Xueguang Zhou and Liren Hou, "Children of the Cultural Revolution: The State and the Life Course in the People's Republic of China," *American Sociological Review* 64, no. 1 (1999): 12–36.

2. Raj Chetty, Will S. Dobbie, Benjamin Goldman, Sonya Porter, and Crystal Yang, "Changing Opportunity: Sociological Mechanisms Underlying Growing Class Gaps and Shrinking Race Gaps in Economic Mobility," NBER Working Paper no. 32697 (2024), http://www.nber.org/papers/w32697.

3. Angela Duckworth, *Grit: The Power of Passion and Perseverance* (New York: Scribner, 2016).

4. As in Chapter 4, this work builds on the analyses in Roland Neil and Robert J. Sampson, "The Birth Lottery of History: Arrest over the Life Course of Multiple Cohorts Coming of Age, 1995–2018," *American Journal of Sociology* 126, no. 5 (2021): 1127–1178.

5. Nancy E. Adler, Thomas Boyce, Margaret A. Chesney, Sheldon Cohen, Susan Folkman, Robert L. Kahn, and S. Leonard Syme, "Socioeconomic Status and Health: The Challenge of the Gradient," *American Psychologist* 49, no. 1 (1994): 15–24.

6. Becky Pettit and Bruce Western, "Mass Imprisonment and the Life Course: Race and Class Inequality in U.S. Incarceration," *American Sociological Review* 69, no. 2 (2004): 151–169.

7. Jason P. Robey, Michael Massoglia, and Michael T. Light, "A Generational Shift: Race and the Declining Lifetime Risk of Imprisonment," *Demography* 60, no. 4 (2023): 977–1003; Christopher Muller and Alexander F. Roehrkasse, "Falling Racial Inequality and Rising Educational Inequality in US Prison Admissions for Drug, Violent, and Property Crimes," *Proceedings of the National Academy of Sciences* 122, no. 4 (2025): e2418077122.

8. Anne Case and Angus Deaton, *Deaths of Despair and the Future of Capitalism* (Princeton, NJ: Princeton University Press, 2020).

9. For an in-depth review, see Ruth Rosner Kornhauser, *Social Sources of Delinquency: An Appraisal of Analytic Models* (Chicago: University of Chicago Press, 1978).

10. Elijah Anderson, *Code of the Street: Decency, Violence and the Moral Life of the Inner City* (New York: W. W. Norton, 2000); Elijah Anderson, *Streetwise: Race, Class, and Change in an Urban Community* (Chicago: University of Chicago Press, 1990); David J. Harding, *Living the Drama: Community, Conflict, and Culture among Inner-City Boys* (Chicago: University of Chicago Press, 2010); Orlando Patterson, "The Social and Cultural Matrix of Black Youth," in *The Cultural Matrix: Understanding Black Youth,* ed. Orlando Patterson (Cambridge, MA: Harvard University Press, 2015), 45–136.

11. William Julius Wilson, *The Truly Disadvantaged: The Inner City, the Underclass, and Public Policy* (Chicago: University of Chicago Press, 1987); Patrick T. Sharkey, *Uneasy Peace: The Great Crime Decline, the Renewal of City Life, and the Next War on Violence* (New York: W. W. Norton, 2018); Bruce Western, *Punishment and Inequality in America* (New York: Russell Sage Foundation, 2006); Elizabeth Hinton, *From the War on Poverty to the War on Crime: The Making of Mass Incarceration in America* (Cambridge, MA: Harvard University Press, 2016).

12. Randol Contreras, *The Stickup Kids: Race, Drugs, Violence, and the American Dream* (Berkeley: University of California Press, 2012).

13. Michael R. Gottfredson and Travis Hirschi, *A General Theory of Crime* (Stanford, CA: Stanford University Press, 1990), 232, emphasis in original; Michael R. Gottfredson and Travis Hirschi, *Modern Control Theory and the Limits of Criminal Justice* (New York: Oxford University Press, 2019).

14. Terrie E. Moffitt, Louise Arseneault, Daniel Belsky, Nigel Dickson, Robert J. Hancox, HonaLee Harrington, Renate Houts, Richie Poulton, Brent W. Roberts, Stephen Ross, Malcolm R. Sears, W. Murray Thomson, and Avshalom Caspi, "A Gradient of Childhood Self-Control Predicts Health, Wealth, and Public Safety," *Proceedings of the National Academy of Sciences* 108, no. 7 (2011): 2693–2698.

15. Duckworth, *Grit.*

16. Per-Olof H. Wikström, Dietrich Oberwittler, Kyle Treiber, and Beth Hardie, *Breaking Rules: The Social and Situational Dynamics of Young People's Urban Crime* (Oxford, UK: Oxford University Press, 2012). On dangerous situations and cognitive decision-making, see also Jens Ludwig, *Unforgiving Places: The Unexpected Origins of American Gun Violence* (Chicago: University of Chicago Press, 2025), 225–231.

17. This analysis extends my earlier work through calendar year 2020, including the pandemic. All measures in the socioeconomic status scale contribute about equally in a principal components analysis (with TANF receipt in the expected opposite direction), and the first component accounts for most of the variation. Though related, individual and neighborhood disadvantage are distinct phenomena, so I do

not incorporate neighborhood measures on theoretical grounds. Nonetheless, results remain consistent when neighborhood poverty is included in the disadvantage index. For more details, see Neil and Sampson, "The Birth Lottery of History."

18. I classify individuals as disadvantaged if they score one standard deviation below the overall mean of the socioeconomic status scale, and as advantaged if they score one standard deviation above the mean. Similar results emerge with alternative definitions, some of them further elaborated in this chapter.

19. For those interested in technical details: the observed interaction is not an artifact of the logistic transformation method, which is inherently interactive. When we subset the data by disadvantage level and fit curves separately for each subset, the results remain qualitatively the same. We can also verify this by avoiding the logistic transformation entirely, instead fitting curves with smoothing splines or polynomials in linear models, with similar results to those presented here. Moreover, the survival analyses in this chapter show a related interaction without using logistic transformation. These robustness checks similarly confirm that the self-control analysis results are not affected by this methodological issue.

20. Following Neil and Sampson, "The Birth Lottery of History," 1157, disadvantage is specifically defined as being in the first quartile, and advantage as being in the fourth quartile of the disadvantage measure. Estimating cumulative arrest quantities requires splitting the sample by disadvantage rather than plotting estimates held at specific values, as in the previous figure. Consequently, the exact disadvantage groups being assessed vary between analyses, in addition to differences in the estimated quantity. (For example, the same person's being arrested at multiple ages can influence Figure 5.1, but not here.) I exclude cumulative prevalence estimates from the oldest two age cohorts (twelve and fifteen) due to concerns about potentially missing arrest data from very early ages before reliable criminal justice record-keeping was established in the mid-to-late 1990s. Including these cohorts nonetheless yields similar results.

21. I also examined the raw data by simply dividing the socioeconomic status measure into low (bottom two quartiles) and high (top two quartiles) classifications. The patterns for Black individuals closely matched Figure 5.3: 55 percent of low-socioeconomic-status Black individuals from the older cohort were arrested during the high-risk ages of seventeen to twenty-four, compared to 26 percent of low-socioeconomic-status Black individuals from the younger cohort. For higher-socioeconomic-status Black individuals, the corresponding figures were 33 percent and 24 percent. Thus, the younger Black cohort shows minimal socioeconomic status difference (26 percent versus 24 percent), again demonstrating a weakening of the status gradient over time. Among Hispanic individuals, both low- and high-socioeconomic-status groups show declining arrest rates in recent cohorts: approximately 37 percent of low-socioeconomic-status Hispanics in the older cohort were arrested compared to 19 percent in the younger cohort, while among higher-socioeconomic-status

Hispanics, 25 percent of the older cohort were arrested compared to only 13 percent of the younger cohort.

22. Although not focused on cohort differences and using arrest data only to 2001, other work on the Chicago dataset shows that neighborhood contextual conditions help explain racial disparities. See David S. Kirk, "The Neighborhood Context of Racial and Ethnic Disparities in Arrest," *Demography* 45, no. 1 (2008): 55–77.

23. These findings are also replicated when limiting analysis to cohorts 0 and 9, which have maximally similar predictor measurement ages and maximal overlap in observed arrest ages.

24. Low self-control similarly predicted arrest in both the full sample and within each cohort, consistent with past research and supporting construct validity. Despite differences in measurement items and ages, the behaviorally based measure of self-control is thus validated in the data. Neil and Sampson, "The Birth Lottery of History," 1145.

25. Because nearly half the sample (46 percent) has a value of "not true" (indicating high self-control) for all three items, I define self-control at age seventeen simply in two categories of high and low, though results are similar for a three-category scale of high ("not true"), medium (at least one response of "somewhat true"), and low self-control (two or more reports of "very true").

26. Rubén G. Rumbaut and Walter A. Ewing, *The Myth of Immigrant Criminality and the Paradox of Assimilation: Incarceration Rates among Native and Foreign-Born Men* (Washington, DC; American Immigration Law Foundation, 2007); Robert J. Sampson, "Immigration and America's Urban Revival," *The American Prospect* 26, no. 3 (2015): 20–24.

6. DISENTANGLING MECHANISMS OF CHANGE

1. For a history of policing in Chicago in this era, especially during the administration of Mayor Richard D. Daley, see John Hagan, Bill McCarthy, and Daniel Herda, *Chicago's Reckoning: Racism, Politics, and the Deep History of Policing in an American City* (Oxford, UK: Oxford University Press, 2022). For other administrations, see Wesley Skogan, *Stop and Frisk and the Politics of Crime in Chicago* (New York: Oxford University Press, 2023).

2. Steven Pinker, *The Better Angels of Our Nature: Why Violence Has Declined* (New York: Penguin, 2012).

3. Michelle Alexander, *The New Jim Crow: Mass Incarceration in the Age of Colorblindness* (New York: New Press, 2012).

4. Michael Tonry, *Malign Neglect: Race, Crime, and Punishment in America* (New York: Oxford University Press, 1995). For a review, see Jeremy Travis, Bruce Western, and Steve Redburn, eds., *The Growth of Incarceration in the United States: Exploring Causes and Consequences* (Washington, DC: National Academies Press, 2014), chapter 3.

5. Jason P. Robey, Michael Massoglia, and Michael T. Light, "A Generational Shift: Race and the Declining Lifetime Risk of Imprisonment," *Demography* 60, no. 4 (2023): 977–1003; Christopher Muller and Alexander F. Roehrkasse, "Falling Racial Inequality and Rising Educational Inequality in US Prison Admissions for Drug, Violent, and Property Crimes," *Proceedings of the National Academy of Sciences* 122, no. 4 (2025): e2418077122.

6. While revealing, this finding doesn't show how large the arrest gap would be if drug charging practices remained constant over time. If drug-war policing had remained consistent, the 1990s cohorts would have experienced drug arrest rates similar to the 1980s cohorts. By combining this counterfactual with the 1990s cohorts' observed non-drug arrests, we can compare the resulting hypothetical total arrest rate to the observed rate for the 1980s cohorts. This hypothetical analysis shows potential arrest rates for the 1980s cohort would be more than 40 percent higher than the 1990s cohort—a large gap, but much smaller than the actual numbers, wherein the 1980s cohort rates are about double the 1990s cohort rates. This means that changing drug arrest patterns explain the majority of the gap but not nearly all of the overall cohort arrest gap between ages eighteen and twenty-two.

7. Although I lack comparable cross-cohort measures of drug use in the PHDCN study, recall that correlates of drug use (delinquency / antisocial behavior and low self-control) were controlled in the analyses. See Delbert S. Elliott, David Huizinga, and Scott Menard, *Multiple Problem Youth: Delinquency, Substance Use, and Mental Health Problems* (New York: Springer-Verlag, 1989).

8. John Hudak, *Marijuana: A Short History* (Washington, DC: Brookings Institution Press, 2020).

9. The normalized trends show levels in each year relative to 1995, enabling comparison across measures. National data come from the Monitoring the Future Study; Chicago data from the CDC's Youth Risk Behavior Survey (YRBS). While not specific to the PHDCN sample, both surveys drew representative samples from the same population at the same ages, suggesting PHDCN children likely followed similar drug use trends. Illinois-wide YRBS data yields identical conclusions despite slight differences from Chicago-specific levels.

10. This test examines all drug arrests as an overall indicator of police drug enforcement trends. Available indicators show declining arrests for other drug types. Not shown in the graph is that cocaine use among Chicago youth trended slightly upward after 2010, making the younger cohort quite similar to older cohorts in usage patterns. Cocaine use among US teens declined after 2007 but stabilized in 2010 and returned to previous levels by 2020. Other drugs, such as amphetamine and heroin, show similar flat trends but with very low usage levels. For further details, see Roland Neil and Robert J. Sampson, "The Birth Lottery of History: Arrest over the Life Course of Multiple Cohorts Coming of Age, 1995–2018," *American Journal of Sociology* 126, no. 5 (2021): 1127–1178.

11. Highlighted here and in the following graphs (and in Chapter 7) are birth cohort years 1981, 1984, 1987, and 1996, because overall they represent the modal birth years for each age cohort (although, for the youngest cohort, late 1995 is the median date of birth). Using other adjacent years does not change the pattern.

12. James Q. Wilson and George Kelling, "Broken Windows: The Police and Neighborhood Safety," *The Atlantic,* March 1982, 29–38.

13. Bernard Harcourt, *Illusion of Order: The False Promise of Broken Windows Policing* (Cambridge, MA: Harvard University Press, 2001), 2; Issa Kohler-Hausmann, *Misdemeanorland: Criminal Courts and Social Control in an Age of Broken Windows Policing* (Princeton, NJ: Princeton University Press, 2018), 1. More generally, see Elizabeth Hinton, *From the War on Poverty to the War on Crime: The Making of Mass Incarceration in America* (Cambridge, MA: Harvard University Press, 2016).

14. Ames Grawert and James Cullen, "Fact Sheet: Stop and Frisk's Effect on Crime in New York City," Brennan Center for Justice, October 2016.

15. On New York City, see Joscha Legewie and Jeffrey Fagan, "Aggressive Policing and the Educational Performance of Minority Youth," *American Sociological Review* 84, no. 2 (2019): 220–247; Andrew Gelman, Jeffrey Fagan, and Alex Kiss, "An Analysis of the New York City Police Department's 'Stop-and-Frisk' Policy in the Context of Claims of Racial Bias," *Journal of the American Statistical Association* 102, no. 479 (2007): 813–823. The definitive analysis of stop and frisk in Chicago is Skogan, *Stop and Frisk.*

16. McCarthy merits particular interest because despite promoting "smart policing" with data, no annual CPD reports were published during his tenure. The Chicago data used in this chapter come from self-reported police information available on the CPD website. These reports date back to 1965 with annual releases except during McCarthy's time as chief.

17. Janet Lauritsen, Maribeth Rezey, and Karen Heimer, "When Choice of Data Matters: Analyses of U.S. Crime Trends, 1973–2012," *Journal of Quantitative Criminology* 32, no. 3 (2015): 335–355. Unfortunately, such victimization data are not available over time for smaller jurisdictions like states and cities.

18. Reginald Hardwick, "By the Numbers: Chicago Murder Count through the Years," *Illinois Public Media News,* July 9, 2020. Chapter 7 presents homicide trends and firearm violence in more detail.

19. While some respondents moved out of Chicago proper after the study began, they remained predominantly within Illinois, particularly metropolitan Chicago. Violent and property crime rates for Illinois as a whole track Chicago trends almost exactly (correlation ≈ 0.99).

20. This analysis extends the counterfactual exercise in Neil and Sampson, "The Birth Lottery of History," 1165–1166.

21. Policing changes are discussed here in detail because the focus is on cross-cohort arrest patterns, and police are the institution most proximate to that process.

Changes in both policing and incarceration may affect aggregate crime rates through deterrence or incapacitation. The research consensus suggests that higher incarceration rates led to modest crime reductions, accounting for approximately 10 percent of the crime decline (Travis, Western, and Redburn, *The Growth of Incarceration*). Improved policing likely explained more of the crime drop than rising incarceration, though a review of estimates suggest they vary considerably. See National Academies of Sciences, Engineering, and Medicine, *Proactive Policing: Effects on Crime and Communities* (Washington, DC: National Academies Press, 2018).

22. Emily A. Shrider and John Creamer, *Poverty in the United States: 2022* (United States Census Bureau, September 2023).

23. For an earlier analysis of poverty exposure up to 2018 using group-based trajectory models, see Jennifer Candipan and Robert J. Sampson, "Diverging Trajectories of Neighborhood Disadvantage by Race and Birth Cohort from Childhood through Young Adulthood," *PLoS ONE* 8 (2023): e0283641. Figure 6.9 shows mean exposure rates by age and cohort using survey weights, but, as in Candipan and Sampson, the patterns are the same for unweighted trajectories.

24. More formally, we can decompose how much of the difference in exposure to high-poverty neighborhoods from childhood to early adulthood is attributable to race versus life trajectories. Nearly all observed differences between white and Black sample members across ages are attributable to baseline neighborhood poverty differences (age nine), with only a small percentage explained by trajectory differences (though trajectory differences explain more for the younger Black-white cohort than for the older one). Similar patterns emerge for Hispanic-white and Hispanic-Black poverty differences. Candipan and Sampson, "Diverging Trajectories."

25. Edward L. Glaeser, *Triumph of the City: How Our Greatest Invention Makes Us Richer, Smarter, Greener, Healthier, and Happier* (New York: Penguin, 2011).

26. Robert J. Chaskin and Mark L. Joseph, *Integrating the Inner City: The Promise and Perils of Mixed-Income Public Housing Transformations* (Chicago: University of Chicago Press, 2015).

27. Analysis of changes in immigrant composition like Figure 6.9 shows relatively parallel patterns across birth cohorts.

28. Robert J. Sampson, "Open Doors Don't Invite Criminals: Is Increased Immigration Behind the Drop in Crime?," *New York Times,* March 11, 2006; Robert J. Sampson, *Great American City: Chicago and the Enduring Neighborhood Effect,* 2nd ed. (Chicago: University of Chicago Press [2012] 2024), 251–260.

29. For a review of the lead exposure literature, and of the crime-decline hypothesis, see Christopher Muller, Robert J. Sampson, and Alix Winter, "Environmental Inequality: The Social Causes and Consequences of Lead Exposure," *Annual Review of Sociology* 44, no. 1 (2018): 263–282. Toxic inequality is further discussed in Chapter 7.

30. Anthony Higney, Nick Hanley, and Mirko Moro, "The Lead-Crime Hypothesis: A Meta-Analysis," *Regional Science and Urban Economics* 97 (2022): 103826.

31. Patrick T. Sharkey, Gerard Torrats-Espinosa, and Delaram Takyar, "Community and the Crime Decline: The Causal Effect of Local Nonprofits on Violent Crime," *American Sociological Review* 82, no. 6 (2017): 1214–1240.

32. See Charles C. Lanfear, "Collective Efficacy and the Built Environment," *Criminology* 60, no. 2 (2022): 370–396.

33. Sampson, *Great American City,* 394–404; Wesley Skogan, "Reflections on Declining Crime in Chicago" (Institute of Policy Research Working Paper, 2007); Wesley Skogan, "Community Organizations and Crime," in *Crime and Justice,* ed. Michael Tonry and Norval Morris (Chicago: University of Chicago Press, 1988). For an example of how cities are trying to evaluate community-based alternatives to policing, see Mark Obbie, "A City Tries to Measure the Violence It's Preventing," *New York Times,* April 22, 2024.

34. David Weisburd, Elizabeth R. Groff, and Sue-Ming Yang, *The Criminology of Place: Street Segments and Our Understanding of the Crime Problem* (New York: Oxford University Press, 2012); Engineering National Academies of Sciences, Engineering, and Medicine, *Proactive Policing: Effects on Crime and Communities* (Washington, DC: National Academies Press, 2018).

35. This is a classic concern of routine activity theory in criminology, which examines the convergence in time and space of motivated offenders, guardianship capacity, and suitable targets. Lawrence E. Cohen and Marcus Felson, "Social Change and Crime Rate Trends: A Routine Activity Approach," *American Sociological Review* 44, no. 4 (1979): 588–608.

36. For further discussion of the technology hypothesis and crime rate changes, see Eric Baumer, María B. Vélez, and Richard Rosenfeld, "Bringing Crime Trends Back into Criminology: A Critical Assessment of the Literature and a Blueprint for Future Inquiry," *Annual Review of Criminology* 1 (2018): 39–61.

37. For an account of unstructured socializing and youth crime, see D. Wayne Osgood, "Delinquency, Unstructured Socializing, and Social Change: The Rise and Fall of a Teen Culture of Independence," *Criminology* 61, no. 4 (2023): 681–704. See also Eric Baumer, Kelsey Cundiff, and Liying Luo, "The Contemporary Transformation of American Youth: An Analysis of Change in the Prevalence of Delinquency, 1991–2015," *Criminology* 59, no. 1 (2021): 109–136.

38. Andrew Perrin, "Social Media Usage: 2005–2015" (Pew Research Center, October 2015). As the prevalence of screen-based leisure activities has grown dramatically for teenagers, their social lives increasingly exist online. According to one leading critic of this trend, the continuous use of screens and social media "has enormous implications for cognition, addiction, and the wearing smooth of paths in the brain, especially during the sensitive period of puberty." Jonathan Haidt, *The Anxious Generation: How the Great Rewiring of Childhood Is Causing an Epidemic of Mental Illness* (New York: Penguin Press, 2024): 34, 118–120.

39. Baumer, Cundiff, and Luo, "The Contemporary Transformation of American Youth."

40. For a focus on explaining and forecasting aggregate crime trends, see Richard Rosenfeld, *Crime Dynamics: Why Crime Rates Change over Time* (New York: Cambridge University Press, 2024).

41. John H. Laub and Robert J. Sampson, "Life Course and Developmental Criminology: Looking Back, Moving Forward," *Journal of Developmental and Life-Course Criminology* 6 (2020): 158–171; Jean Twenge and Heejung Park, "The Decline in Adult Activities among U.S. Adolescents, 1976–2016," *Child Development* 90, no. 2 (2019): 638–654.

7. GUNS, VIOLENCE, AND POISONED DEVELOPMENT

1. Patrick T. Sharkey and Robert J. Sampson, "Violence, Cognition, and Neighborhood Inequality in America," in *Social Neuroscience: Brain, Mind, and Society,* ed. Russell K. Schutt, Larry J. Seidman, and Matcheri S. Keshavan (Cambridge, MA: Harvard University Press, 2015).

2. Patrick T. Sharkey, "The Acute Effect of Local Homicides on Children's Cognitive Performance," *Proceedings of the National Academy of Sciences* 107 (2010): 11733–11738.

3. David S. Kirk and Margaret Hardy, "Acute and Enduring Consequences of Exposure to Violence on Youth Mental Health and Aggression," *Justice Quarterly* 31 (2014): 539–567.

4. Patrick T. Sharkey, Nicole Tirado-Strayer, Andrew V. Papachristos, and C. Cybele Raver, "The Effect of Local Violence on Children's Attention and Impulse Control," *American Journal of Public Health* 102, no. 12 (2012): 2287–2293. See also Sharkey's broader discussion of exposure to violence in *Uneasy Peace: The Great Crime Decline, the Renewal of City Life, and the Next War on Violence* (New York: W. W. Norton, 2018).

5. Julia Burdick-Will, Jens Ludwig, Stephen W. Raudenbush, Robert J. Sampson, Lisa Sanbonmatsu, and Patrick Sharkey, "Converging Evidence for Neighborhood Effects on Children's Test Scores: An Experimental, Quasi-Experimental, and Observational Comparison," In *Whither Opportunity? Rising Inequality, Schools, and Children's Life Chances,* ed. Greg Duncan and Richard Murnane (New York: Russell Sage Foundation, 2011), 255–276.

6. This argument aligns with evidence showing poverty and scarcity's effects on short-sighted decision-making and time-discounting. See Johannes Haushofer and Ernst Fehr, "On the Psychology of Poverty," *Science* 344 (2014): 862–867.

7. This section and Figures 7.1 and 7.2 draw from Charles C. Lanfear, Rebecca Bucci, David S. Kirk, and Robert J. Sampson, "Inequalities in Exposure to Firearm Violence by Race, Sex, and Birth Cohort from Childhood to Age 40, 1995–2021," *JAMA Network Open* 6, no. 5 (2023): e2312465. Because I am primarily interested in cumulative prevalence estimates here, these figures are weighted to reflect population estimates based on PHDCN+ sampling design and attrition. The patterns,

especially for witnessing shootings (a more common event with more precise estimates), nonetheless mirror the unweighted patterns in the JAMA paper.

8. As noted in Chapter 3, the original data collection scheme rotated across several years at each wave. For example, members of the nine-year-old cohort were born between 1986 and 1988. I typically refer to modal birth year for each cohort. Note that being shot is rare, limiting precision in estimating cohort differences that are substantively but not statistically different.

9. Being shot by eighteen and witnessing a shooting by eighteen are both significant predictors of death after eighteen at conventional levels ($p < .01$ for being shot and for witnessing), constituting a very small probability that this finding would be obtained if there were null relationships between violence exposure and death. Death rates reflect individuals surviving to at least eighteen, using sampling and attrition weights. Unweighted rates are nearly identical: 3.3 percent vs. 15 percent for being shot before eighteen, and 2.3 percent vs. 5.5 percent for witnessing shootings before eighteen in the 1981 and 1984 cohorts.

10. The hazard ratio of combined violence exposure before eighteen (being shot or witnessing shooting), calculated using a Cox Proportional Hazard Model without sampling or attrition weights, was significant at the $p < .05$ level for the 1981 cohort and the $p < .10$ level for the 1984 cohort. Incorporating weights led to similar hazard ratios but weaker significance levels. No additional controls were included because the focus is on differences between 1981 and 1984 cohorts in violence exposure. These cohorts showed no significant differences in key variables except neighborhood poverty percentage, which didn't significantly relate to mortality.

11. These mortality data aren't subject to attrition as they cover deaths through age forty (2023) for all wave 1 respondents. When comparing overlapping years (ages fifteen to forty), weighted death rates were 3.5 percent for the 1981 cohort and 4.1 percent for the 1984 cohort. Homicide rates in this age range were 0.27 percent for the 1984 cohort versus 1.41 percent for the 1981 cohort, a significant difference ($p < .01$) after adjusting for race and sex.

12. Charles C. Lanfear, David S. Kirk, and Robert J. Sampson, "Dual Pathways of Concealed Gun Carrying and Use from Adolescence to Adulthood over a 25-Year Era of Change," *Science Advances* 10 (2024): eadp8915.

13. Unlike measures of witnessing shootings or being shot, the gun use measure for the 1984, 1987, and 1996 cohorts is limited to the 2021 wave 5 sample, restricting comparative analyses. For the fifteen-year-old cohort (born 1981), wave 3 data allow measuring self-defense gun use before age twenty-one. Using a gun in self-defense by twenty-one is associated with a threefold increase in later mortality risk in this cohort, though this doesn't reach statistical significance, likely due to the imprecision of this one-time measure limited to self-defense.

14. Note that the age curve in Figure 7.3 and the year curve in Figure 7.4 do not necessarily align precisely because the year estimates were calculated from respondents of different ages, even within cohorts.

15. For more details, see Lanfear, Kirk, and Sampson, "Dual Pathways of Concealed Gun Carrying and Use," 6–7.

16. Christopher Muller, Robert J. Sampson, and Alix Winter, "Environmental Inequality: The Social Causes and Consequences of Lead Exposure," *Annual Review of Sociology* 44 (2018): 263–282.

17. For example, see Ellen Gabler, "How 2 Industries Stymied Justice for Young Lead Paint Victims," *New York Times,* March 29, 2022; Emily Anthes, "More Childhood Lead Poisoning Is a Side Effect of Covid Lockdowns," *New York Times,* March 11, 2021; Michael Hawthorne, "Brain-Damaging Lead Found in Tap Water from Most Illinois Communities during the Past 6 Years, Tribune Analysis Finds," *Chicago Tribune,* March 19, 2021.

18. Michael J. McFarland, Matt E. Hauer, and Aaron Reuben, "Half of US Population Exposed to Adverse Lead Levels in Early Childhood," *Proceedings of the National Academy of Sciences* 119, no. 11 (2022): e2118631119; Robert J. Sampson, "Legacies of Inequality, Legacy Lead Exposures, and Improving Population Well-Being," *Proceedings of the National Academy of Sciences* 119, no. 14 (2022): e2202401119.

19. Yvette Cabrera, "The Lead Crisis: Tackling an Invisible, Dangerous Neurotoxin," ThinkProgress, July 15, 2017.

20. Yvette Cabrera, "Ghosts of Polluters Past," *Grist,* January 13, 2022. See also Scott Frickel and James R. Elliott, *Sites Unseen: Uncovering Hidden Hazards in American Cities* (New York: Russell Sage Foundation, 2018).

21. Shannon Heffernan, "EPA Cleans up Lead Contaminated Lot in Pilsen," WBEZ Chicago, June 25, 2013; Michael Hawthorne, "Cleanup of Lead-Polluted Yards Begins in Pilsen," *Chicago Tribune,* December 26, 2016.

22. Abby Goodnough, "Their Soil Toxic, 1,100 Indiana Residents Scramble to Find New Homes," *New York Times,* August 30, 2016, A1.

23. Jessica Sauve-Syed, "Lead Exposure and Student Outcomes: A Study of Flint Schools," *Health Economics* 33, no. 3 (2024): 432–448.

24. See the review in Muller, Sampson, and Winter, "Environmental Inequality." See also Anna Aizer and Janet Currie, "Lead and Juvenile Delinquency: New Evidence from Linked Birth, School, and Crime Records," *Review of Economics and Statistics* 101, no. 4 (2019): 575–587.

25. For further discussion, see Alix S. Winter and Robert J. Sampson, "From Lead Exposure in Early Childhood to Adolescent Health: A Chicago Birth Cohort," *American Journal of Public Health* 107, no. 9 (2017): 1496–1501; Sampson and Winter, "Poisoned Development."

26. Geoffrey T. Wodtke, Sagi Ramaj, and Jared Schachner, "Toxic Neighborhoods: The Effects of Concentrated Poverty and Environmental Lead Contamination on Early Childhood Development," *Demography* 59, no. 4 (2022): 1275–1298.

27. Robert Manduca and Robert J. Sampson, "Punishing and Toxic Neighborhood Environments Independently Predict the Intergenerational Social Mobility of

Black and White Children," *Proceedings of the National Academy of Sciences* 116, no. 16 (2019): 7772–7777.

28. Robert Manduca and Robert J. Sampson, "Childhood Exposure to Polluted Neighborhood Environments and Intergenerational Income Mobility, Teenage Birth, and Incarceration in the USA," *Population and Environment* 42, no. 4 (2021): 501–523. For other work showing the deleterious effects of pollution on well-being, see Joshua Graff Zivin and Matthew Neidell, "Air Pollution's Hidden Impacts: Exposure Can Affect Labor Productivity and Human Capital," *Science* 359, no. 6371 (2018): 39–40; Adam Isen, Maya Rossin-Slater, and W. Reed Walker, "Every Breath You Take—Every Dollar You'll Make: The Long-Term Consequences of the Clean Air Act of 1970," *Journal of Political Economy* 125, no. 3 (2017): 848–902; Geoffrey T. Wodtke, Kerry Ard, Clair Bullock, Kailey White, and Betsy Priem, "Concentrated Poverty, Ambient Air Pollution, and Child Cognitive Development," *Science Advances* 8, no. 48 (2022): eadd0285.

29. Ted Schwaba, Wiebke Bleidorn, Christopher J. Hopwood, Jochen E. Gebauer, P. Jason Rentfrow, Jeff Potter, and Samuel D. Gosling, "The Impact of Childhood Lead Exposure on Adult Personality: Evidence from the United States, Europe, and a Large-Scale Natural Experiment," *Proceedings of the National Academy of Sciences* 118, no. 29 (2021): e2020104118; Aaron Reuben, Avshalom Caspi, Daniel W. Belsky, Jonathan Broadbent, Honalee Harrington, Karen Sugden, Renate M. Houts, Sandhya Ramrakha, Richie Poulton, and Terrie E. Moffitt, "Association of Childhood Blood Lead Levels with Cognitive Function and Socioeconomic Status at Age 38 Years and with IQ Change and Socioeconomic Mobility between Childhood and Adulthood," *JAMA* 317, no. 12 (2017): 1244–1251.

30. James J. Feigenbaum and Christopher Muller, "Lead Exposure and Violent Crime in the Early Twentieth Century," *Explorations in Economic History* 62 (2016): 51–86; Joseph R. McConnell, Nathan Chellman, Andreas Plach, Sophia M. Wensman, Gill Plunkett, Andreas Stohl, Nicole-Kristine Smith, Bo Møllesøe Vinther, Dorthe Dahl-Jensen, Jørgen Peder Steffensen, Diedrich Fritzsche, Sandra O. Camara-Brugger, Brandon T. McDonald, and Andrew I. Wilson, "Pan-European Atmospheric Lead Pollution, Enhanced Blood Lead Levels, and Cognitive Decline from Roman-Era Mining and Smelting," *Proceedings of the National Academy of Sciences* 122, no. 3 (2025): e2419630121.

31. For details, see Robert J. Sampson and Alix Winter, "The Racial Ecology of Lead Poisoning: Toxic Inequality in Chicago Neighborhoods, 1995–2013," *Du Bois Review: Social Science Research on Race* 13 (2016): 261–283. See also Andrew Zaleski, "The Unequal Burden of Urban Lead," Bloomberg CityLab, January 2, 2020.

32. Manduca and Sampson, "Punishing and Toxic Neighborhood Environments Independently Predict."

33. Data on lead exposure by race that could be geo-coded to each neighborhood in Chicago were not available after 2013.

34. Anna Aizer, Janet M. Currie, Peter Simon, and Patrick Vivier, "Do Low Levels of Blood Lead Reduce Children's Future Test Scores?," *American Economic Journal: Applied Economics* 10, no. 1 (2018): 307–341.

35. Robert J. Brulle and David N. Pellow, "Environmental Justice: Human Health and Environmental Inequalities," *Annual Review of Public Health* 27 (2006): 103–124.

36. Amanda Friedman, "Trump Removes Gun Violence Public Health Advisory," Politico, March 17, 2025.

8. THE REIGN OF PROPENSITY AND THE CHARACTER TRAP

1. Robert J. Sampson and L. Ash Smith, "Rethinking Criminal Propensity and Character: Cohort Inequalities and the Power of Social Change," *Crime and Justice* 50 (2021): 13–74.

2. Michael R. Gottfredson and Travis Hirschi, *A General Theory of Crime* (Stanford, CA: Stanford University Press, 1990), 177.

3. Gottfredson and Hirschi, *A General Theory of Crime*, 90. Though Gottfredson and Hirschi advocate for behavioral indicators of low self-control, as analyzed in this book, many studies use attitudinal scales measuring risk-seeking, physical activities, self-centeredness, and temper. See, for example, Bruce J. Arneklev, Lori Elis, and Sandra Medlicott, "Testing the General Theory of Crime: Comparing the Effects of 'Imprudent Behavior' and an Attitudinal Indicator of 'Low Self-Control,'" *Western Criminology Review* 7 (2006): 41–55, 44.

4. Callie H. Burt, "Self-Control and Crime: Beyond Gottfredson and Hirschi's (1990) Theory," *Annual Review of Criminology* 3 (2020): 43–73. Burt argues that self-control involves more external influences than previously recognized, including neighborhood poverty and crime, reflecting complex interactions between situational stimuli and individual dispositions. She defines self-control as individuals' ability to engage in "effortful inhibition of impulse" by "forgoing short-term pleasures that conflict with enduring higher-order goals" (45, 59). In a later work, Gottfredson and Hirschi acknowledge that "life circumstances" like school completion, employment prospects, and residence may affect criminal activity through mutual interactions with self-control capabilities (*A General Theory of Crime*, 75–77). For other reviews of self-control theory, see Travis C. Pratt and Francis T. Cullen, "The Empirical Status of Gottfredson and Hirschi's General Theory of Crime: A Meta-Analysis," *Criminology* 38 (2000): 931–964; Erich Goode, *Out of Control: Assessing the General Theory of Crime* (Stanford, CA: Stanford University Press, 2008); Carter Hay and Ryan Meldrum, *Self-Control and Crime over the Life Course* (London: Sage Publications, 2016).

5. For example, see Ronald L. Simons, Christine Johnson, Rand D. Conger, and Glen Elder Jr., "A Test of Latent Trait Versus Life-Course Perspectives on the

Stability of Adolescent Antisocial Behavior," *Criminology* 36, no. 2 (1998): 217–243; Daniel Nagin and Raymond Paternoster, "Population Heterogeneity and State Dependence: State of the Evidence and Directions for Future Research," *Journal of Quantitative Criminology* 16 (2000): 117–144. Other examples of latent traits posited in a prominent text include high impulsivity and low conscience; James Q. Wilson and Richard Herrnstein, *Crime and Human Nature* (New York: Simon and Schuster, 1985). Alleged psychopathic personalities—"characterized by distinctive affective, behavioral, lifestyle, and interpersonal features"—constitute another such trait, particularly common among "serious, violent, and chronic" criminals. See Bryanna H. Fox, Wesley G. Jennings, and David P. Farrington, "Bringing Psychopathy into Developmental and Life-Course Criminology Theories and Research," *Journal of Criminal Justice* 43 (2015): 274–289, 276.

6. See Robert J. Sampson, "The Characterological Imperative: On Heckman, Humphries, and Kautz's *the Myth of Achievement Tests: The GED and the Role of Character in American Life*," *Journal of Economic Literature* 54 (2016): 493–513, 495, 509, on the age-graded theory.

7. Per-Olof H. Wikström, Dietrich Oberwittler, Kyle Treiber, and Beth Hardie, *Breaking Rules: The Social and Situational Dynamics of Young People's Urban Crime* (Oxford, UK: Oxford University Press, 2012), 15, 140–141. For a later analysis of longitudinal data from England that emphasizes the situational and moral aspects of character, see Per-Olof Wikström, Kyle Treiber, and Gabriela Roman, *Character, Circumstances, and Criminal Careers: Towards a Dynamic Developmental and Life-Course Criminology* (Oxford, UK: Oxford University Press, 2024).

8. Terrie E. Moffitt, "Male Antisocial Behaviour in Adolescence and Beyond," *Nature Human Behaviour* 2, no. 3 (2018): 177–186, 177. See also Terrie E. Moffitt, "Adolescence-Limited and Life-Course-Persistent Antisocial Behavior: A Developmental Taxonomy," *Psychological Review* 100, no. 4 (1993): 674–701.

9. David Farrington, "The Integrated Cognitive Antisocial Potential (ICAP) Theory: Past, Present, and Future," *Journal of Developmental and Life-Course Criminology* 6 (2020): 172–187, 178.

10. Daniel Nagin and Raymond Paternoster, "On the Relationship of Past and Future Participation in Delinquency," *Criminology* 29 (1991): 163–190.

11. Travis Hirschi, *Causes of Delinquency* (New Brunswick, NJ: Transaction Publishers, 2002 [1969]), 3.

12. Thomas J. Reed, "Trial by Propensity: Admission of Other Criminal Acts Evidenced in Federal Criminal Trials," *University of Cincinnati Law Review* 50 (1981): 713–739. Propensity evidence may encompass everything from prior bad acts or misconduct (legal or illegal), to prior arrests, to prior convictions. See Nikos Harris, "Evidence of Propensity in a Criminal Proceeding: Admissible, Inadmissible, or Something in Between," *Advocate* 57, no. 4 (1999): 563–570. Courts, too, have defined it rather leniently—for instance, as "any kind of evidence of a defendant's evil character to establish a probability of his guilt" (Michelson v. United States, 335

US 469, 475–476, 1948); or any "propensity to commit acts similar to those charged" (United States v. LeMay, 260 F.3d 1018, 1033 (9th Cir. 2001)).

13. Allan G. King and Syeeda S. Amin, "The Propensity to Stereotype as Inadmissible Character Evidence," *ABA Journal of Labor and Employment Law* 27 (2011): 23–42, 24.

14. See also Charles A. Wright and Kenneth W. Graham, *Federal Practice and Procedure* (Eagan, MN: West, 1978), 346.

15. Josephine Ross, "'He Looks Guilty': Reforming Good Character Evidence to Undercut the Presumption of Guilt," *University of Pittsburgh Law Review* 65 (2004): 227–279; Thomas J. Reed, "The Development of the Propensity Rule in Federal Criminal Causes 1840–1975," *University of Cincinnati Law Review* 51 (1982): 299–325, 306. These exceptions are extensive. In Langbord v. US Department of Treasury (832 F.3d 170, 193 (3rd Cir. 2016)), the court admitted propensity evidence to support claims that the defendant concealed coins because he had previously forfeited illegal coins. Similarly, in United States v. Beechum (582 F.2d 898 (5th Cir. 1978)), evidence of previously stolen credit cards was admitted in a stolen silver dollar case because it "lessened the likelihood" of innocent intent—leading Judge Goldberg (920) to dissent: "How this differs from reasoning that the defendant has a 'propensity' to act with evil intent . . . is beyond reason."

16. Ross, "'He Looks Guilty,'" 247. The rule governing the exceptions to the propensity rule—Rule 404(b)—is so widely invoked that it "is the most litigated Federal Rule of Evidence," according to Daniel J. Capra and Liesa L. Richter, "Character Assassination: Amending Federal Rule of Evidence 404(B) to Protect Criminal Defendants," *Columbia Law Review* 118 (2018): 769–832.

17. Richard B. Kuhns, "The Propensity to Misunderstand the Character of Specific Acts Evidence," *Iowa Law Review* 66 (1981): 777–810, 789. See also David Hamer, "The Legal Structure of Propensity Evidence," *International Journal of Evidence and Proof* 20 (2016): 135–161, 141.

18. See Note, "Procedural Protections of the Criminal Defendant: A Reevaluation of the Privilege against Self-Incrimination and the Rule Excluding Evidence of Propensity to Commit Crime," *Harvard Law Review* 78 (1964): 426–451; David Ring, "Rush to Judgment: Criminal Propensity Clothed as Credibility Evidence in the Post-Proposition 8 Era of California Criminal Law," *Whittier Law Review* 15 (1994): 241–269, 241.

19. United States v. Foskey, 636 F. 2d 517, 523 (DC Cir. 1980).

20. Mike Redmayne, *Character in the Criminal Trial* (New York: Oxford University Press, 2015), 6; John Henry Wigmore, *A Treatise on the System of Evidence in Trials at Common Law: Including the Statutes and Judicial Decisions of All Jurisdictions of the United States,* vol. 3 (Boston: Little, Brown, 1904).

21. H. Richard Uviller, "Evidence of Character to Prove Conduct: Illusion, Illogic, and Injustice in the Courtroom," *University of Pennsylvania Law Review* 130 (1982): 845–891.

22. John Rawls, *A Theory of Justice* (Cambridge, MA: Harvard University Press, 1971 [1999]), 277, 89. In this sense, Rawls is similar to Gottfredson and Hirschi's self-control theory, which simultaneously recognizes and brackets the external environment.

23. Some state courts have expressly equated character with personality. For example, Freeman v. State, 486 P.2d 967, 972 (Alaska 1971).

24. Barrett J. Anderson, "Recognizing Character: A New Perspective on Character Evidence," *Yale Law Journal* 121 (2012): 1912–1968, 1915–1916. He also argues that courts fail to distinguish between character and other propensity qualities like "habits, mental illnesses, genetic attributes, skills, abilities, or personality traits." *Black's Law Dictionary* (9th ed.) similarly defines character evidence vaguely as that "regarding someone's general personality traits or propensities, of a praiseworthy or blameworthy nature; evidence of a person's moral standing in a community" (St. Paul, MN: West, 2009), 636.

25. Miguel A. Mendez, "Character Evidence Reconsidered: People Do Not Seem to Be Predictable Characters," *Hastings Law Journal* 49, no. 3 (1998): 871–894, 893.

26. Character criminalization has evolved with changing ideas about identity, responsibility, and punishment. The rise in status offense legislation, for example— similar, in its assumption of a stable personality, to three-strikes laws or dangerous offender statutes—reflects these developments. Nicola Lacey, *In Search of Criminal Responsibility: Ideas, Interests, and Institutions* (Oxford, UK: Oxford University Press, 2016), 40, 47.

27. United States Sentencing Commission, *Special Report to the Congress: Mandatory Minimum Penalties in the Federal Criminal Justice System,* August 1991, 24, https://www.ojp.gov/pdffiles1/Digitization/137910NCJRS.pdf.

28. California's "Three Strikes Law" (1994) assumes three-time offenders are likely to reoffend yet allows courts to determine whether "in light of the nature and circumstances of present felonies and prior convictions, and particulars of background, character and prospects, the defendant may be deemed outside the . . . spirit [of the Law] in whole or in part" (People v. Williams, 948 P.2d 429, 1998).

29. Donald J. Black and Abert J. Reiss Jr., "Police Control of Juveniles," *American Sociological Review* 35 (1970): 63–77.

30. Redmayne, *Character in the Criminal Trial.*

31. Mirko Bagaric and Kumar Amarasekara, "The Prejudice against Similar Fact Evidence," *International Journal of Evidence and Proof* 5 (2001): 71–98, 93.

32. Character considerations appear in bail laws in in the District of Columbia (DC Code § 23-1322(e)), Indiana (Ind. Code Ann. § 35-33-8-4 (West)), New York (NY Crim. Proc. Law § 510.30 (McKinney)), and Wisconsin (Wis. Stat. Ann. § 969.01 (West)). Additionally, pretrial risk assessment instruments—a burgeoning algorithmic technology now at use in most US states—often take into account considerations of a defendant's character (typically criminal records, but also "antisocial"

behavioral histories, antisocial peers, "criminal thinking," and socialization failures), in outputting a risk score that recommends release or detention to the presiding judge. Bernard E. Harcourt, *Against Prediction: Profiling, Policing, and Punishing in an Actuarial Age* (Chicago: University of Chicago Press, 2007); Northpointe, *Practitioners Guide to COMPAS,* August 17, 2012, https://njoselson.github.io/pdfs/FieldGuide2 _081412.pdf. D. A. Andrews, James Bonta, J. Stephen Wormith, Lina Guzzo, Albert Brews, Jill Rettinger, and Rob Rowe, "Sources of Variability in Estimates of Predictive Validity: A Specification with Level of Service General Risk and Need," *Criminal Justice and Behavior* 38, no. 5 (2011): 413–432.

33. Dunn v. Edwards, 569 S.E.2d 525, 526 (Ga., 2002).

34. Commenting on the 2018 Bail Reform Act of Delaware, an editor notes: "The term 'character' is subjective, has no reliable benchmark, and overlaps with many factors already taken into account by a defendant's criminal record, which is a major input [already.] [A]ny consideration of that factor is suspect" (DE Interim Special Rules of Crim. R., Schedule 5.2B). Moreover, the rise in police and prosecutors' discretionary powers, from the late twentieth into the early twenty-first centuries, has likewise enhanced the odds that character evidence is invoked in the pretrial stages of criminal justice; Lacey, *In Search of Criminal Responsibility.* The rise in plea bargaining enables prosecutors' unchecked assumptions about criminal character to permeate criminal convictions—without even the check of a democratically accountable trial jury.

35. Roughly 97 percent of criminal cases end in guilty pleas and therefore never go to trial. Innocence Staff, *Report: Guilty Pleas on the Rise, Criminal Trials on the Decline,* Innocence Project, August 7, 2018, https://innocenceproject.org/guilty -pleas-on-the-rise-criminal-trials-on-the-decline/. For these cases, notions of criminal character under law are more salient insofar as they impact recidivist statutes leading to plea deals in the first place, or post-conviction decisions (such as sentencing and parole, which are taken up later).

36. Redmayne, *Character in the Criminal Trial.*

37. Haley v. State, 173 S.W.3d 510, 517 (Tex. Crim. App. 2005); Charles A. Wright and Victor J. Gold, *Federal Practice and Procedure* (Eagan, MN: West, 1993), 6113.

38. Federal Rule of Evidence 406.

39. For example, the prosecutor can inquire into relevant specific instances of the defendant's prior criminal conduct on cross-examination of a defendant-character witness (Federal Rule of Evidence 405(a)). See also Redmayne, *Character in the Criminal Trial.*

40. United States v. Blackwell, 853 F.2d 86, 88 (2nd Cir. 1988).

41. Quoted in Booth v. Maryland, 482 US 496, 497 (1987). There are limits to the admissibility of the victim's character evidence in the case of sex offenses. Rape shield laws, for example, "prohibit the accused from raising the sexual 'character' of

the victim in a rape case," notes Aviva Orenstein, "No Bad Men! A Feminist Analysis of Character Evidence in Rape Trials," *Hastings Law Journal* 49, no. 3 (1998): 663–716, 669; see also Fed. R. Evid. 412. Again, however, certain exceptions exist (Fed. R. Evid. 412) such that character judgments may enter the deliberative process, even here.

42. Joe Frankel, "Payne, Victim Impact Statements, and Nearly Two Decades of Devolving Standards of Decency," *N.Y. City Law Review* 12, no. 1 (2008): 87–128. While about victims and not defendants, *Payne* illustrates the pervasiveness of constructs of moral character in the US criminal justice system, and it has raised concerns of wrongful convictions in capital cases—for example, Erin McCampbell, "Tipping the Scales: Seeking Death through Comparative Value Arguments," *Washington and Lee Law Review* 63 (2006): 379–420. *Payne* thereby illustrates the problems with a character-infused criminal justice system—sacrificing accuracy and justice for a moral, character-infused narrative of crime and punishment.

43. Edward J. Imwinkelried, "Undertaking the Task of Reforming the American Character Evidence Prohibition: The Importance of Getting the Experiment Off on the Right Foot," *Fordham Urban Law Journal* 22 (1995): 285–304; David P. Leonard, "In Defense of the Character Evidence Prohibition: Foundations of the Rule against Trial by Character," *Indiana Law Journal* 73 (1998): 1161–1215; James S. Liebman, "Proposed Evidence Rules 413 to 415—Some Problems and Recommendations," *University of Dayton Law Review* 20 (1995): 753–762; Mark A. Sheft, "Federal Rule of Evidence 413: A Dangerous New Frontier," *Criminal Law Review* 33 (1995): 57–87.

44. Robert D. Dodson, "What Went Wrong with Federal Rule of Evidence 609: A Look at How Jurors Really Misuse Prior Conviction Evidence," *North Carolina Central Law Review* 23, no. 1, article 4, https://archives.law.nccu.edu/ncclr/vol23/iss1/4. See also Frankel, "Payne, Victim Impact Statements"; Mendez, "Character Evidence Reconsidered."

45. This may occur through one of two mechanisms: "reasoning prejudice," by which "the fact-finder giv[es] too much weight to bad character evidence" against a defendant; or "moral prejudice," by which "the fact-finder . . . give[s] the correct weight to the evidence, but take[s] a dislike to the defendant on the basis of his past criminal record and therefore convict[s] him when not convinced beyond reasonable doubt that he is guilty"; Redmayne, *Character in the Criminal Trial,* 33. See also Anderson, "Recognizing Character," 1917–1929, which additionally raises the concern of "nullification prejudice," by which jurors may "justify a verdict 'irrespective of guilt'" based on character evidence (good or bad) alone—with potentially discriminatory results (1911).

46. Janice Nadler, "Blaming as a Social Process: The Influence of Character and Moral Emotion on Blame," *Law and Contemporary Problems* 75, no. 2 (2015): 1–31;

Janice Nadler and Mary-Hunter McDonnell, "Moral Character, Motive, and the Psychology of Blame," *Cornell Law Review* 97, no. 2 (2012): 255–304.

47. For examples, see E. Gill Clary and David R. Shaffer, "Effects of Evidence Withholding and a Defendant's Prior Record on Juridic Decisions," *Journal of Social Psychology* 112, no. 2 (1980): 237–245; E. Gill Clary and David R. Shaffer, "Another Look at the Impact of Juror Sentiments toward Defendants on Juridic Decisions," *Journal of Social Psychology* 125, no. 5 (1985): 637–651; Roselle L. Wissler and Michael J. Saks, "On the Inefficacy of Limiting Instructions: When Jurors Use Prior Conviction Evidence to Decide on Guilt," *Law and Human Behavior* 9, no. 1 (1985): 37–48; Edith Greene and Mary Dodge, "The Influence of Prior Record Evidence on Juror Decision Making," *Law and Human Behavior* 19, no. 1 (1995): 67–78.

48. Federal Sentencing Guidelines 2005, 459.

49. 28 U.S.C.A. § 994 (West). Although they can be considered by sentencing judges, such facts "are not ordinarily relevant in determining whether a departure [from the Federal Sentencing Guidelines] is warranted," per the US Sentencing Guidelines Manual §§ 5H1.2, 5H1.5, 5H1.6, 5H1.12, US Sentencing Commission, *US Sentencing Guidelines Manual* (2009). This ambiguity leaves open a path toward discretionary, inconsistent, and discriminatory impositions of sentencing departures based on generally impermissible factors—left almost entirely to the discretion of the trial judge (subject to reversal on appeal). For a review of how sentencing guidelines have evolved in recent decades from mandatory to advisory, see Michael Tonry, "Federal Sentencing 'Reform' since 1984: The Awful as Enemy of the Good," in *Crime and Justice,* vol. 44, *A Review of Research,* ed. Michael Tonry (Chicago: University of Chicago Press, 2015).

50. Morris B. Hoffman, "Booker, Pragmatism and the Moral Jury," *George Mason Law Review* 13 (2005): 455–510. The comparative advantage of the Federal Sentencing Guidelines is "flexibility . . . in making fine distinctions between the relative blameworthiness of various offenders," according to Carissa Byrne Hessick, "Motive's Role in Criminal Punishment," *Southern California Law Review* 80, no. 1 (2006): 89–149. But considering moral blameworthiness is making a character-infused morality judgment in criminal sentencing, as Erin Kelly argues in *The Limits of Blame: Rethinking Punishment and Responsibility* (Cambridge, MA: Harvard University Press, 2018). To be sure, the Federal Sentencing Guidelines did not begin this trend. The indeterminate sentencing scheme that existed prior to the guidelines' enactment was similarly problematic: judges' discretionary determinations regularly turned on evaluations of defendants' characters. See Meg E. Sawyer, "The Prior Convictions Exception: Examining the Continuing Viability of Almendarez-Torres under Alleyne," *Washington and Lee Law Review* 72, no. 1 (2015): 409–466, 413–414.

51. Edward E. Rhine, Joan Petersilia, and Kevin R. Reitz, "The Future of Parole Release," in *Crime and Justice,* vol. 46, *Reinventing American Criminal Justice,* ed. Michael Tonry and Daniel S. Nagin (Chicago: University of Chicago Press, 2017).

52. This may entail a risk assessment that takes into account an offender's history of convictions, incarceration, employment, and institutional adjustment. Those deemed high-risk will likely be deemed ineligible for parole, while high-medium-risk individuals might be granted parole (usually requiring intensive supervision); medium-risk individuals may be granted parole with conditions, and low-risk individuals may be subjected to a standard parole plan. Utah's guidelines specifically build out a "criminal history category," which ranges from "poor" to "excellent," in advising eligibility in parole. Both focus heavily on criminal history in determining "risk." Victoria J. Palacios, "Go and Sin No More: Rationality and Release Decisions by Parole Boards," *South Carolina Law Review* 45, no. 3 (1994): 567–615.

53. Gilbert Harman, "Moral Philosophy Meets Social Psychology: Virtue Ethics and the Fundamental Attribution Error," *Proceedings of the Aristotelian Society* 99 (1999): 315–331.

54. Susan M. Davies, "Evidence of Character to Prove Conduct: A Reassessment of Relevancy," *Criminal Law Bulletin* 27, no. 6 (1991): 504–537, 517.

55. Walter Mischel, *Personality and Assessment* (New York: Wiley, 1968), 177.

56. Justin Sevier, "Legitimizing Character Evidence," *Emory Law Review* 68 (2019): 441–508.

57. Lacey, *In Search of Criminal Responsibility*, 4, 47. As Lacey further notes, this perspective tends to view character as a "settled disposition" that is deserving of "moral indignation" and societal punishment. Bad character also implicates a presumed propensity towards engaging (and reengaging) in such behaviors; and if enough individuals of a particular group are seen to share such criminality, then a given status can be viewed as criminal per se. The result, she argues, is a form of responsibility attribution that focuses on character-essentialism and risk propensity, which in turn influences ideas (social narratives and normative understandings) and societal institutions, including "the political system, economic institutions, courts, trial processes, and judicial systems" (3, 25–26, 36, 40, 82–87, 107–109). Character becomes all-infusing.

9. HOW A CHANGING SOCIETY DEGRADES PREDICTION

1. The reform bill calls for developing an "objective and statistically validated tool" to assess "the risk that a prisoner will recidivate upon release from prison." First Step Act of 2018, Public Law No. 115-391, 132 Stat. 5194, 38.

2. For a critical assessment of the reach of prediction, see Bernard E. Harcourt, *Against Prediction: Profiling, Policing, and Punishing in an Actuarial Age* (Chicago: University of Chicago Press, 2007).

3. Richard Berk, *Machine Learning Risk Assessments in Criminal Justice Settings* (New York: Springer, 2018); Jens Ludwig and Sendhil Mullainathan, "Fragile Algorithms and Fallible Decision-Makers: Lessons from the Justice System," *Journal of Economic Perspectives* 35, no. 4 (2021): 71–96.

4. Erika Montana, Daniel S. Nagin, Roland Neil, and Robert J. Sampson, "Cohort Bias in Predictive Risk Assessments of Future Criminal Justice System Involvement," *Proceedings of the National Academy of Sciences* 120, no. 23 (2023): e2301990120. This chapter summarizes and builds on this work.

5. Zhiyuan "Jerry" Lin, Jongbin Jung, Sharad Goel, and Jennifer Skeem, "The Limits of Human Predictions of Recidivism," *Science Advances* 6, no. 7 (2020): eaaz0652.

6. Rolf Loeber and David P. Farrington, "Young Children Who Commit Crime: Epidemiology, Developmental Origins, Risk Factors, Early Interventions, and Policy Implications," *Development and Psychopathology* 12, no. 4 (2000): 737–762.

7. Ludwig and Mullainathan, "Fragile Algorithms and Fallible Decision-Makers"; Julia Dressel and Hany Farid, "The Accuracy, Fairness, and Limits of Predicting Recidivism," *Science Advances* 4, no. 1 (2018): eaao5580. One study that drew widespread attention on predictive instruments' bias by race is Julia Angwin, Jeff Larson, Surya Mattu, and Lauren Kirchner, "Machine Bias: Here's Software Used across the Country to Predict Future Criminals. And It's Biased against Blacks," ProPublica, May 23, 2016, https://www.propublica.org/article/machine-bias -risk-assessments-in-criminal-sentencing. For a critique, see Anthony W. Flores, Kristin Bechtel, and Christopher T. Lowenkamp, "False Positives, False Negatives, and False Analyses: A Rejoinder to 'Machine Bias: There's Software Used across the Country to Predict Future Criminals. And It's Biased against Blacks,'" *Federal Probation* 80, no. 2 (2016): 38–46.

8. Further details on variable measurement and analytic models can be found in Montana et al., "Cohort Bias." To be consistent with how risk assessment instruments and prediction models are typically used in the real world, we do not include population or attrition weights in making estimates. Our empirical quantity of interest is a measure of how well we can predict arrest among study participants.

9. Robert J. Sampson and John H. Laub, *Crime in the Making: Pathways and Turning Points through Life* (Cambridge, MA: Harvard University Press, 1993); David P. Farrington, "Individual Differences and Offending," in *The Handbook of Crime and Punishment,* ed. Michael Tonry (New York: Oxford University Press, 1998).

10. The models evaluated a binary outcome (1 = arrested, 0 = not arrested) using various techniques, including logistic regression, lasso and ridge regularized logistic regressions, and random forests. Lasso and ridge regression shrink coefficients associated with correlated predictors to improve predictive performance for new cases by preventing overfitting (fitting noise in the training sample). Random forests are ensemble decision tree algorithms allowing highly nonlinear and interactive predictions with low overfitting risk. Trevor Hastie, Robert Tibshirani, and Jerome H. Friedman, *The Elements of Statistical Learning: Data Mining, Inference, and Prediction* (New York: Springer-Verlag, 2009).

11. Because the slope estimate is .53, if 100 individuals in the younger cohort were predicted to be arrested, only about 53 would have actually been arrested. Thus, the prediction of 100 individuals would have been 188.7 percent of the actual number of 53 arrested individuals—an overprediction of 88.7 percent. The full feature model, using lasso logistic regression to enhance prediction accuracy with numerous predictors, performs better but still overpredicts by over 50 percent.

12. As a confirmation test, we compared risk rankings of older cohort members using the same four methods and two feature sets. This analysis produced much higher overlaps in the top risk quartile than the across-cohort analysis (65 percent to 98 percent), with rank-order correlations between 0.77 and 0.99. This indicates that the decline in rank-ordering performance stems from cohort bias rather than inherent sensitivity of rank orderings across model specifications.

13. The third test, defining "high risk" as anyone who has been arrested between the ages of ten and seventeen, compared the infant and age nine cohorts, because of partial data censoring of official records prior to age seventeen for the age twelve and age fifteen cohorts.

14. Montana et al., "Cohort Bias," Supporting Information (SI) Appendix, figure S7.

15. Jean Twenge and Heejung Park, "The Decline in Adult Activities among U.S. Adolescents, 1976–2016," *Child Development* 90 (2019): 638–654; Lloyd D. Johnston, Richard A. Miech, Patrick M. O'Malley, Jerald G. Bachman, John E. Schulenberg, and Megan E. Patrick, *Monitoring the Future: National Survey Results on Drug Use, 1975–2020: Overview, Key Findings on Adolescent Drug Use* (Ann Arbor: Institute for Social Research, University of Michigan, 2021), https://monitoringthefuture.org/wp-content/uploads/2022/08/mtf-overview2020.pdf.

16. William A. Knaus, Elizabeth A. Draper, Douglas P. Wagner, and Jack E. Zimmerman, "Apache II: A Severity of Disease Classification System," *Critical Care Medicine* 13, no. 10 (1985): 818–829; Matthew DeMichele, Peter Baumgartner, Michael Wenger, Kelle Barrick, Megan Comfort, and Shilpi Misra, "The Public Safety Assessment: A Re-Validation and Assessment of Predictive Utility and Differential Prediction by Race and Gender in Kentucky," *SSRN Elecronic Journal* (2018), http://dx.doi.org/10.2139/ssrn.3168452.

17. Lawrence J. Schweinhart, Helen V. Barnes, and David P. Weikart, *Significant Benefits: The High/Scope Perry Preschool Study through Age 27* (Ypsilanti, MI: High/Scope Press, 1993).

18. Luminosity and University of Chicago's Crime Lab New York, *Updating the New York City Criminal Justice Agency Release Assessment: Maintaining High Court Appearance Rates, Reducing Unnecessary Pretrial Detention, and Reducing Disparity,* June 2020, https://www.nycja.org/assets/Updating-the-NYC-Criminal-Justice-Agency-Release-Assessment-Final-Report-June-2020.pdf.

19. David Lazer, Ryan Kennedy, Gary King, and Alessandro Vespignani, "The Parable of Google Flu: Traps in Big Data Analysis," *Science* 343, no. 6176 (2014): 1203–1205.

10. DEFINING CHARACTER UP

1. Nicola Lacey, *In Search of Criminal Responsibility: Ideas, Interests, and Institutions* (Oxford, UK: Oxford University Press, 2016), online edition, 135.

2. Norman Ryder, "The Cohort as a Concept in the Study of Social Change," *American Sociological Review* 30 (1965): 843–861.

3. Andrew Abbott, "The Historicality of Individuals," *Social Science History* 29 (2005): 1–13. See also Andrew Abbott, *Processual Sociology* (Chicago: University of Chicago Press, 2016).

4. Akiva Liberman, David S. Kirk, and KiDeuk Kim, "Labeling Effects of First Juvenile Arrests: Secondary Deviance and Secondary Sanctioning," *Criminology* 52 (2014): 345–370.

5. See especially the results and description of research from PHDCN+ studies in Chapters 4 and 7 on these and related issues.

6. Stephen W. Raudenbush, "How Do We Study 'What Happens Next'?," *Annals of the American Academy of Political and Social Science* 602, no. 1 (2005): 131–144.

7. Khalil Gibran Muhammad, *The Condemnation of Blackness: Race, Crime, and the Making of Modern Urban America* (Cambridge, MA: Harvard University, 2011), 271.

8. The most recent incarceration statistics can be found in Christopher Muller and Alexander F. Roehrkasse, "Falling Racial Inequality and Rising Educational Inequality in US Prison Admissions for Drug, Violent, and Property Crimes," *Proceedings of the National Academy of Sciences* 122, no. 4 (2025): e2418077122. See also Jason P. Robey, Michael Massoglia, and Michael T. Light, "A Generational Shift: Race and the Declining Lifetime Risk of Imprisonment," *Demography* 60, no. 4 (2023): 977–1003. Despite absolute declines in incarceration, the rate of incarceration is still substantially higher among Black individuals, at about 5:1 in 2019 compared to about 9:1 in 1999—although for drug offenses the racial disparity is nearly gone. On life expectancy, see Patrick T. Sharkey and Michael Friedson, "The Impact of the Homicide Decline on Life Expectancy of African American Males," *Demography* 56, no. 2 (2019): 645–663. Rajiv Sethi discusses what he calls "essentialist causal misattributions" in "Crime and Punishment in a Divided Society," in *Difference without Domination: Pursuing Justice in Diverse Democracies,* ed. Danielle Allen and Rohini Somanathan (New York: Oxford University Press, 2020).

9. Patrick T. Sharkey and Alisabeth Marsteller, "Neighborhood Inequality and Violence in Chicago, 1965–2020," *University of Chicago Law Review* 89, no. 2 (2022): 349–381. Among middle-aged adults, especially white Americans with no college degree, there has also been a rise in recent decades in so-called deaths of despair from suicide, drug overdose, and alcoholism. See Anne Case and Angus Deaton, *Deaths of Despair and the Future of Capitalism* (Princeton, NJ: Princeton University Press, 2020).

10. Christopher Wildeman, "The Intergenerational Transmission of Criminal Justice Contact," *Annual Review of Criminology* 3, no. 1 (2020): 217–244; Christopher Wildeman, Robert J. Sampson, and Garrett Baker, "Adult Children of the Prison Boom: Family Troubles and the Intergenerational Transmission of Criminal Justice Contact," *Demography* 61, no. 1 (2024): 141–164.

11. Christopher Wildeman and Robert J. Sampson, "Desistance as an Intergenerational Process," *Annual Review of Criminology* 7, no. 1 (2024): 85–104.

12. Nathan Wilmers, "Declining Inequality," paper presented at the Russell Sage Foundation, January 15, 2025; Clem Aeppli and Nathan Wilmers, "Rapid Wage Growth at the Bottom Has Offset Rising US Inequality," *Proceedings of the National Academy of Sciences* 119 (2022): e2204305119.

13. On intergenerational mobility, see Raj Chetty, Will S. Dobbie, Benjamin Goldman, Sonya Porter, and Crystal Yang, "Changing Opportunity: Sociological Mechanisms Underlying Growing Class Gaps and Shrinking Race Gaps in Economic Mobility," NBER Working Paper no. 32697 (2024), http://www.nber.org/papers/w32697.

14. Karl Mannheim, "The Problem of Generations," in *Essays on the Sociology of Knowledge: Collected Works,* vol. 5, ed. Paul Kecskemeti (New York: Routledge, [1928] 1952); Howard Schuman and Jacqueline Scott, "Generations and Collective Memories," *American Sociological Review* 54, no. 3 (1989): 359–381.

15. On these points, see the rich discussions in Mario Small, "Culture, Cohorts, and Social Organization Theory: Understanding Local Participation in a Latino Housing Project," *American Journal of Sociology* 108, no. 1 (2002): 1–54; Felton Earls and Mary Carlson, *Voice, Choice, and Action: The Potential of Young Citizens to Heal Democracy* (Cambridge, MA: Harvard University Press, 2020). Cohort studies can also help illuminate aggregate crime and incarceration trends. See, for example, William Spelman, "How Cohorts Changed Crime Rates, 1980–2016," *Journal of Quantitative Criminology* 38, no. 3 (2022): 637–671; Philip J. Cook and John H. Laub, "After the Epidemic: Recent Trends in Youth Violence in the United States," *Crime and Justice* 29 (2002): 1–37; Yinzhi Shen, Shawn D. Bushway, Lucy C. Sorensen, and Herbert L. Smith, "Locking Up My Generation: Cohort Differences in Prison Spells over the Life Course," *Criminology* 58, no. 4 (2020): 645–677.

16. Rodrigo Pérez Ortega, "Half of Americans Anticipate a U.S. Civil War Soon, Survey Finds," *Science* 377 (2022): 357; Garen J. Wintemute, Andrew Crawford, Sonia L. Robinson, Elizabeth A. Tomsich, Paul M. Reeping, Julia P. Schleimer, and Veronica A. Pear, "Firearm Ownership and Support for Political Violence in the United States," *JAMA Network Open* 7 (2024): e243623; Robert J. Sampson and Charles C. Lanfear, "Disentangling Gun Ownership and Leanings to Political Violence in Unstable Times," *JAMA Network Open* 7 (2024): e245066; Maggie Haberman, Charlie Savage, and Jonathan Swan, "Trump Suggests No Laws Are Broken if He's 'Saving His Country,'" *New York Times,* February 15, 2025.

17. On the case of Jon Burge and his reign of torture that has only recently been clearly documented, see the Chicago Police Torture Archive, https://chi cagopolicetorturearchive.com/; and Sam Charles, "New 'Chicago Police Torture Archive' Details Acts of Jon Burge and Underlings," *Chicago Sun Times,* February 3, 2021. On legal cynicism about racism and policing in Chicago more generally, including a history of the Burge case and his protection by political institutions, see John Hagan, Bill McCarthy, and Daniel Herda, *Chicago's Reckoning: Racism, Politics, and the Deep History of Policing in an American City* (Oxford, UK: Oxford University Press, 2022).

18. Control variables include demographic factors (race, sex, immigrant generation); family socioeconomic factors (parental education levels, welfare receipt in childhood, whether parents were married, cohabitating, or single, parental employment status, whether family owned a home, household income); family criminality and problems (frequent legal trouble, arrest, treatment for substance or emotional issues, alcohol issues, drug use issues, and general trouble with the law, fights, jobs, or school); childhood neighborhood factors (percent poverty, percent unemployment, percent Black, percent Hispanic); individual levels of self-control, anxiety / depression, and aggression; being arrested during ages seventeen to twenty-four; and differences from the mean age at the age twenty-five interview. Adjusted differences between cohorts are statistically significant. Interestingly, although members of the mid-1990s cohort are less trusting of neighbors and the police, when asked how many people they can talk to about private matters or call for help, they had a higher reported number at age twenty-five than the mid-1980s cohort. Both the trust and personal ties differences are significant after adjusting for the full list of covariates used in Figure 10.1, and significance holds whether or not sampling and attrition weights are used.

19. Robert Putnam, *Bowling Alone: The Collapse and Renewal of American Community* (New York: Simon and Schuster, 2000). For the 1987 cohort where we have the same measures at waves 4 and 5, or between ages twenty-five and thirty-four, trust in police decreased 12 percentage points compared to the 30-point gap between the 1987 and 1996 cohorts in their mid-twenties. According to Johnathan Haidt, as parents lose trust in the other adults in their neighborhood, they also become more fear-driven and more prone to "paranoid parenting," wherein children are allowed even less unsupervised time away from their parents. Jonathan Haidt, *The Anxious Generation: How the Great Rewiring of Childhood is Causing an Epidemic of Mental Illness* (New York: Penguin Press, 2024), 87–88.

20. C. Wright Mills, *The Sociological Imagination* (New York: Oxford University Press, 1959).

21. Robert J. Bursik, "Erickson Could Never Have Imagined: Recent Extensions of Birth Cohort Studies," *Journal of Quantitative Criminology* 5 (1989): 389–396.

22. See, for example, Marvin E. Wolfgang, Robert M. Figlio, and Thorsten Sellin, *Delinquency in a Birth Cohort* (Chicago: University of Chicago Press, 1972);

Lyle W. Shannon, *Criminal Career Continuity: Its Social Context* (New York: Human Sciences Press, 1988); David Huizinga, Terence Thornberry, Kelly Knight, and Peter Lovegrove, "Disproportionate Minority Contact in the Juvenile Justice System: A Study of Differential Minority Arrest/Referral to Court in Three Cities," Office of Juvenile Justice and Delinquency Prevention, National Criminal Justice Reference Service, document 219743 (2007).

23. Stephen Farrall, "Politics, Research Design, and the 'Architecture' of Criminal Careers Studies," *British Journal of Criminology* 61, no. 6 (2021): 1575–1591; Stephen Farrall and Emily Gray, *The Politics of Crime, Punishment and Justice: Exploring the Lived Reality and Enduring Legacies of the 1980s Radical Right* (London: Routledge, 2024).

24. An example of comparing studies across international contexts that were designed for different purposes is Izabela Zych, David P. Farrington, Denis Ribeaud, and Manuel P. Eisner, "Childhood Explanatory Factors for Adolescent Offending: A Cross-National Comparison Based on Official Records in London, Pittsburgh, and Zurich," *Journal of Developmental and Life-Course Criminology* 7, no. 3 (2021): 308–330. As if to make my point, however, while this study is admirably comparative in nature, like most research efforts it sets aside social change and focuses on common risk-factor predictors.

25. Stephen Farrall, Felipe Estrada Dörner, and Robert J. Sampson, "Changes in Society, Welfare, Penalty, Law, and Justice: Implications for the Future of Criminological and Socio-legal Theorising," Workshop, International Institute for the Sociology of Law, Oñati, Spain, May 16–17, 2024.

26. For further discussion on this issue, see Daniel S. Nagin and Robert J. Sampson, "The Real Gold Standard: Measuring Counterfactual Worlds That Matter Most to Social Science and Policy," *Annual Review of Criminology* 2 (2019): 123–145; Robert J. Sampson, Christopher Winship, and Carly Knight, "Translating Causal Claims: Principles and Strategies for Policy-Relevant Criminology," *Criminology and Public Policy* 12 (2013): 1–30.

27. The White House, "Strengthening and Unleashing America's Law Enforcement to Pursue Criminals and Protect Innocent Citizens," Executive Order, April 28, 2025. On fear of crime relative to current conditions, see also Isabelle Taft and Kate Selig, "The Number of Murders Kept Falling This Year, but Fear of Crime Persists," *New York Times,* December 30, 2024.

28. If we are to predict, we should do so at the societal level and improve our forecasting models, which in turn would aid in planning for the future. For a defense of forecasting crime dynamics, see Richard Rosenfeld, *Crime Dynamics: Why Crime Rates Change over Time* (New York: Cambridge University Press, 2024).

29. See for example, the *Merriam-Webster Dictionary* and the *Oxford English Dictionary.*

30. Although he meant something very different, Daniel Patrick Moynihan's influential essay provoked my thinking about matters of character. See "Defining Deviancy Down," *The American Scholar* 62 (1993): 17–30.

31. Robert J. Sampson, "The Characterological Imperative: On Heckman, Humphries, and Kautz's *The Myth of Achievement Tests: The GED and the Role of Character in American Life*," *Journal of Economic Literature* 54 (2016): 493–513.

32. Ekaterina Botchkovar, Ineke Haen Marshall, Michael Rocque, and Chad Posick, "The Importance of Parenting in the Development of Self-Control in Boys and Girls: Results from a Multinational Study of Youth," *Journal of Criminal Justice* 43, no. 2 (2015): 133–141.

33. Charles C. Branas, Eugenia South, Michelle C. Kondo, Bernadette C. Hohl, Philippe Bourgois, Douglas J. Wiebe, and John M. MacDonald, "Citywide Cluster Randomized Trial to Restore Blighted Vacant Land and Its Effects on Violence, Crime, and Fear," *Proceedings of the National Academy of Sciences* 115, no. 12 (2018): 2946–2951; John MacDonald, Charles Branas, and Robert Stokes, *Changing Places: The Science and Art of New Urban Planning* (Princeton, NJ: Princeton University Press, 2019).

34. On community organization, collective efficacy, and environmental action, see Christopher Muller, Robert J. Sampson, and Alix Winter, "Environmental Inequality: The Social Causes and Consequences of Lead Exposure," *Annual Review of Sociology* 44 (2018): 263–282; Charles C. Lanfear, "Collective Efficacy and the Built Environment," *Criminology* 60 (2022): 370–396; Yvette Cabrera, "The Lead Crisis: Tackling an Invisible, Dangerous Neurotoxin," ThinkProgress, July 15, 2017; Robert J. Sampson, *Great American City: Chicago and the Enduring Neighborhood Effect*, 2nd ed. (Chicago: University of Chicago Press, [2012] 2024), 432–433.

35. There is urgency to taking collective action, especially community based. As of spring 2025, decades of environmental science and public health regulations are being dismantled by the government, setting in motion a likely return to long-term harms to children's development. See for example, Lisa Friedman, "Trump Administration Aims to Eliminate E.P.A.'s Scientific Research Arm," *New York Times,* March 17, 2025. Matthew Daly, "Trump Environmental Rollbacks Would Boost Pollution and Endanger Lives, Former EPA Heads Say," Associated Press, March 14, 2025; Julia Bosman, "With C.D.C. In Retreat, Lead Crisis Grows in Milwaukee," *New York Times,* April 20, 2025.

36. National Research Council, *Proactive Policing: Effects on Crime and Communities* (Washington, DC: National Academies Press, 2018).

37. Monica Bell, "Next-Generation Policing Research: Three Propositions," *Journal of Economic Perspectives* 35 (2021): 29–48. For an assessment of community alternatives, see National Academies of Sciences, Engineering, and Medicine *Reducing Racial Inequality in Crime and Justice: Science, Practice, and Policy*

(Washington, DC: National Academies Press, 2023), chapters 6 and 7. Measurement is critical to progress in this area, which practitioners on the ground are increasingly recognizing. See for example, Mark Obbie, "A City Tries to Measure the Violence It's Preventing," *New York Times,* April 22, 2024.

38. On childhood intervention programs, see James J. Heckman, "Skill Formation and the Economics of Investing in Disadvantaged Children," *Science* 312, no. 5782 (2006): 1900–1902; Jorge Luis García and James J. Heckman, "Parenting Promotes Social Mobility within and across Generations," *Annual Review of Economics* 15, no. 1 (2023): 349–388. Heckman's argument is consistent with the idea that character is not inherent to individuals but can be socially induced and is changeable.

39. For a discussion of social support and collective efficacy theory, see Francis Cullen, "Social Support as an Organizing Concept for Criminology: Presidential Address to the Academy of Criminal Justice Sciences," *Justice Quarterly* 11 (1994): 527–559; Robert J. Sampson, Stephen W. Raudenbush, and Felton Earls, "Neighborhoods and Violent Crime: A Multilevel Study of Collective Efficacy." *Science* 277, no. 5328 (1997): 918–924; Sampson, *Great American City,* chapter 7. On the need to shore up the social safety net, especially with the aim to reduce concentrated disadvantage and resulting crime and punishment, see David Garland, *Law and Order Leviathan: America's Extraordinary Regime of Policing and Punishment* (Princeton, NJ: Princeton University Press, 2025). Another reason for optimism here is that macrolevel policies to reduce poverty have been more effective than commonly realized. The late Christopher Jencks pointed this out over a half-century ago, in "Did We Really Lose the War on Poverty?," American Enterprise Institute Lecture, May 13, 1996, https://www.youtube.com/watch?v=563La9N3k0Q.

40. Robert M. Sapolsky, *Determined: A Science of Life without Free Will* (New York: Penguin Random House, 2024).

41. The Teague doctrine of the Supreme Court limits the retroactive application of new constitutional rules of criminal procedure in habeas corpus petitions. Teague v. Lane, 489 US 288 (1989). Exceptions exist—those sentenced under anti-sodomy statutes could have sentences vacated after *Lawrence v. Texas* (2003) ruled these laws unconstitutional. The legal distinction is that anti-sodomy laws criminalized an entire category of conduct, whereas crack/cocaine laws applied different mandatory minimums to the same conduct (drug use). I thank Ash Smith for this clarification (personal communication). For a passionate argument on the necessity of repairing the harms of disadvantage in the criminal justice system, especially among African Americans, see Bryan Stevenson, *Just Mercy: A Story of Justice and Redemption* (New York: Spiegel and Grau, 2014). For a more philosophical take on justice, responsibility, and forgiveness, see Erin I. Kelly, *The Limits of Blame: Rethinking Punishment and Responsibility* (Cambridge, MA: Harvard University Press, 2018); Martha C. Nussbaum, *Anger and Forgiveness: Resentment, Generosity, Justice* (New York: Oxford

University Press, 2018). See also Michael Tonry on legal prospects for adversity mitigation by the courts in *Doing Justice, Preventing Crime* (New York: Oxford University Press, 2020), 91–94.

42. Ta-Nehisi Coates brought widespread attention to addressing slavery's legacy in "The Case for Reparations," *The Atlantic,* June 2014. For a definitive sociological and historical analysis of slavery across temporal and cultural contexts, see Orlando Patterson, *Slavery and Social Death: A Comparative Study* (Cambridge, MA: Harvard University Press, 1982).

43. Reinhold Niebuhr, *Moral Man and Immoral Society: A Study in Ethics and Politics* (New York: Charles Scribner's Sons, 1932). For a more recent emphasis on inner moral character, see David Brooks, *The Road to Character* (New York: Random House, 2016). To clarify, I don't argue against inner character but advocate reorienting the goal toward building the social foundations where character can truly flourish. On this argument, consistent with community-based theories of collective efficacy and social capital, the development of inner character is fundamentally dependent on, or at least most effectively cultivated through, robust social institutions.

44. John Rawls, *A Theory of Justice* (Cambridge, MA: Harvard University Press, 1971 [1999]). From the impartial "original position," he argued rational individuals would select principles ensuring fairness and equality.

Acknowledgments

This book brings together in one place my research and thinking about the importance of social change in transforming our lives. The bulk of the work I describe here was supported by a series of additions to the Project on Human Development in Chicago Neighborhoods that, combined, produced what is now a thirty-year effort (the study I refer to as the PHDCN+). It is remarkable to me that I started work on this project when I was at the University of Chicago in the early 1990s. I am grateful to my many collaborators on it over the decades.

I particularly want to thank the people who have worked on PHDCN+ or associated papers with me since 2012, when *Great American City: Chicago and the Enduring Neighborhood Effect* was first published. Since that book, I have been lucky to work with a stellar group in probing new issues, including (in alphabetical order) Garrett Baker, Rebecca Bucci, Emily Buff, Jennifer Candipan, Dave Kirk, Charles Lanfear, Brian Levy, Robert Manduca, the late Robert Mare, Erika Montana, Daniel Nagin, Roland Neil, Amelia O'Halloran, Ann Owens, Kristin Perkins, Stephen Raudenbush, Ash Smith, Christopher Wildeman, and Alix Winter. Rebecca and Amelia deserve special notice for their efforts in data coordination and analyses for the PHDCN+ team.

I also thank Lisa Albert at Harvard University, Julia Kirby at Harvard University Press, and Thomas LeBien at Moon and Company for editorial assistance; Sharmila Sen, editorial director at the Press, for her work advancing the book; and friends, family members, colleagues, and anonymous reviewers for constructive comments on various chapters or analyses along the way. Instead of a long and necessarily incomplete list, please accept my gratitude—you know who you are!

Funding for data collection, analysis, and writing was provided in part by the John D. and Catherine T. MacArthur Foundation, the National Collaborative on Gun Violence Research, the National Science Foundation, the National Institute of Justice, a Guggenheim Fellowship, the Milgrom Family Supporting Foundation at the University of Chicago, and Harvard University. Without their collective financial support, the data and this book would not have been possible. I gratefully acknowledge all these institutions.

Research Support Services and NORC at the University of Chicago were instrumental in fielding the fourth and fifth waves of the longitudinal surveys, respectively, and the Chicago Department of Public Health and the Illinois Criminal Justice Information Authority graciously provided access to administrative records.

Portions of Chapters 4, 5, and 6 include text first published in Roland Neil and Robert J. Sampson, "The Birth Lottery of History: Arrest over the Life Course of Multiple Cohorts Coming of Age, 1995–2018," *American Journal of Sociology* 126, no. 5 (2021): 1127–1178. Chapter 8 includes portions of text that first appeared in Robert J. Sampson and L. Ash Smith, "Rethinking Criminal Propensity and Character: Cohort Inequalities and the Power of Social Change," *Crime and Justice* 50 (2021): 13–76.

Index